BISON
BOOKS

Baseball and the Media

How Fans Lose in Today's Coverage of the Game

George Castle

University of Nebraska Press

Lincoln and London

♾

Library of Congress
Cataloging-in-Publication Data
Castle, George.
Baseball and the media : how fans lose in today's coverage of the
game / George Castle.
p. cm.
ISBN-13: 978-0-8032-6469-4 (pbk. : alk. paper)
ISBN-10: 0-8032-6469-0 (pbk. : alk. paper)
1. Baseball—Social aspects—United States.   2. Mass media and
sports—United States.   I. Title.
GV867.64.C37 2006
796.3570973—dc22   2006015462

Set in Janson Text by BookComp, Inc.

Contents

Preface

Baseball is the eternal game, melding past, present, and future in a sport that never dies. In fact our oldest professional sport prospers after all the knocks it takes—labor disputes, greed, venality, management incompetence, and petty politics—through the decades.

No wonder we talk about baseball 24/7/52/365. The free-agent era brought the end of the off-season as traditionally perceived. But if truth be known, baseball fans never took a month or two off. We've always talked, debated, and argued baseball year-round, even if the news slowed to a trickle. We could always time-travel to some previous era to compare present achievers with those in the good old days, which often seem more glamorous in hindsight. Now the never-ending parade of player movement and related developments provide fresh fodder even during the traditional downtime between Christmas and New Year's. As a result, for sheer athletic entertainment value, the sport provides conversational grist and analogies for other parts of life like no other. Baseball terminology pervades so many facets of life, from politics to sex.

Measure its competitors—many say its superiors. The NFL is a white-hot focus of office-cooler talk when betting pools are set up on Fridays and settled on Mondays, sandwiched around the social event of sixteen Sunday games. In between, however, these amateur gamblers are not exactly talking up the merits of the slant play. Most who call themselves NFL fans probably could not name their favorite team's starting offensive linemen or top defensive reserves. "If gambling could somehow be outlawed, football would dry up," sportswriter-pundit-turned-travel-writer Alan Solomon said around

1988, a feeling seconded by those who can see beyond the NFL's intensely choreographed marketing and media machine.

The betting aspect isn't as prevalent in the NBA, whose fine points of the give-and-go and the triangle offense are not chewed over by the average league follower. Aerial artistry, slamma-jamma, and other deft body English are the main lures here. Professional basketball is intensely visual, a perfect made-for-TV winter game where the players wear less than any other sport and whose identities are not obscured by helmets. But the NBA has been a big deal for only a generation. "I'd love to have the history baseball possesses," NBA commissioner David Stern once said. Indeed, when Joe DiMaggio was captivating the country and building up mythic legend by hitting in fifty-six in a row, what passed for pro basketball were vagabond teams playing for coffee money in small industrial cities of the Northeast and Midwest.

Hockey? Remember that winter sport? After a brief upsurge in the 1970s and into the 1980s, the Canadian import was steadily reduced to cult status long before labor squabbles cashed in its 2004–5 season. Hockey faded behind other individual sports in popularity, falling totally off the table.

Golf, tennis, and NASCAR are all good visual theater. But they don't cut to the base loyalties of the average sports consumer like baseball does. In the end—and despite the criticism battering it from non-fans and football lovers—baseball remains the one sport so closely intertwined with other classic Americana.

To be sure, the game was overromanticized by too many authors and essayists. They read into it far more than it is. *Field of Dreams* was well-made Hollywood fantasy, but that's all it was. Don't try to whip up assorted allegories for deeper human meanings. The game does have some social significance. Jackie Robinson's color-line busting of 1947 was a true landmark in American history, with a baseball player representing progress that presidents and Congresses before and after 1947 shamefully refused to foster. And in some cases, a winning team is a psychological salve, uniting a disparate community and temporarily healing wounds, a function served by the world-champion 1968 Detroit Tigers a year after their city burned in horrific riots. Yet to apply all kinds of links to the human soul that might puzzle Freud himself is unsuitable.

Simply put, baseball is the first sport we usually love. And if a gaggle of propagandists don't convince us we should have a passion for other sports or forsake baseball entirely, it's a game that sticks with us a lifetime, passing down to our heirs in the process.

Baseball is a game we pursue at many levels. Almost all of us have played it or its variant, softball, at the very least at a basic level. Beyond park-league, flag-and-touch contests, football winnows out most competitors with its jarring contact, equipment requirements, and sheer brute strength. Basketball has approached baseball in the last two decades in year-round participation by both adults and those at the formative stages of their sports loyalties, yet height and quickness absent in most competitors will prevent it from being pursued at a truly competitive level.

Most sandlotters and park-district participants waive themselves out by the time serious interscholastic competition begins. Yet the love of the game simply is transformed into day-to-day interest in the Major Leagues via the media, the prism through which we truly get to know the game and its stars. Long before the inception of the Internet, that gateway usually was provided through published accounts of games near and far, along with the ubiquitous box score, the collection of baseball hieroglyphics and codes that got more detailed as the twentieth century progressed. Poring over the box scores and game stories was a morning ritual of countless millions, with even more up-to-the-minute accounts of day games featured in afternoon newspapers before that genre began slipping away in post–World War II America.

The newspaper and magazine coverage of the game was joined around 1930 by radio play-by-play accounts. Fans' favorite teams were augmented by loyalties to announcers, who like hitters' stances and pitchers' deliveries offered up a myriad of well-remembered styles. Voices of the greats still resound in millions of memory banks. They range from the exciting, tell-it-like-he-thought-it-was warbling of Harry Caray, with Stan Musial conquering the pavilion wall in old Busch Stadium; to the poetry-in-motion of Vin Scully as Sandy Koufax channeled other-world lightning through his left arm to throw a perfect game; to the vocal-chords-busting deliveries of Jack Brickhouse, Jack Quinlan, and Vince Lloyd when beloved Ernie Banks hit another out of Wrigley Field.

Print and radio were joined by TV by 1950. At first restricted by cumbersome equipment, the video presentation of baseball soon became a classic directors' game. Be it Harry Coyle's capturing of Carlton Fisk trying to gesture his home run fair in the 1975 World Series or Arne Harris working magic with just four cameras and one replay machine in Chicago, baseball's daily personality came alive in living color. Advancements in replays, camera lenses, and other equipment dissected the sport up close and personal as never before.

And, in turn, the march forward of broadcast coverage improved the print coverage. Instead of sometimes purple prose offering up a mere play-by-play of the game, quotes began to pepper game stories. Notebooks and "sidebar" stories were added to coverage packages, taking the reader inside the clubhouse and executive suite to explain the "whys" of the game. Clashes and divisions erupted between print and broadcast, the former considering itself the old guard protecting its turf, the latter demanding, but not always getting, equal access despite the mega-millions pouring into the game through broadcast rights fees.

By the 1990s, the Internet finally grabbed a toehold in the baseball prism. But if in the early twenty-first century the online purveyors were about as advanced as radio was in, say, 1928 or TV in about 1953, the cyberspace coverage of the game was not yet on equal footing with the older forms of media.

Baseball and the media cannot get along without each other. From the very day the National League opened for business in the Grant administration, team owners could not afford to purchase the space that newspapers allotted for baseball coverage, for which they paid in writers' and editors' salaries. Nearly a century later, owners depended upon raking in seven figures in revenue from radio and TV rights. But it would have been unthinkable for the lords of the game to have paid the broadcast outlets for three hours a day, at some 190 games a year (including spring training and the postseason). Baseball has wised up in the nascent Internet era, owning a portion of the leading online purveyor of baseball information.

Without the media conduits to the fans, who talk up the game and eventually are its paying customers, baseball would go the way of a gambling-free football. So you'd figure the sport and those who cover it would be one big, happy family. Figure again. Rather than keep the slow, loving embrace going, baseball and the media have allowed a gulf to grow between them. Both parties are still in it together, but increasingly at arm's length. And the consumer at home is the loser in the end.

Players and executives, in whose best interest it lies to make their personas accessible through the media, are increasingly keeping their distance. Soaring salaries allow players to morph into Hollywood celebrities with a careful filter masking what they're really like, if not an outright wall around them. A careful corporate mentality has enveloped much of baseball. Fans have always felt close to their baseball heroes, even if they've never met them, but now they are increasingly light years' removed. Trust has been replaced by bitterness.

But the media itself also has had a big hand in the breakdown. Baseball writers don't stay at their jobs long anymore, disrupting the continuity of coverage demanded by fans. Many on the beat eschew relationships with players in favor of roaming clubhouses and foul territory in packs or cliques in what one writer calls "socialized journalism." Elitism and arrogance, as bad as any practiced by wealthy players, exist among the pen-and-mike crowd. Columnists and radio sports-talk-show hosts often don't show up at the ballpark. That in turn creates ill will among baseball folk when the opinion-meisters craft their output on the basis of second- and thirdhand information to which their readers and listeners already have access. "Entertainment" is liberally substituted for accurate journalism by ratings-hungry broadcast executives. The presentation, or the "sizzle," is perceived as more important than the truth, or the "steak."

The fans deserve better, as they do from their politicians and business executives. After all, baseball is supposed to be a passionate escape from everyday worries. Instead the outside world intrudes into the toy factory. Politics is political, sport is more political than politics, and media is worse than both of them.

How things came to be, and how things could be better in how baseball is perceived through the media, will be detailed in the next couple of hundred pages. But there's one reassuring certainty. The game goes on. It's so tough, it always gets up after being knocked down. It's been buried and pronounced dead so many times that you'd scarcely pay attention to the next such proclamation.

In an era of bullpen specialization, of five-and-fly starters, baseball itself still goes the distance. Harry Caray once said the names change, die, and fade away, but the game continues on. Thank goodness for such small favors in a tough, tough world.

Baseball and the Media

Introduction

Even though he was surrounded by a score of people, Wendell Kim looked lonely as he stood, almost lost in his thoughts, to the dugout side of the door to the weight room in the Chicago Cubs clubhouse late on the night of July 19, 2004, in Wrigley Field.

Kim, the diminutive Cubs third-base coach, no doubt had a feeling of dread about his employment for the following season after the events that had just transpired. The Cubs had just lost a tough 5–4 game to the archrival St. Louis Cardinals. Cubs starter Carlos Zambrano had an emotional meltdown at the wrong time, foolishly aiming his pitches at parts of St. Louis slugger Jim Edmonds' body, as the Cards widened their first-place lead over a team that had been favored to reach the World Series this season.

But Kim, whose reckless gambles sending runners home earned him the nickname "Wavin' Wendell" from Cubs announcers Chip Caray and Steve Stone, lived up to his reputation on this night. Third baseman Aramis Ramirez was still gimpy from a groin injury suffered two weeks previously. Ramirez doubled to lead off the sixth in a 3–3 tie. Catcher Michael Barrett then blooped a single to right. Kim waved Ramirez around rather than holding him up, which would have fashioned a men-on-first-and-third, no-out situation. Cardinals right fielder Reggie Sanders cleanly picked up the ball and gunned a huffing Ramirez out at the plate. Moments later, Alex Gonzalez hit into an inning-ending double play, drawing boos from the standing-room-only crowd of 40,033.

Zambrano's histrionics had attracted the main attention of the media. Edmonds had clubbed a two-run homer off the strapping right-hander in the fourth, prompting Zambrano to jaw at Edmonds as he rounded the bases. "He didn't say nothing," Zambrano said. "I just told him to run the bases, don't be cocky." Cubs pitching coach Larry Rothschild quickly lectured Zambrano out of sight of the throng.

But the lecture did not stick. Zambrano appeared to shake a finger in Edmonds's direction when he struck him out in the sixth. Then in the eighth, after Zambrano served up Scott Rolen's two-run homer that gave the Cardinals a 5–3 lead, the pitcher plunked Edmonds on the hip. Since a warning had been issued by the umpires, Zambrano and Cubs manager Dusty Baker were ejected.

That appeared to be the main storyline of the evening. Zambrano and Baker addressed their parts in the passion play in the postgame interview room, a stifling little cubbyhole reachable by a tunnel from both the dugout and ballpark main concourse. There was little other information to garner about the incident when the media then moved en masse into the clubhouse.

The regular beat writers, radio reporters, a stray TV crew, and a couple of other hangers-on gathered at one end of the clubhouse, near the dual exits to the dugout and concourse, with the weight room off to the side. I joined them in my role of covering the game for the *Times of Northwest Indiana*, the Chicago area's fourth largest daily newspaper. I thought the presence of Kim among the media was quite curious. Thirteen months earlier, Kim had foolishly waved slow-footed catcher Damian Miller into a sure out at home plate in a one-run loss to the White Sox at Wrigley Field. After Baker had defended longtime chum Kim in his postgame talk in the cubbyhole, I raced into the clubhouse in an attempt to snare Kim for his version. But the coach had quickly ducked out, not 'fessing up to his mistake until the next day.

So in light of that earlier incident the sight of Kim standing among the media was amazing. He wasn't talking to a fellow coach or player. About two minutes transpired while I kept looking at Kim. All the other media members' collective gaze was focused on the center of the clubhouse, perhaps waiting for Barrett or another player to appear. Nobody seemed to notice Kim. He could well have stood in that spot until hell froze over.

Finally I approached him. "Wendell, can you comment on that play with Aramis?" I asked.

"That's why I'm here," Kim responded.

As if given a Pavlovian cue, a whole mess of tape recorders, note-pads, and microphones swung around 180 degrees and enveloped Kim.

"I caused the loss," he said. "I was aggressive at the wrong time. I apologize to all the Cubs fans, the front office, and my teammates."

Kim's mea culpa wasn't as astounding as another double-barreled aspect of that scene. First, Kim had bridged the widening chasm between baseball figures and the reporters who cover the game by seeking the media out. Secondly, when presented a key figure in a dramatic game for interviews on a silver platter, the assembled media did not make the first move, only asking questions when a group formed and someone else took the initiative to start the interview—almost as if there was a "safety in numbers" attitude.

I had seen innumerable examples of such passive behavior among colleagues going back some fifteen years. Back on September 8, 1989, at the other end of the clubhouse in the manager's office, Don Zimmer looked even more agitated than usual, his expressive eyes bulging as the media assembled around him. Cubs general manager Jim Frey, his lifelong friend and sponsor, shuffled about at the back of the media cluster, looking at the floor. The Cubs had just lost a crucial game 11–8 to these same Cardinals, who cut the hosts' first-place lead to half a game. Pedro Guerrero had slugged a three-run homer off Cubs closer Mitch Williams to enable the Cards to rally from a 7–1 deficit.

Zimmer had started journeyman lefty Paul Kilgus, who had been demoted to the bullpen, then to the minors, a couple of months earlier. Kilgus had not been stretched out in a game in a while. I remarked to radio reporter Bruce Levine in the press box that after Kilgus had limited the Cardinals to just one run in five innings, Zimmer should pat him on the rear, say, "Good game," and not press his luck. But Zimmer, no handler of pitchers, let Kilgus go further, and the Cardinals started their rally as a result.

As Zimmer stared into space in his office, the only sound in the room was nervous shuffling, maybe a cough or throat-clearing. A minute or more passed without one question directed at Zimmer. Nobody, not even the beat guys from the downtown Chicago papers, wanted to make the first move. Perhaps they realized Zimmer wasn't really the cuddly baseball lifer popularly portrayed. He had a horrible temper, as I would find out a decade later when he lit after me in the U.S. Cellular Field's visitors' dugout without any provocation. But in that 1989 gathering, a palpable fear factor pervaded the assembled media. It shouldn't have. What was Zimmer going to do? Lash out and bite them like a rabid dog?

I couldn't take the silence any longer. "What went into your thinking of stretching out Kilgus?" I asked Zimmer. That broke the ice. He answered in a reasonable manner. Other questions, asked sheepishly, then came forth from the group.

The Kim and Zimmer incidents were telling about the state of courage and perception among those covering baseball. They also gave clues as to the product that the consuming public receives each day in print, broadcast, and Internet form. The experiences I would endure weren't what I expected when I first dreamed of baseball writing back in high school, more than three decades before Wendell Kim crossed the barrier and reached out to an unwilling media throng.

ONE

A Long, Strange Journey to the Press Box and Clubhouse

The path to a Major League clubhouse is decided early in life. A select few have the natural gift to play baseball, sport's most mentally challenging game, at its highest level. A larger group is athletically challenged, but either talented enough or lucky enough or both to end up in the locker room with pen and notebook or tape recorder.

But it's not certain where a dual passion for writing and baseball originates.

Some of it is environmental. Your mother brings home two newspapers each day and you learn writing style by osmosis and repetition. The local team, in this case the Chicago Cubs, starts winning after two decades' wandering in baseball's desert, with saturation TV coverage providing an easily opened window for you to get close to the game.

Perhaps the rest is just embedded deep within you. Those who are fated to be good in math go on to clean up in the tough courses and, in many cases, help rule the world because they can work the numbers so well. Baseball and basketball mogul Jerry Reinsdorf was surely a math whiz in school back in Brooklyn. Those less fortunate go into literary or creative pursuits. I liked history and current events, so naturally I'd read and follow the news.

In my formative 1960s, Chicago was blessed with four distinctive daily newspapers—the *Tribune*, *Sun-Times*, *Daily News*, and *American*. By age thirteen, while living in West Rogers Park, five miles northwest of Wrigley Field, I read three of the papers daily, the *Tribune* excepted because it was reflexively conservative and Republican. Reading became a true gateway to the greater world in a tumultuous era.

When the *Tribune* started moving toward the center under editor Clayton Kirkpatrick in 1969, I began reading the giant daily regularly. Soon I'd get an even closer view during my first entrée into the business around April Fool's Day, 1974, while finishing up my freshman year in college. A friend of my mother's friend worked as an executive in the *Tribune*'s insurance subsidiary. An opening for a copy clerk on the 11:30 p.m. to 7:00 a.m. shift Fridays and Saturdays was available. In true Chicago and media fashion, the word was put in and I journeyed through the front door at 435 N. Michigan Avenue.

Strolling into the fourth-floor *Tribune*'s city room was like taking a trip through a modern-day Wonderland. I had my more mundane gofer's duties such as answering the switchboard, stripping the AP and UPI wires every half hour or so, moving copy from desk to desk, and fetching coffee from the mailroom downstairs. The camaraderie was special on the night shift, also called the "dog watch." The daytime caste system broke down to a degree. The old sea-dog desk guys would talk to you. Emphasize "guys." In 1976, LeAnn Spencer became the first woman to work such late weekend hours on the desk, her cries of "Copy!" many octaves above the typical bullfrog-level summonses of the night crew.

Telegraph editor Bob Seals tipped me $20 every Christmas, a handsome sum for a college student making $4.60 an hour (double the minimum wage at the time). Veteran copyeditor Bob Corbet advised me to leave the paper eventually, work my way up elsewhere in the business, and "come back here a star." Falstaffian deskman Bob Hughes rumbled down the aisles in the middle of the night, singing "Amelia Earhart, Where Have You Gone?" When he wasn't laying out the final replate edition, George Schumann talked about how he could "sleep in shifts" during the day to handle the overnight hours while making a 120-mile round trip from his New Buffalo, Michigan, home.

The secrets of the night shift stayed there, like inside-baseball clubhouse information. The entire cadre of city-room copyeditors was scheduled to work from 11:00 p.m. to 7:00 a.m. starting Friday night. However, their editing completed about 3:30 or 4:00 a.m., they began drifting home one by one. I could even steal away one of the nights around 4:30 a.m. during the baseball season to get a few more hours' sleep in order not to be totally bleary-eyed going to the 1:15 p.m. ball game at Wrigley Field. "We don't pay people now for not working," thundered Jim Dowdle, the number two Tribune Company executive, when I told him of this featherbedding situation twenty-five years later.

The *Tribune* sports department was off to one side of the newsroom. It might as well have been in a different world. If it took an executive's recommendation to get a part-time job on the city-side dog watch, what kind of internal politics did it take to become a member of the sports department? The all-male staff of the time certainly wore their elitism proudly, if not arrogantly. Men in their late twenties and thirties, even the summer intern, walked around with mammoth, dirigible-shaped cigars stuffed in their mouths, the kind of smoking accessory only the wise-guy types a generation older at Friedman's or at the Devon-Western newsstand logically would savor. The stogies were seemingly a combination of macho, member-of-the-club rite of passage and a showcase of smug satisfaction with their employment.

Sports obviously operated in a different world than the rest of the paper, oriented toward a deadline dash when game results would come in all within about a ninety-minute period. On Friday night, August 30, 1974, I found Bob "Lefty" Logan, Cubs and Bulls beat writer and top punster in Chicago sports, typing furiously on an Underwood manual. Logan watched the Cubs-Padres twinight doubleheader from San Diego on sports editor Cooper Rollow's office color TV. In those days, if a Chicago baseball team was well under .500 and out of the race later in the season, the local dailies cut out much of the road travel for their writers. Logan had not been sent to the West Coast with the Cubs, forcing him to cover games off TV, a not uncommon practice in the era. The next morning, the game story was datelined "San Diego" with a "Special to the *Tribune*" byline. Logan's name was nowhere to be found. It would not be the first time, and is still far from the last, that baseball fans were not getting the whole story—or truth in packaging—about their teams from the media.

At age twenty, my own work would soon appear in the sports section under another man's byline. Gary Deeb was the new tv-radio critic, imported from Buffalo. He soon became an overnight sensation and the most talked-about columnist in town this side of Mike Royko with his take-no-prisoners criticism of bad programming, talent, and executives along with some sharp broadcast-industry scoops. *Time Magazine* called Deeb "the terror of the tube." But Deeb had also started a Tuesday sports tv-radio column in the jock pages and needed someone steeped in Chicago sports knowledge to do the legwork. I became that person, having met and conversed with Deeb on the dog watch. He was a lone-wolf worker, prowling in at night to type his column for the advance features-section deadline after doing a first draft in longhand at his nearby apartment.

Deeb paid me out of his own pocket. I assisted him by researching critical columns on Howard Cosell and White Sox color announcer J. C. Martin and a praiseworthy piece on the Cubs radio teaming of Vince Lloyd and Lou Boudreau. But the best-remembered Deeb column, to this day, was his 1975 satire on Bears radio announcers Jack Brickhouse and Irv Kupcinet. I gathered 90 percent of the information in that piece, with Deeb using many of the lines I submitted in a preliminary column form. "Dat's right, Jack," Kup's typical response to Brickhouse's request for analysis, became a catchword in Chicago sports. Brickhouse had helped develop an entire city's enthusiasm, me included, for its often-losing teams. Yet he was unintentionally comical working an NFL game as the public's only live media conduit during an era of home-game tv blackouts.

Decades later I'd become friends with Brickhouse and even put together an historical exhibit on his career for the Museum of Broadcast Communications. Still the mid-1970s was a time when Brickhouse, who had close business ties to Chicago's sports owners and thus was never wholly objective, deserved some knocks. He was a mediocre football announcer. Vince Lloyd told me in 2003 that Brickhouse, to whom baseball and basketball broadcasting back in his native Peoria were almost his birthrights, really did not understand football's intricacies.

Deeb even persuaded the features department to run my own bylined piece, appearing in his column space during his July 1976 vacation, on the lack of science-fiction tv shows in the gap between the original *Star Trek*'s cancellation and the advent of *Star Wars* mania.

The continuation of this apparent first big break came when John Waggoner, the *Tribune*'s news editor and number three man in the editorial department, offered me a summer internship for 1976. I had gotten to know Waggoner as I started my Friday night shifts while he was finishing up his deadline work. An internship was a good entrée to being hired full time later on at the *Tribune*; if not, it was certainly a sterling section on a résumé that would impress another sizeable newspaper. Inexplicably, though, I froze up, telling Waggoner I needed more published experience before I could work as an intern. I had needed someone to get in my face to counsel me that a phalanx of assistant city editors and copyeditors provided layers of protection for my copy, and I wasn't going to be assigned to national politics or City Hall. A year later, with more published clips at a college daily, I approached Waggoner to ask if the internship offer was still good for 1977. "It's a tough world out there," he said in telling me "no."

That bad news took place after the Deeb work connection also had been severed, due to a disagreement over assigned research not used and, in turn, not compensated. With the twice-a-week all-nighters finally getting to me physically, I left the *Tribune* in April 1977 to assume a $135-a-week summer news internship at the *Decatur Herald and Review*, 180 miles south of Chicago. I probably learned more at the smaller daily than I would have at the colossus on Michigan Avenue. But a request for full-time employment at the *Herald and Review* when I graduated from Northern Illinois University in 1978 had been nixed by my supervising city editor, who felt he was stuck in the agribusiness-industrial city and did not wish the same on me.

As life progressed, the alternate road I took became the only sure way into the press box and locker room.

Following two other writing-related positions after college, I learned a friend was leaving a part-time sports job at the weekly Lerner Newspapers' Chicago North Side main office, recommending me as his successor. I started in April 1980, glorying in what I thought was my good fortune. It was not the *Tribune*, but it was a sportswriting job in my hometown.

I soon began a sports column, which I tabbed "The Bleacher

Bench," after my summertime ballpark roost. My first effort was about finding Mr. Cub, Ernie Banks, working as a management trainee at the Bank of Ravenswood on Lawrence Avenue, two miles from Wrigley Field. Banks was not exactly overworked while I talked to him. In the middle of the bank lobby, he intently listened to decade-old audio highlights of his teammates I had provided to him.

The value of my Lerner sports position appeared to inflate even more when I obtained my first press credential to cover games at Wrigley Field. However the credential was only a daily pass. And it had restrictions imposed by Cubs media-relations director Buck Peden, mindful that I only worked for a weekly. I could not gain access to the tiny, inadequate home clubhouse down the left-field line. I also could not eat a pregame lunch in the Pink Poodle, the media dining room behind home plate. However, in a twist, I was allowed to use the Poodle's kitchen phone to feed interview tape to an Evanston radio station for which I aired a daily sportscast during the 1980 season. When I'd enter the Pink Poodle a half hour after games, the place had an open bar with hard liquor, one or two or more for the road for the thirsty media. But in 1981, after Peden was transferred to another job, a more friendly media-relations type finally granted me my first season credential with full clubhouse and dining-room access.

The 1980 credential squeeze by the Cubs did not compare to what I encountered back at 7519 N. Ashland Avenue as a first career lesson in the kind of media management that negatively impacts baseball coverage. Company owner Lou Lerner had just acquired full ownership of the chain from his mother, sister, and brother. Lerner also had dabbled as a petty Democratic Party activist who was rewarded for early support of Jimmy Carter with the ambassadorship to Norway in 1977. But Lerner's political and financial passions did not extend to the team at Clark and Addison. I did not know whether Lerner hated the Cubs (one report had the West Rogers Park native a White Sox fan) or hated the Tribune Company, formerly the archconservative antithesis to his late, liberal father-publisher Leo Lerner. Maybe he just hated ambition among his help.

Whatever the motivation, Lerner certainly did not want any straight-on coverage of the Cubs even though the team played smack-dab in the middle of his circulation area. I had to come up with a "local angle" for any Cubs-related story—the batboy hailing from a local high school, community opposition to the installation of lights in Wrigley Field, and so on. Management's lame excuse was that the dailies covered baseball so well that a weekly should cover what the dailies didn't. Yet if a murder occurred outside the ballpark (as actually took place two decades later), the downtown print and broadcast outlets would cover it just the same as the local weekly.

Lerner and his puppet editorial director, Charles Mouratides, ignorantly demanded coverage of micro-interest, high-school sports and summer-park district softball without ever being in touch with what their readers really desired. This was the first indication to me that media coverage of any event, baseball included, often is determined by the whims and fancies of the boss. In this mediawide trend, baseball coverage sometimes yields to lesser, "local" sports, even in newspapers not far from the teams' home ballparks. Barred from more than scattershot Cubs coverage, I sought out some freelance baseball writing opportunities, but instead I ended up authoring a TV-radio column for *Pro Football Weekly* and taking other freelance work.

An attempt to blast myself out of Lerner failed in 1984 when Rupert Murdoch swooped in to buy the *Sun-Times* after Ted Field, half-brother of primary owner Marshall Field, wanted to cash out to finance his movie production company. Scores of news-side and feature department staffers, worried about Murdoch's low-rent reputation in publishing tabloids, bailed out of the *Sun-Times*. Columnist Mike Royko led the exodus, joining the *Tribune*, a paper he had long baited in print.

There was one catch. Only three sports department staffers, including sports editor Marty Kaiser and assistant sports editor Mike Davis, departed. There was only so much more sensationalism Murdoch could inject into sports coverage. Besides, writers are usually out of the office and divorced from the petty day-to-day office politics. Desk editors tend to work at night when the honchos are not around. Employment at a big-city sports department was a sweet plum, indeed, no matter who signed the checks.

The four hundred dollars I spent to buy a new suit, figuring I had some angles to get a job interview at the *Sun-Times*, went to waste. Other attempts to move on to bigger, better jobs in the Chicago market fell short. Editors at dailies had a haughty attitude toward writers on weeklies, wrongly believing they either weren't good enough or could not handle daily deadlines. The Newspaper Guild's contract for Lerner Newspapers' editorial employees prohibited any work for "competing" publications, thus precluding slipping in to the downtown dailies or the suburban *Daily Herald* via the side door of part-time gigs or stringing. This situation was exacerbated when the Guild failed to secure a cost-of-living increase in the five years an apparently cash-strapped Lou Lerner ran the paper. The Guild went all-out for its "glamour" contract at the *Sun-Times* when the crying need for improved wages and benefits was at smaller publications such as mine.

Why not simply leave the job, you say? I was advised by too many pundits to move away from Chicago, the stereotyped manner to move up in journalism and one that negatively impacts the wanderers' acumen in covering each new market. But move to where? Staffers of dailies from smaller cities throughout the Midwest were willing to move down in class at a weekly such as mine just to live in a big city. Not everyone can uproot their family. In addition, Lerner Newspapers provided a steady, albeit modest wage with benefits, the two most important factors when you have a young child. And there was that not-insignificant fringe benefit of season Cubs and White Sox credentials as sports editor of the North Side editions. A quarter-loaf was better than none at all.

Still, continued confinement at Lerner Newspapers got ever more stifling as the years progressed. An announcement was made early in 1984 that for the first time in TV history, several Cubs home games would be blacked out locally to enable NBC to have an exclusive audience for its Saturday *Game of the Week*. That was historic—two generations of Chicago fans had grown up never further from the Cubs than their TV sets. I called Brickhouse, a North Side resident, and several others for their reactions. Lou Lerner was so incensed by the story that he crafted a memo to Mouratides that "no coverage of professional sports" was to be permitted in the paper. Later, in August 1984, Lerner spotted me in the basement composing room. "Why don't you go to [get a job at] the *Tribune* so you can get World

Series tickets?" he huffed, mindful that the Cubs had just taken over first place in the National League East. "If I could, I would," I responded. The Cubs barely missed the World Series in 1984.

Lerner, only forty-nine, died of a brain tumor a few months later. His widow, Susan, soon sold the chain to Pulitzer Publishing of St. Louis. The new management was a little more flexible. I soon gained the support of Nick Van Hevelingen, Pulitzer's executive dispatched from St. Louis to run Lerner Newspapers. A format change in 1988 enabled me to write a weekly sports-media celebrity column in the lakefront editions of the chain. Combined with freelance work for the Cubs publications department, *Sport* magazine and several other local and national publications, I wrapped up the 1980s more or less covering the majority of home games at Wrigley Field.

More evidence of the whims and fancies of media management became apparent, though, when I began doing fill-in baseball and basketball work for the *Daily Southtown*, a daily circulating on Chicago's Southwest Side and southwest suburbs. *Southtown* covered the home games of all the city's teams and had also had been bought by Pulitzer.

Some noneditorial people moved from Lerner to the daily, but not a single writer or editor switched. Van Hevelingen, who knew I was frustrated at a weekly, had put in a good word at the daily to get me the freelance fill-in gig. After a year, I called up *Southtown* editor Michael Kelley to pitch him on the idea of joining the staff. He would hear nothing of it. "You're a magazine writer," the overopinionated Kelley told me. He also used the magazine-writer put-down to Ted Cox, a *Southtown* copyeditor who wanted to switch to writing. Five years later, Cox was TV-radio columnist of the larger *Daily Herald* in Chicago's northwest suburbs. Yet in 1991, after the sports newspaper the *National* had folded, Kelley moved money around in the midst of a recession to create a columnist's position that previously did not exist. Kelley liked the *National*, so he snapped up Tom Keegan, one of its writers in dire need of employment, for the bargain salary of thirty-eight thousand dollars.

When I was not asked to stay on when Pulitzer Publishing came within days of closing Lerner Newspapers before selling it to a local investor in the fall of 1992, I actually got a huge break. I had built up a portfolio of regular freelance assignments over the years and simply went to work on my own, making an aggregate fourteen thousand dollars more than my base Lerner salary. Besides, I no longer would be dragged down writing poorly read high-school sports or having any artificial restrictions on baseball coverage, the latter of which never totally went away long after Lou Lerner's passing.

Within a year, I began my own weekly radio show, *Chicago Baseball Weekly*, on suburban FM station WCBR. I strongly believed that baseball was undercovered by the newly hot format of sports-talk radio, which went gaga first over Mike Ditka, then the NFL overall. Besides, WGN Radio, a logical originator for a weekly baseball magazine show, restricted the amount of sports programming other than its live baseball and football play-by-play, the better to protect its perennial number one ratings position.

I paid two hundred dollars for the hour of live airtime at WCBR and somehow rustled up enough advertisers to more than cover the cost. Former Philadelphia Phillies manager John Felske was a sponsor with his chain of quick oil-change outlets. Surviving the 1994–95 baseball strike, I took the show to the Illinois Radio Network for production and distribution, renamed it *Diamond Gems*, and put it into syndication via satellite as a taped program. By 1997 I had persuaded eighteen stations to carry the seasonal offering, which ran from Opening Day till the end of the World Series. Two years later, the affiliate count climbed to twenty-five, airing on stations as far away as Anchorage and Honolulu, while I entered into a better and less expensive production deal with SRN Broadcasting of Lake Bluff, Illinois. All along I somehow managed to snare enough advertising to keep the program going. In 2006, *Diamond Gems* marked its thirteenth season on the air—three or four lifetimes by radio standards.

At the same time I began the radio show in 1994, I began covering Cubs games for the *Times of Northwest Indiana*, based in Munster, just a half mile east of the Illinois state line, thirty miles southeast of downtown Chicago. The newspaper found it more convenient and cost effective to employ a Chicago-based writer than dispatch one of their staffers daily for the traffic-clogged drive to Wrigley Field. Periodically I was used to back up on White Sox home games, and even some of the dynastic Bulls NBA Finals contests. Although the per-story compensation certainly did not match the security of a staffer's regular paycheck and benefits, the arrangement was better than I had enjoyed previously. I was working for a daily newspaper, which is generally treated better than most other media genres by the powers that be in baseball.

Factoring in other magazines and publications, for whom I had already been covering baseball, I figured I had achieved my dream. Sure, I lacked the pay and sheer circulation of the most privileged baseball journalists. Some of my more arrogant colleagues held my part-time *Times* status and representation of—horrors, an out-of-state, Indiana paper—against me. Welcome to the politics of big-city media, more political than the pols themselves.

In addition to the baseball figures with whom I forged some important relationships while out at the ballpark almost daily, I began noticing how the game was being covered—or not covered. Changes were afoot in the news business. Newspapers were losing circulation at a time when stockholders demanded instant gratification and ownership was being consolidated. Sports-talk radio had burst onto the scene. TV stations and cable sports outlets sent more video cameras into the locker room. The average person covering baseball was getting younger and probably less knowledgeable. Putting all these factors together, I persuaded the *Times of Northwest Indiana* sports editor Dave Campbell to let me write the following feature. Appearing on October 8, 1995, the story is reprinted courtesy of the *Times*:

CHICAGO—Cubs manager Jim Riggleman stands in a corner of his clubhouse, running the gauntlet of postgame questions. One long-faced young man, appearing hardly older than senior-prom fodder, thrusts a microphone toward Riggleman.

"Well, Coach, what did you think of . . ." begins his question as the assembled reporters' eyes roll.

The very junior radio reporter leaves to gather another sound bite elsewhere.

Riggleman's a low-key guy and just smiles slightly as someone says, "Well, Coach, who's going to start at running back next week?"

This image is a reminder of one of the worst downer years in baseball history.

How our most traditional game is portrayed in the media has a lot to do with its image in the fractured 1994 and 1995 seasons. Two separate but connected themes in crafting that image have emerged in newspapers and on radio and TV stations:

(1) In an unsettled time when the game has enough off-the-field troubles, baseball is being enthusiastically bashed, most often by columnists, essayists, and sports-talk-show hosts who usually stay away from the ballparks.

(2) In a trend long predating the 1994–95 strike, baseball has been undercovered or miscovered, particularly by the broadcast media. The quality and quantity of reporting on the game has dipped sharply as early twenty-something rookies are sent out to cover events formerly reserved for the most experienced old hands.

Baseball offers by far the most access of any sport. Yet only a minority of media outlets and reporters take advantage of that open-door policy, with superficial postgame sound bites comprising the sum total of a lot of broadcast coverage.

White Sox manager Terry Bevington was the latest baseball figure to point out the clubhouse and dugout absences of prominent opinionists.

Meanwhile, in a far more stage-managed sport where access is tightly controlled, every last Bears' utterance was duly documented at summer camp in Platteville.

"The Bears are the most overcovered team in this town," said WMVP-Radio host Les Grobstein, one of the minority of sports-talk types to regularly cover Chicago baseball games in person.

Baseball right now is like a bloodied boxer taking cheap shots without out a referee to step in. And the sport seems to have few advocates among sports-media honchos.

"It's fashionable," said WMVP-Radio reporter Bruce Levine, for fifteen years by far the most active Chicago radio reporter covering the game. "The reason why is because baseball hasn't stood up for itself."

"Baseball is down, so it's a good time to get another punch in," said the *Chicago Tribune*'s Jerome Holtzman, a Hall of Fame enshrinee who has been on the beat since 1957.

Mind you, the game deserves plenty of knocks as it is. The senseless strike, self-serving owners and union officials, boorish players, a bungled TV contract, the hyperinflation of ticket prices, and lack of a coordinated marketing plan all make easy and legitimate targets.

But often-absentee columnists and talk-show hosts seem to take special glee in trying to lead public opinion into believing baseball is dying.

Columnists showed up more often at baseball games in past years than now. The *Tribune*'s *Odds & Ins* columnist Fred Mitchell, a Gary native and present-day south suburbanite, said columnists were much more frequently in attendance in the mid-1980s when he handled the Cubs beat.

Columnists and beat writers have had to share their influence on the public with sports-talk-show hosts, benefiting from the radio industry's fastest-growing format of the 1990s.

Opinions, no matter how outlandish or misinformed, are put at a premium over inside, information-style analysis. It's "entertainment."

Thus there's little motivation for talkfest practitioners to work the clubhouses to find out the real story.

"My stance is you should make the occasional visit to the ballpark, and maybe visit the clubhouse once in awhile," said Jim Memolo, The Score's morning co-host, who grew up a Yankees fan in New York. "But it's human nature to start going soft on people. They become your friends while you're going hard on other people."

A contrasting view was offered by Homewood's Bill Motluck, a ballpark frequenter in hosting and producing *Talking Sports* for the past six years on WCGO-AM (1600) in Chicago Heights.

"I still believe that your job is to put your listeners inside the locker room or dugout," said Motluck. "Otherwise, you're no different than the listener. What new can you offer them? You're just reading the paper or watching TV like they are."

In fairness to many of the Chicago talk-show hosts, they face schedule crunches in attempts to visit baseball locker rooms. Many, like Memolo, work live studio shifts six days a week, an old radio tradition. If they have families, they have to come home sometime.

Some talk-station executives don't put a premium on baseball knowledge anyway.

Several past and present workers at The Score say top management called the studio in the middle of a show while the flow of calls centered on baseball. The management edict: Book a basketball guest, now! A writer out East was hurriedly called, and talk shifted to the NBA. But the same sources said an orgy of pro football talk would not have prompted a mid-show demand for a basketball guest.

With the talk-show hosts studio-bound, the flow of good baseball information is cut off even more with the increased dispatching of young, inexperienced reporters to cover baseball.

Most do not bother to talk to players before the game. They also act timidly after the game, particularly in a losing clubhouse.

"I think the work ethic leaves a lot to be desired," said Levine, often the first in the clubhouse each day. "Many seem to think their workday begins with the first pitch, if then."

Those who grew up with the game are out covering it. Those who offer opinions do so in hit-and-run fashion. And many who call the shots may know the way to the nearest Soldier Field skybox, but not to the Wrigley Field bleachers entrance.

Beyond the precepts of the *Times* feature, there'd be a telling truth uttered by baseball lifer Jim Riggleman, a virtual saint in a sinner's business, who still ranks as the most decent man among all the managers and coaches I've covered. If all baseball people and reporters could follow his simple advice, the game and its media conduits would be a near-paradise.

"It does not have to be an adversarial relationship," Riggleman said. "The media is an opportunity to promote your ball club. The way I put it to the Mets GM, when I interviewed for the managing job there, was: 'I look at the media not as a problem, but as an opportunity. We have free advertising every day, a chance to talk about our ball club. You could promote your players in the media.'"

Required to carry out this simple concept are talent, common sense, and passion for the game. I would sometimes find all three in short supply in a journey through baseball before and after the millennium.

TWO

Old-Time Players and Scribes

Baseball is all about truth. Yet myths comfortably coexist with black-and-white facts.

The fans always deserve the truth about their most traditional game, though they haven't always gotten it. On the other hand, they would not have fallen in love with baseball without its excess of myths.

A core of hard-bitten, almost elitist writers brought forth dollops of the truth, a heavy dose of myth, and a lot of gray-area material in between, ever since baseball became America's first mass spectator sport in the mid-nineteenth century. It was a three-way relationship—between players, writers, and readers—that worked far more often than it didn't for more than a century until exploding player salaries, burgeoning new media, rising costs, declining circulation, a thirst for profit margins, and an overemphasis on "local" coverage made serious dents in the traditional way of conveying baseball news through daily print journalism.

Indeed, where would baseball be without myths such as Babe Ruth's "called shot" in the 1932 World Series—a seeming invention by newspaper lyricist Paul Gallico? How about the standoffish Joe DiMaggio's supposed regal elegance? Even in a more cynical world, the Red Sox's Curse of the Bambino and the Cubs' Billy Goat Curse—both of which were utter nonsense—give color to the sport that simply doesn't exist in baseball's more expertly packaged athletic competitors like the NFL and NBA.

"One of the great things about baseball is that it's everyday and it's accessible," said Scott Reifert, Chicago White Sox director of communications. "It's built this myth about baseball that's existed forever. Football doesn't have it."

The long, long season has always lent itself to a kind of living passion play, full of heroes and (yes) goats, saints and sinners, good guys and bad guys, that the consuming public eats up. For the majority of baseball's existence, the primary conduits for this were writers who traveled with the teams, becoming virtually extensions of those teams. They revealed some truths, but held back a lot more, and played along with the mythmaking that developed into a cottage industry. Loyal baseball fans hung on almost every word of these writers through long decades of purple play-by-play prose that eventually yielded to quote-filled stories. It seemed like a dream existence for fans desiring to nudge up to their heroes. They could have gotten a lot closer had the knights of the keyboard taken full advantage of their inside-out vantage point in baseball for the first seven decades of the twentieth century.

You're a baseball writer? What fun it must be! The image was established eons ago and has never left. I've had attorneys and others out-earning me by tens of thousands of dollars saying they wish they could have my job, with free admission to the ballpark and up-close-and-personal access to ballplayers.

In truth, baseball writing was never as glamorous as it was made out to be. The tedium, routine, and strains of the job often outweighed its joys for those who undertook the profession. Nevertheless, the job's perceived glamour was an irresistible lure to writers for several generations and never more so than in the era when newspapers were still the country's predominant medium.

"It was the paradigm job at the paper," Reifert said. "It was the job everyone wanted."

By the mid-twentieth century, the writers were buttressed by radio broadcasts. But the broadcast play-by-play went in one ear and out the other, in one dimension. Two other dimensions were always available with the printed word, which could always be analyzed and chewed over further before the newsprint became birdcage liner.

The image of the baseball writer was as an extension of the team—real and perceived. "They were like our twenty-sixth, twenty-seventh, and twenty-eighth players," former Minnesota Twins ace Bert Blyleven said of the three beat writers who covered him in the early and mid-1970s. That image never really died long after the gulf between the scribes and the players began to grow into a chasm.

"A lot of them feel like we're paid by the team," said veteran writer Larry LaRue of the *Tacoma News Tribune*. "There hasn't been a year gone by in the last ten years where a rookie doesn't ask me if I make the (Major League player) minimum. I tell them three to four guys on the beat, pooled, might make the minimum. They're making the least they can make in the majors, and they think you're on that level."

Hal McCoy, the Major League's senior beat writer with the *Dayton Daily News*, also has heard the players' belief that the writers are on the team payroll. "You'd criticize them and they'd say, 'How can you do that? You're paid by the team.' " he said. "You'd have to correct that impression."

Several generations of La Rue's and McCoy's predecessors comported themselves as if they indeed drew paychecks from the teams they covered. The traditional baseball writer enjoyed privileges granted by both their teams and their own newspapers that few other journalists could access.

The writer—usually a man (no women, period), thirty-five or older—traveled on the team train, then plane, along with the team buses from the hotel to the ballpark, and then to the train station or airport.

"We'd hold the team bus for the writers [on getaway day]," Blyleven said. "We flew mainly commercial flights. They were with us at the airport at 5:00, 6:00 a.m. after a night game."

The traveling writer roomed in the team hotel, his luggage was handled along with that of the players, and he socialized with the players in transit and after hours. He consumed free food and liquor at the teams' expense throughout ballparks during spring training and the regular season. Such freebies, along with the convivial atmosphere of a boys' club or stag party, often wedded writers to the owners' line even into a supposedly more enlightened era.

"Most of them did side with Calvin Griffith more than the players," Blyleven said of his former, penurious (to players) owner. "He was feeding them and gave them luxury box seats for their use. The owners took care of writers. Calvin had one of the best postgame places, a bar downstairs. He made sure the writers drank as much as they wanted and ate as much as they wanted. Billy Martin hung out in the press room after the game. Some of the older, more established players went in there to talk to the writers and Calvin. But when it came down to a battle between the players and Calvin Griffith, he made it known he wanted those writers to side with him, not the players."

Management was used to doling out gifts to writers. Raised in baseball and with Bill Veeck his idol, the late Bob Logan remembered the Christmas holidays when Pat Williams, raised in baseball and with Bill Veeck as his idol, was general manager of the Chicago Bulls in the early 1970s.

"Pat handed me a one-hundred-dollar gift certificate as a 'Christmas present,'" remembered longtime Chicago sportswriter Bob "Lefty" Logan. "He seemed surprised when I handed it back, saying, 'Ed Stone and the other (beat men) took it.'

"I never regarded a seat on the team plane or bus, or a free meal, as a privilege. The paper paid for transportation and if food wasn't available in the press box, I would have gone to a concession stand."

Press-box food was free well into the 1990s before rising player salaries and other operating costs forced charges of five dollars to eight dollars per meal. Even the famed brats dipped in "secret stadium sauce," previously free and often consumed in triplicate at Milwaukee County Stadium, were only available with a full meal purchase at spanking-new Miller Park starting in 2001. And as a sign that the good old days were gone in an era of Mothers Against Drunk Driving, the open pressroom bars disappeared. Alcohol was not served or welcomed anymore in the press box, although into the mid-1990s I'd see warhorse columnist Bill Gleason quaffing something held in a paper bag.

Further examples of Williams's holiday good cheer also came to an end. The Cubs used to send out Christmas gifts to media. One December a very efficient, soft-cover black briefcase came in the mail with the Cubs logo on the side. I still use it, almost twenty years later. But the briefcase was the last of its line.

Logan's ethical stance was in the minority. A baseball writer's job in the good ol' days was akin to a ward committeeman. He was a man who received and dispensed favors, a man to whom it was vital to get close if you liked baseball.

At the newspaper, the beat writer, more often than not virtually appointed for life in the manner of a Supreme Court justice, had what was perceived to be the plum job. To his colleagues and friends he was a source of both free tickets and inside information about baseball. He could use his position to gain favors and obtain some services free. In his seminal book *The Summer of '49*, David Halberstam told of one New York writer who traded favors to get the phone company to install without charge an expensive monitoring system connected to a neighbor's apartment. This way, the writer and his wife could go out for the evening while not having to pay for a babysitter. If the writer's kids woke up, the neighbors thus would be summoned. That's child neglect in both 1949 and the twenty-first century, but a tactic one could more likely get away with in the earlier year.

The scribes all belonged to the Baseball Writers Association of America, which was begun early in the twentieth century to improve sometimes-terrible working conditions at the ballpark. Eventually, though, it morphed into a powerful, exclusionary group that seized control of voting for the Hall of Fame and postseason awards and overall media access to press boxes into the 1970s. Manning a baseball beat also meant a shot at automatic outside income for the game's "bible," *The Sporting News*, which received a subsidy from Major League Baseball.

The working conditions for the old-time writer outwardly were punishing. Garbed in tie even in hot weather, he worked spring training and then every regular-season game, 154 and then 162 games, just like the players he covered. He usually did not get off-days at home on weekends. In the off-season he was switched to football, basketball, or hockey with little rest. There was only the occasional wintertime trade or press luncheon story to write.

Despite the grind, the beat man often manned his post for fifteen, twenty-five, even forty years till he simply wore out. He had built-in breaks, though—better deadlines and few of the off-the-field stories with which his present-day counterparts must deal. Uncommon was the advance story about a trade or manager hiring before it was officially announced. In the days prior to Leo Durocher's startling appointment as Cubs manager on October 25, 1965, the Chicago daily newspapers had no advance word that the hiring was imminent, even though it had been discussed earlier in the month at the World Series.

"We didn't have the business side of the sport to write about," said John Kuenster, baseball beat man for the *Chicago Daily News* in the 1950s and 1960s, before he left to become editor of the monthly *Baseball Digest*.

"They put me on the hockey beat in the off-season," Kuenster said. "My vacation would be in December for two or three weeks. During the season, road trips were much longer, three weeks. You did that a couple of times a year. I had eight children and a wonderful wife who took care of the kids."

The same mentality to endure the travel and hardships lasted through the 1980s, when Tacoma's LaRue came onto the beat.

"A lot of the early sportswriters and to a degree us old-timers were mavericks in journalism," La Rue said. "We didn't like working in offices. We didn't like working with a sports editor or news editor looking over our shoulder."

But through his labors and time away from the family, the baseball writer of baseball's so-called golden age did not have a horrific daily deadline grind.

"Our workload was easier," Kuenster said. "You didn't have the laptops you have now. We had our typewriters. We'd punch out the story and hand it to a Western Union operator to transmit. It was a little slower process."

If he was employed by a morning paper, the beat writer simply crafted up to two versions of a game story containing play-by-play only, without quotes. Notebooks, accompanying stories, features, and other "inside-baseball" pieces by the beat writer were scarce. Through the 1960s such a style prevailed. When Roger Maris was zeroing in on sixty-one homers for the Yankees at the end of the 1961 season, veteran *New York Times* baseball man John Drebinger simply wrote the play-by-play. Maris's reaction to each game was segregated into a sidebar story by Louis Effrat. As late as June 11, 1967, a day Adolfo Phillips slugged four homers for the Cubs in a Wrigley Field doubleheader sweep of the Mets, no Phillips quotes were featured in Jerome Holtzman's game story in the *Chicago Sun-Times* the next morning. One sparse Phillips quote was featured in a short sidebar that included the reaction of his more glib teammates.

Writers for afternoon papers, such as Kuenster's, would pen a "running" story with play-by-play only for their final editions if covering a daytime game. After the game, day or night, the "PM" writer could more leisurely craft a "featurized" version of the story to hand in, in the middle of the night, for his first edition that came out late morning. Kuenster had the luxury of typing such a story on the team train or plane on getaway day, then filing it when he reached the next city.

But the story behind the story often would not be covered. Off-the-field escapades, racial and ethnic discrimination, management ineptitude, and all the other elements of baseball Babylon often were kept out of the public view. Babe Ruth's profligate off-the-field lifestyle would stock tabloid newspapers and TV along with sports-talk radio now, but in the 1920s it was soft-pedaled, if not ignored. Hence the real malady—a case of venereal disease—behind the Babe's famed 1925 "bellyache" did not make print by writers with whom the slugger had generally good relations. Ford Frick, later commissioner of baseball, was Ruth's confidant and ghost-writer as a scribe, keeping the faith for the Babe's home run record when Frick decreed an asterisk for Maris's record, accomplished in 162 games to Ruth's 154.

Despite their desire to work independently of newspaper office routine and distance themselves from day-to-day office politics, the average baseball writer was no flaming revolutionary on his beat. His publishers were more often than not conservative Republicans, rich men who did not encourage crusades. The culture of sports, particularly baseball, was more conservative and slower to change than the country at large. With the writers as virtual extensions of the team, they were not going to vary from their routine of chronologically written game stories to toss journalism bombs around.

"I knew quite a bit about their peccadilloes," Kuenster said of the players. "I didn't write that stuff. I told those guys if I saw them out after curfew, that's their business. However, if I found out you seriously broke curfew and the next day you goof up mentally on the field, I'm going to get on you really good. They understood where I was coming from. In Washington DC, I saw a White Sox player sneaking out the side door. He didn't come back till 7:00 a.m. They played a doubleheader that day, and it was hot as hell. The guy comes up to pinch hit. I'm thinking he'll get killed, he probably doesn't even see the ball. He hits a double, scored the tying run, and his tongue is hanging out."

The seminal change in baseball history, its integration by Jackie Robinson in 1947, was covered largely in down-the-middle fashion. Daily updates of Robinson's progress in spring training of '47 were duly reported, but without much hype in the one-story-a-day ration typical of newspapers of the time. Robinson's progress was confined to the sports section. Page 1 had yet to glom onto sensational sports stories to lure readership.

At a couple of points, though, the reporting drifted to the borderline of controversy. That quality could not be avoided with the breaking of the color line at hand.

"No player on this club will have anything to say about who plays or does not play on it," Dodgers president Branch Rickey was quoted by the *New York Times*'s Roscoe McGowen on March 31, 1947. "I will decide who is on it and (Leo) Durocher will decide who of those who are on it does the playing."

But then McGowen penned a forerunner of decades-later "inside" reporting with this sentence on the politically astute Rickey's actions, albeit with the turgid copy so common to baseball writing of the era: "It is pertinent to interpolate here that if the Dodger president has no concern about what his players think, why has he asked many of them how they regard the idea of the Negro star joining the club?"

When Robinson was officially purchased by Rickey from triple-A Montreal on April 10, 1947, the news did not make page 1 of the *New York Times*, the serious rock of American journalism being more concerned with issues of the world. The promotion was the lead headline on page 20. Louis Effrat's story called Robinson a "well-proportioned lad." Then Effrat reported what would dog Robinson for his debut season and years afterward—the evidence of prejudice from fellow big leaguers: "He may run into antipathy from Southerners who form about 60 percent of the league's playing strength. In fact, it is rumored that a number of Dodgers expressed themselves unhappy at the possibility of having to play with Jackie."

Robinson's actual big league debut on April 15, 1947, also was kept off page 1 of the *Times*. The advance stories that day and the

Dodger game piece on April 16 were not focused on Robinson. The play-by-play style held sway despite the earth trembling. It was left up to Arthur Daley in his *Sports of the Times* column to analyze the implications of Robinson's arrival and reveal more inside information, just at the time of another controversy—Durocher's suspension from baseball due to alleged associations with shady characters.

On April 15, Daley wrote:

> Did you notice, by the way, the deft manner in which the Deacon (Rickey) of the Dodgers brought up Robinson? He practically smuggled him in. Just as the excitement of the Durocher episode reached its apex, Rickey quietly announced that Jackie was being signed to a Dodger contract. Thus did he hope that the precedent-shattering implications of Robbie's promotion would be smothered by the publicity engendered by the Lip's suspension.
>
> It is merely an attempt to lighten the pressure on Robinson's shoulders . . . Yet nothing actually can lighten that pressure, and Robbie realizes it full well. There is no way of disguising the fact that he is not an ordinary rookie and no amount of pretense can make it otherwise.

On April 16, Robinson's debut was only the third headline in a multisegmented Daley column:

> The muscular Negro minds his own business and shrewdly makes no effort to push himself. He speaks quietly and intelligently when spoken to and already has made a strong impression. "I was nervous in the first play of my first game at Ebbets Field," he said with his ready grin, "but nothing has bothered me since."
>
> A veteran Dodger said of him, "Having Jackie on the team is still a little strange, just like anything else that's new. We just don't know how to act with him. But he'll be accepted in time. You can be sure of that. Other sports have had Negroes. Why not baseball? I'm for him, if he can win games. That's the only test I ask." And that seems to be the general opinion.

In Chicago, John Kuenster faced some similar editorial indifference as the reporting of race relations in sports lagged behind the news side of newspapers in this era as the civil rights movement got underway in earnest.

"The Sox were training in Florida," Kuenster said. "Four black players on the team had to get off a bus in the pouring rain to stay in the black neighborhood in Tampa. They had to stay in private homes. I wrote stories about the situation, but the paper buried it on page 2 and trimmed it. I was surprised at that."

Even with gatekeepers often shutting the door to controversial stories, the writers themselves acted as their own self-censors, and not just concerning accounts of after-hours high jinks. Sometimes the relationship between players and writers prior to the 1970s got amazingly close. In her 2002 book *Sandy Koufax: A Lefty's Legacy*, author Jane Leavy described how the families of Jack Lang of the *Long Island Press* and Dodgers catcher Roy Campanella babysat for one another during spring training at Dodgertown in Vero Beach, Florida. Later in Koufax's career, Leavy detailed the friendship between the left-hander and Phil Collier, Dodgers beat writer for the *San Diego Union-Tribune*. Koufax confided in Collier in the middle of the 1965 season that he would play only one more year due to his aching elbow. Collier kept the confidentiality and then was rewarded with the official scoop when Koufax finally pulled the plug on his career after the 1966 season. Koufax supposedly wanted to announce his retirement on the plane returning to Los Angeles from the 1966 World Series, but Collier dissuaded him on the grounds that it would "screw" every morning newspaper in the country. Such a dynamite scoop couldn't be sat upon for more than a year in today's media climate—and it's doubtful a player the caliber of Koufax would whisper it to a media member anyway.

When Frank Thomas (not the White Sox all-time batsman) came to the Cubs in 1960, he had dinner at Kuenster's house. "He'd get out on the street and hit fly balls to kids," Kuenster said. "Ernie Banks came over to my house when I was working on a story. It was more of a personal relationship then." Such rapport was still possible all the way up to the early 1980s.

Hal McCoy worked all sides of baseball starting in 1973, when he was placed on the Reds beat by the *Dayton Daily News*. More than three decades later, his eyesight fading due to a rare virus, McCoy soldiered on at the same beat, able to out-report and outlast colleagues despite his narrowing vision. Like a predator being able to sniff out its prey without seeing it, McCoy can sense a story at fifty paces.

He began by simply signing up almost the entire Reds clubhouse as sources. Sometimes there would be conflicts. Almost always McCoy and the players he covered enjoyed mutual respect.

"I did associate more with players," McCoy said of his early days on the beat. "I used to play tennis with them in the mornings. I traveled on the charter and spent more time with them. Still, if you're a professional, you know the line and don't cross it."

McCoy quickly fell into the cookie jar for writers—the famed Big Red Machine of the 1970s. The star-studded team was a journalist's dream with a story by every locker and master storyteller Sparky Anderson holding court in his manager's office.

"Sparky would lay out by the swimming pool and all the writers would be out there with him, every day," McCoy said. "It was the best team I ever covered. Ask Pete Rose one question and that's all you needed—he'd fill up your notebook. Joe Morgan and Johnny Bench were the same way. [Tony] Perez and [Davey] Concepcion had the [Spanish] language barrier, but they were cooperative."

Pitcher-turned-author Jim Brosnan defined such connections. "It was an older-brother relationship, and they were the older brother," he said of the writers of bygone days. "They knew more about what baseball was about than what we did—or so they thought."

"At that time the media kind of protected the players," Blyleven said. "They knew what the players were going through. They knew it wasn't an easy haul over 180 days with all the traveling. You had a closer relationship with the writers. I became friends with Sid Hartman [later the mainstay Twin Cities sports columnist]. I used to tackle Sid in the clubhouse. One day I hid his tape recorder in Boston. He was steaming in the press box. In the eighth inning, I put the tape recorder back to where it was on the table."

Brosnan, finishing his career with the White Sox in 1963, endured a rough flight to Baltimore next to a sportswriter. "We thought we'd crash," he said, so he and the writer decided to ensure a farewell drink. "I was sharing some sort of his bourbon, Virginia Gentleman or something." Brosnan also hoisted a few with legendary *Los Angeles Times* columnist Jim Murray.

Sportswriters and baseball players enjoyed closer relationships in the fifties and sixties for another reason. The wage gap between writers and players was close—and sometimes went in favor of the writer. Rookies made a six-thousand-dollar minimum salary through much of the 1960s—less than senior beat writers. Both groups of men were working stiffs.

Having seen baseball from the inside-out as a pitcher with the Cubs and Cardinals, Brosnan believed that the reticent nature of the baseball writing of the time needed supplementing. Possessed of his own literary bent, he authored *The Long Season* and *Pennant Race*, in 1959 and 1961, respectively. These were the first two books that took a realistic, honest look at big league life, sans the profanities.

"They weren't [bugging the players for quotes], but they should have," he said of the writers who covered him. "The reason why the books came out is I didn't believe what I was reading [about the daily news in baseball]."

Brosnan's books made a small impact, but nothing would change and improve baseball print journalism like effective daily media competition. The newspapers had the only daily conduit for baseball information besides live play-by-play broadcasts of games. Some changes took place from within—the *New York Daily News*'s Dick Young began regularly working the clubhouse for quotes. "He always told me, give them something no one else has," sportscaster George Grande said of his own youthful advice from Young. A group of iconoclastic New York writers, branded the "chipmunks" for one guy's toothy grin, began to ask tougher questions of players.

But increasingly sophisticated live TV coverage and game highlights on the 6:00 and 10:00 p.m. news forced sports editors to mandate their writers to follow Young's lead and start stocking game stories with quotes, while adding regular multi-item notebooks with further clubhouse and dugout comments. Some writers grumbled at the extra work. But they more loudly resisted the first incursions of tape-recorder-toting radio reporters who the writers feared would "steal" their quotes in putting them on the air soon after they were recorded.

The late Red Mottlow was one of the pioneers of recording the pre- and postgame comments of baseball figures for Chicago's WCFL-Radio, starting in 1965. Mottlow was the only day-in, day-out radio regular at Wrigley Field covering the Cubs' aborted pennant run in 1969. When the Cubs played the Mets at Shea Stadium in the ill-fated "black cat" series in September of '69, Mottlow obtained proper credentials from the Mets. But when he attempted to enter the Shea press box, Jack Lang, by then a Baseball Writers Association of America heavyweight, blocked his path. "This is *my* press box," Lang told Mottlow, reasoning that radio people did not belong in the same work quarters with writers. Mottlow was relocated nearby and got his tape, but the hidebound writers continued to object to radio's encroachment for the next two decades. They would try to force the broadcasters into inferior press-box seating while preserving instances of superior access to sources. Well into another century, the BBWAA held onto its favored position with baseball's establishment.

"It really is kind of unfair they wield that much power," said Sharon Pannozzo, media relations director of the Cubs and a twenty-three-year veteran of baseball public relations. "TV people had no say, radio people have little say. The BBWAA is the only organized group, a very powerful lobby. The broadcast people never organized themselves. The BBWAA in the early 1980s could almost prevent you from being in the press box. The BBWAA could say radio people can't sit in a certain area. It was one of those long-standing traditions that carried over, which is what a lot of things are."

Radio men weren't the only ones who found the press-box doors barred when they first tried to enter. Women made their initial attempts to cover baseball from the accustomed ballpark perch at the end of the 1960s. The traditionalists also kept them locked out, at least for another half-decade.

But while they crabbed at the new media and the other gender for trying to gain an entrée, the writers' output dramatically improved as the 1970s got underway. Competition, in the form of media that could deliver more immediate information, was good overall for the industry. The writers had to report realistically on baseball. They could tap into the same kind of clubhouse access and relationships they had long enjoyed. Despite some wear around the edges, the 1970s and most of the 1980s might be called a golden age of baseball reporting for newspapers. Some old-timers used to simply writing a play-by-play game story groused, but were forced to adapt. The reader got more for his money with the dramatic increase of daily notebooks and features, while the gap had not yet formed between multimillionaire players and media. Baseball's inside story was covered like never before, to the benefit of fans.

Many of the writers maintained their close relationships with players and managers. They still flew on the team plane and rode the team bus. Even the newly arrived radio reporters traveled with the players. The late Red Mottlow recalled that he got into a little tiff with Durocher while riding the team bus in 1972 in St. Louis.

Still, familiarity did not usually breed contempt.

"I flew with the team when I started," the *Detroit News*'s Tom Gage said of his debut season (1979) on a Tigers beat he still held down twenty-six years later. "It allowed the players to see you in a different setting. You were more relaxed and you weren't always needing something from them. They didn't look at you as someone they had to put up with. I think we got to know the players a lot better than now. They just accepted you more as a presence than you are now."

In addition to the traditional relationship with players, the writers' responsibilities expanded as the labor side of baseball began to heat up with the first strike in 1972 and the subsequent advent of arbitration and free agency. The management side of the game began to be scrutinized as never before, as all aspects of baseball began to be well documented in print. Hard on their heels were hard-working radio reporters like Mottlow, battling access issues on top of trying to snare interviews and report on the game.

Those executives who tried to hang on to the good old days of the reserve system bumped into reporters, like Hal McCoy, who always tried to report honestly. At the cusp of the 1980s, McCoy ran afoul of Reds general manager Dick Wagner, a true front-office martinet. Decades later, the two still have not spoken. But McCoy wasn't finished clashing with the brass.

McCoy chronicled the travails of the Marge Schott ownership regime, in which the frustrated widow kept the entire front office on edge. Schott figured the way to a man's heart was through his stomach.

"Marge banned me from the [Riverfront Stadium] dining room four years in a row, when meals were free," he said. "In those days we had a dining-room card. After I wrote anything critical, she'd have a PR guy come up to me, hold out his hand and say, 'You know what I want.' She banned [fellow writers] Jerry Crasnick and Rob Parker. Eric Davis and Tim Belcher sent up pizzas to me in the press box. The other writers took up a canned-goods collection and put the cans in my seat. I just bought my lunch from Subway."

The bonds of friendship were torn asunder when the gambling cloud began to engulf Rose, by then the Reds' manager, in 1989.

"After every game, the PR director would stand and monitor questions and say, 'Baseball questions only,'" McCoy recalled of Rose's media sessions. "As soon as a nongame question was asked, the interview would be over. It was the toughest year of my life. Every day I had to take the information we learned and ask Pete about it. He would deny it every day, but we still had to ask it. That cost me a pretty good friendship, because Pete and I were pretty close. It was a kill-the-messenger mentality. He looked upon me as the enemy after that."

But the contentious relationships that McCoy endured as the 1980s progressed still were the exception in baseball.

"If I pitched poorly and the next day I picked up a newspaper, then what I read was I pitched poorly," former Tigers pitcher Dan Petry said. "Somebody didn't take a shot at me. The next day, I'd run into him and say, 'How ya doin', Tom Gage?' Nobody shied away from anybody because nobody ever said something that was not true. They just reported what they saw and that's all you could ever ask of anybody."

"I sensed more collegiality when I broke in [as a Cub] in 1986," ancient Mariners lefty Jamie Moyer said in 2004. "The beat writers were on the plane. They were respecting our space. There was a professional side and a friendship side. There was a balance between the two."

Two years before Moyer came up, Cubs general manager Dallas Green invited the Chicago media to travel on the team plane to the National League Championship Series (NLCS) in San Diego. Red Mottlow, along for the ride for Chicago station WFYR-FM, recalled the treatment as "first class."

But as the 1980s drew to a close, the old system of athlete-media relationships—and the benefits the fans derived from the improvements of the previous two decades—began to break down. When the Cubs flew to San Francisco for the NLCS in 1989, the media was barred from the team plane to prevent distractions. As more TV money flowed into the game, with the first billion-dollar network contract from CBS taking effect in 1990, salaries skyrocketed. The way media began to do business also began to change with more cost controls, more sophisticated TV coverage, and the onset of sports-talk radio.

"The attitude really began to change in 1988–89, when the money really began to flow," said John Hickey, then a young baseball writer in Oakland who would move on to the *Seattle Post-Intelligencer*.

Lasting two decades in the game, Moyer can only shake his head at the contrast of the people who now want a minute of his time for one quote or a sound bite. "Now I sense the attitude of 'I gotta get in to get what I need, and I don't care how I get it or where I got it,'" he said.

Moyer made that statement with a sense of regret. The journalistic professionalism and insight to which he was first exposed at career's start would not always be matched by the people who covered the game or those who, in turn, hired them during Moyer's sunset journey in baseball.

THREE

The Baseball Beat Writer

Tongues were wagging in press boxes all over the country in mid-summer 2004. Some of that verbiage suggested that Murray Chass was almost blasphemous in the acceptance speech he had just given for the Spink Award, given annually to a veteran baseball writer during the Hall of Fame induction ceremonies.

Chass had dedicated his long *New York Times* career, in which he was recognized as one of the game's preeminent baseball writers, to searching for the truth in the game. Now he believed he spoke of the same in his own business. "I covered baseball and pro football, but there came a time when I had to choose between them," Chass told the multitudes in Cooperstown. "It was an easy choice. With games every day and news developing year-round, baseball was the more legitimate and challenging beat to cover.

"Unfortunately, too many baseball writers of recent vintage don't want to cover the beat. So many of them don't like the daily grind or don't like all the off-the-field developments that have intruded on the game on the field. I feel I [thrived] on the off-the-field part of the game. I thoroughly enjoyed [covering] nongame issues as well as nonbaseball stories, the World Series earthquake, for example, because they challenged me as a reporter and I thought of myself as a reporter who happened to cover baseball. I would encourage young baseball writers to adopt that attitude. They will be better for it."

Then Chass suggested that not all that many of his junior colleagues might heed his advice. "But the first thing they have to do is cover the beat for more than the few years, if that long, that they cover it these days. In New York, for example, the turnover has been startling. In recent years, baseball writers for the major newspapers have averaged two years or less on the beat. In many instances before they've learned much, even though they think they know everything, they want to become columnists. Then when they write columns, instead of picking their spots to criticize, they often display their ignorance, or worse, show a mean-spirited attitude toward the people they write about. Their style shows a decided lack of professionalism and that absence hurts all of us with the people we cover."

Finally, Chass decried the insular nature of many writers in not extending their scope of coverage. "There was an instance some years ago when the Yankees were on the road and one of the veteran reporters, Ross Lee of the [Newark] *Star-Ledger*, was talking to an official of the home team before a game. When he was finished, one of the other writers asked who he had been talking to. None of them knew or even recognized Bud Selig."

Hitting a lot of folks right between the eyes, Chass accurately summed up the changes—many for the worse—since he had started in the business. Instead of a lifetime, Supreme Court–like appointment, many baseball writers viewed their jobs as a way station to something better. The baseball beat, once thought of as each newspaper sports department's preeminent job, if not for the entire paper, had been greatly devalued. It was a stressful position in which an ambitious writer would put in his time until he could move up to a columnist's gig or, failing that, the easier, more choreographed beat of an NFL writer.

To be sure, baseball writing could not duplicate the conditions of the mid-twentieth century, when the position was glamorized to young journalists coming up through the ranks. The demands for copy are so much greater now. Writers must "feed the monster" with almost nonstop copy every day in-season and frequently in the fall and winter, instead of a more leisurely pace of updated game stories and very occasional off-season contributions. Athletes and baseball officials alike are less accessible and amenable to conversations. Travel is tougher, particularly in a post–9/11 era, when writers no longer can hop the team chartered plane. They are squarely on the ballplayers' schedules and itineraries without their exclusive privileges and, certainly, their salaries.

Even with the hassles of life covering baseball in the twenty-first century, aren't there thousands of worse ways to make a living? After all, isn't it glamorous to hang around some of the most famous celebrities in the country, be admitted to the ballpark free, and get to attend postseason baseball every now and then? Some writers with seniority make more than one hundred thousand dollars a year. Top scale at most unionized newspapers of size is bumping a thousand dollars a week or more. I've had attorneys who probably earned four times my pay drooling over the thought of switching jobs.

That was observing the job at face value, though. The covetous would-be writers never considered the standing-around time, the frustration, the stay-at-your-post through three-hour rain delays and eighteen-inning marathons, the inability to have much of a personal life, even during a homestand, and the brutal travel for the decreasing number of writers dispatched on road trips through the six-month season, on top of the six weeks away from home in spring training.

The answers for the skeptical baseball rooter are simpler than he'd believe. If vastly increased turnover, growing cynicism, and lack of passion envelop the beat-writer jobs, the resulting lack of continuity hurts the overall coverage of baseball. That statement is stark. Despite the explosion of newer media, the old-fashioned newspaper still remains the most unfettered conduit of information about the game.

"I have a bias," Bob Dvorchak, former Pirates beat writer for the *Pittsburgh Post-Gazette*, said of his status as a print journalist for nearly forty years. "There's no better media to cover baseball than print media. There's more space, more time. As much as we compete with broadcast, it's still the best, most complete, in-depth way to cover baseball."

An inherent cynicism drifts into baseball coverage, past and present. Some of the old-time writers were hard-bitten, two-fisted drinker types. Others toadied up to management. Yet some level of baseball knowledge and instinct, plus an overall love of the game, had to filter in to their work. Same with the best of the latter-day writers. If they stick with covering baseball, they must have started out as a fan of the game. Why else would they put up with what they do? Obviously the lack of continuity that Chass decried stems partially from the fact that the job-changers can take baseball or leave it (and often do).

Months after his speech, Chass expounded at length about his beloved business and why so many others don't share his longtime passion.

"Things started with the creation of free agency in 1976," he said at the end of 2004. "There always were off-season trades being made. But free agency made the off-seasons much busier. It demanded more time of baseball writers. Depending on how you reacted to that, the writer either liked or disliked the job.

"I enjoyed all the off-season stuff, and I was in the minority. To me, it was being a reporter. There was so much more of the games to cover. I remember in the 1981 players' strike, the [New York] *Daily News* had three baseball writers who wanted no part of [covering] the strike. They called in a labor writer, who was at a disadvantage with a lack of connections.

"It's not the preeminent [sportswriting] job anymore. That happened when other sports became big time. The NFL was not big time before TV. The NBA didn't exist sixty years ago."

Chass may be a bit cloistered as a national writer who does not have to jump on planes every other week as a harried beat writer. Down in the trenches, Drew Olson, formerly of the *Milwaukee Journal Sentinel* and former president of the Baseball Writers Association of America, summarized the reasons why the traveling baseball writer turns over every few years.

"The travel is worse," Olson said. "There are fewer day games because of TV. There are Sunday night games. There is the Internet to deal with, which creates a constant thirst for scoops and new analysis. The off-season never ends. There was a time when a lot of papers didn't even feel compelled to have an off-day story when the team wasn't playing. That isn't the case now.

"For people with families—or even a desire to lead something close to a 'normal' and balanced life, the baseball beat is very demanding."

One poster to SportsJournalists.com in 2005 summed up the stresses of baseball travel. "It's a marriage-killer," he wrote.

A diminishing number of writers hang on with multiple-decade service, but younger colleagues are not following in their wake.

"You don't see many guys with even fifteen-plus years," said the *Detroit News*'s Tom Gage, who started on the Tigers' beat in 1979. "When I was first on the beat, there were people on the beat who were there forever. It was considered a plum job."

The writer who both sticks around and does consistent good work is someone who wanted to be there from day one.

"People come into the beat not wanting to be a baseball writer," said the *Dayton Daily News*'s Hal McCoy, the game's senior traveling writer. "I grew up wanting to be a baseball writer and nothing else. I had opportunities to be a columnist, be other things. I didn't want them. I was lucky enough to get a job and keep it. Others want to do it two, three years and do something else.

"They don't have the passion and don't take the time to gain the knowledge, and don't stick around long enough to make the contacts. I can pick up a telephone and call about any general manager in baseball, and he'll take my call. You take someone on the beat two years, a lot of guys [baseball executives] say, 'Who is this guy?' And if they do take their call, they won't be forthcoming."

Even before the baseball writer knifes through the thick office politics of media and the vagabond, rootless existence required to rise in the business, he ought to have an affinity for the game. Jerome Holtzman insisted there was no cheering in the press box, but no demerits were given to starting out life as a fan, rooting from the cheap seats, and soaking up the nuances of baseball through osmosis. After all, bard-of-writers Holtzman recalled sneaking into Wrigley Field during the Great Depression to avoid the admission charge.

Larry La Rue, another two-decade veteran covering the Mariners with the *Tacoma News-Tribune*, started with a good base of interest and added on.

"It hurts that they don't learn," La Rue said of younger writers. "All of us came to this beat thinking we knew baseball. And most of us learned a lot on the beat talking to the people who played it and managed it, past, present, and future. We try to understand their game. No matter how much we know about the game, it's theirs. We're here to describe the game."

Wrigley Field was as good of a place as any to learn about baseball close-up, growing up. I did so, from every vantage point, including the $1.25 bleacher seats. Mike Klis, former Rockies beat writer and national baseball writer of the *Denver Post*, enjoyed some of the same views on youthful excursions from Oswego, Illinois, forty-five miles west of Chicago.

"I'm not sure of the percentage of ball writers who grew up ball fans," Klis said. "None of my friends was as devoted a Cubs fan as I was. I thought I was the biggest Cubs fan ever until I met you [the author] and you told me, at a moment's notice, the score of the game late in the 1966 season when Kenny Holtzman, a rookie for the last-place Cubs, beat Cy Young Award winner and soon-to-retire Sandy Koufax of the first-place Los Angeles Dodgers. That was the first game I ever saw as a seven-year-old watching a black-and-white TV."

Former sportswriter Drew Olson was not as big of a born fan as others he knew in the business. "My appreciation of the game has grown during the time I have covered it," Olson said. "There are a few hardcore 'seamheads' who are now working the beat. I'd say Tyler Kepner of the *New York Times* fits that description. As a kid, he and his family published a baseball newsletter. The job is really all he wanted to do. Others, like myself, are simply newspaper sports guys who happen to cover baseball."

But even a youthful love for the game often isn't enough to overcome the increasing negatives of writing baseball on a daily basis. Brian Hanley of the *Chicago Sun-Times* appeared to achieve his dream job in his early thirties in 1992. He and his family had owned Cubs season tickets. Hanley, whose father was a stockbroker, even owned one share of Cubs stock under the former Wrigley family ownership.

"The last stockholders meeting [to approve the sale of the team to Tribune Company in 1981], there were four hundred of us in a room downtown. Gene Siskel, who also owned stock, was two rows behind me. The four hundred of us all say no to the sale, but the lawyers came out with written proxies. The sale had been [temporarily] screwed up."

Politics of another nature marked his ascension to the Cubs beat more than a decade later.

"That was the sad part of it, going on the baseball beat, and then finding out how it burns you out pretty quickly," Hanley said. "The White Sox were good to be around, but the Cubs under [manager

Jim] Lefebvre were a disjointed team, a divided clubhouse. Lefebvre surrounded himself with those [players] who he thought could save his job. It was a miserable team to be around. After just a year, I said I'm not enjoying it. It was a grind.

"The sad part of covering baseball is you realize as much as you love the sport, you don't love the people involved. It turned me off to baseball the next couple of years."

Leaving the beat after the 1993 season, Hanley pulled a quicker hook on himself than most of his contemporaries. They usually last two to three full years before the weariness sets in. Even more so than the distasteful personalities Hanley and others claim they encounter, the grinding nature of travel through the long seasons that often causes ballplayers to pull the plugs on their careers in their thirties pushes writers away from baseball.

If a writer develops a wealth of knowledge about a particular team growing up, that fountain of information sometimes goes to waste when he follows the mandated path for advancement—moving from market to market in search of the better job. Shortcuts are taken by those who play the relationship game the best and thus don't have to perform like a military family with a different posting every year or so. But for those not as lucky, the business seems to demand such wanderings.

But the rootlessness that results is never good for anyone—writer, reader, even employer, who has stored away the moving-van company number. In the mid-1980s, then-ESPN-sportscaster George Grande summed it up best: "You move from one city to another, keep moving, and after ten years you look up and ask yourself: Where am I and where am I going?"

Susan Goldberg, executive editor of the *San Jose Mercury News*, likes what she termed "institutional knowledge." "It makes us a smarter newspaper. Every now and then, we make a hire from the outside, feeling maybe this is an excellent journalist. Having that home-team knowledge is helpful."

Even so, when their Oakland Athletics beat [since discontinued] opened up before the 2004 season, the *Mercury News* hired Chris Haft, who had a decade-long run in Cincinnati shuttling between the *Enquirer* and MLB.com. Haft had previously covered the Houston Astros. Haft, now covering the Giants, is a quality writer. Sports editors often won't look from within, however, instead tapping into the networking of the business to snare a beat writer who already has experience covering a team—even if he has to start stone cold over again when relocating.

"I think people feel they can get a bigger and better opportunity elsewhere," Goldberg said. "The only way to get that next step is to change your newspaper. Other people have been here twenty or thirty years, and have reinvented themselves. I've been here two different times. Some journalists have itchy feet."

Bottom line—when a freshly arrived writer begins covering a team, he often does not possess the historical track about how that team got to where it is. Baseball is the one sport that melds past and present. Years of management changes and the ebb and flow of good fortune determine the fate of a team. Coming in cold, no matter how skilled the reporter is as a scribe, affects the continuity of coverage for the reader. And the moving from city to city plays havoc on family life, if the writer indeed possesses one. It's a precursor to the stresses suffered when traveling with a team through the long season.

Greg Couch, columnist for the *Chicago Sun-Times*, hopped on the advancement railroad after growing up a Cubs fan in Chicago's western suburbs. He journeyed to papers in Savannah, Georgia; Wichita, Kansas; and Akron, Ohio, before pestering the *Sun-Times* to finally allow him to come home in 1997.

Couch does not believe readers lose out when an outsider comes into the market and must play catch-up ball in debriefing himself about the nuances of his adopted home's teams.

"When I was a columnist in Akron, people knew more about Cleveland sports than I did," he said. "But you try to immerse yourself. You can research things quickly. You do get up to speed, but not right away. You start providing an outsider's perspective. Give them a fresh set of eyes. You can get too much in the woods. It's okay to have an outsider's look at things."

But can a newly arrived writer really catch up on what makes a team—and a town—tick when he has to rush to catch the next plane? The original glamour angle of baseball writing was traveling with the players on the Pullman sleeper trains, sharing card games, half pints, and overall camaraderie. When airplanes replaced trains in the 1950s, travel time was cut dramatically, but the writer-player road bond continued.

"My friend Phil Collier did it twenty-five years and he went to the Hall of Fame," said Tom Krasovic, a veteran of a decade as the Padres' beat writer for the *San Diego Union-Tribune*. "His line was, 'When I did it, there was a lot less heavy lifting.' He traveled on chartered planes and the bus with the team. Travel was much better."

When airline supersaver fares and mileage points became commonplace in the 1990s, combined with some teams' reluctance to keep allowing writers such up-close-and-personal travel arrangements, the writers were on their own. They had to book their own flights and tote their own luggage from airport to hotel instead of having it delivered with the team's directly to the hotel room. Now the writers usually do not stay at the team hotel. It became more important to amass Marriott bonus points.

The on-your-own system meant harried and hurried efforts to catch the last flight out Sunday night on the road, or working on short rest to get one of the first flights out the morning of a game in another city. Not to mention extended separation from families.

"Travel shreds the home life," said Krasovic. "Guys can do it only so much. Six weeks in spring training, winter meetings, GM meetings, the postseason.

"Being single most of those years was probably an advantage. If I had had a couple of kids and a wife, it would have been a lot harder. That's the bottom line. I was married in November of 2000. My wife would prefer if there was less travel. She would prefer the Padres play 162 games in San Diego. Travel some day will knock me off the beat. When that day comes, I don't know. But I won't do it as long as Phil [Collier]."

By virtue of his longevity, Hal McCoy has endured more than any other writer.

"It's tough on family life," he said. "You need a special wife. You don't see your family growing up. Both my sons were good baseball players, but I never got to see them play. I was married twenty-two years to my first wife and to my second wife for sixteen years."

Paul Hoynes of the *Cleveland Plain Dealer* surprisingly does not mind the travel.

"My kids are twenty-six and twenty-four," he said in 2004. "It was tough. I had a great wife. I'm just lucky. My kids understood and my wife understood I liked the job. They never asked me to come off the beat."

While Tom Gage said the Detroit Tigers bar writers from flying on the team plane, the Indians still permit their presence, although it is more expensive than traveling commercial with the airline frequent flyer miles.

"After 9/11 it became tougher," Hoynes said. "You're in line and strip-searched. Planes are so crowded now. You've got to get the aisle seat. It's really changed the way you travel."

Hopping the team train or chartered plane, the present writers' forebears often typed out their stories en route. But their overall workload was much less. They might do two versions of a quoteless game story and no notes or sidebars. They quickly filed their stories on getaway days and traveled with the team rather than sweating out finishing their stories so they could catch the last commercial train or flight out of town—or rise early the next morning to do the same.

"It's a lot of work," said Michael Morrissey, former Mets beat writer for the *New York Post*. "It's not an easy job to do. Just as I can't join a construction crew and pave a highway, not everyone can carve out a notebook along with early and late 'gamers.' Over the course of the years, it wears you down. With the Internet, there's a huge amount of reading you must do. I know guys who read virtually everything that's written [about baseball daily on the Internet]. There's the sheer number of phone calls you have to make."

"Feeding the monster" means several versions of a game story, notes (sometimes revised), a match-ups box, scouting report, and a "how they score" play-by-play that ends up in small type.

"The high turnover can be attributed to the work grind," Denver's Mike Klis said. "I've said this many times: the laziest beat writer works harder than anyone else at his newspaper. The travel, the heavy off-hour workload, and small pay diminishes the quality of life to one week of winter Marriott hotel points. It's not a good life."

The beat writer cannot afford not to be at the ballpark from the moment the first player reports for the day. "In those days, it was not uncommon to get to the ballpark at five o'clock or five thirty," was the 1980s memory of covering the Oakland Athletics for John Hickey, now Mariners writer for the *Seattle Post-Intelligencer.* "I leave for the ballpark today at two o'clock."

Dayton's Hal McCoy does the work of two writers. He is so popular with west-central Ohio baseball fans that he takes over large news holes of the sports section on Saturday and Sunday. He writes a Saturday column, then fronts a forty-inch *Baseball Insider* notes column and a thirty-inch *Ask Hal* feature in which readers e-mail him questions.

"I used to do just a 'gamer' and notes each day, no columns," McCoy said. "Friday is a nightmare, with the 'gamer' and notes and all the weekend material. I write two hundred inches of copy on Friday."

Larger papers employ national writers like Chass, who write big-picture stories, focus on other teams, pen features about players in their own markets, and sometimes fill in for their beat writers. Part of the monster they must feed weekly are Sunday notes columns—McCoy thus is doing double or triple duty—first popularized by Peter Gammons in the *Boston Globe* more than two decades ago.

However, no individual national writer could be everywhere at once, covering the entire Major Leagues. So as part of the built-in clubbiness and networking in their business, they began sharing notes over the phone. With the development of the Internet, the notes became institutionalized. All the writers had access to a common file to which they had contributed.

But there were inherent drawbacks. The lack of originality and the possibility that notes items could be inaccurate, then spread throughout the country in that form, was very real.

"It's the worst thing," Chass said of the notes package. "I have not participated for years. I've never done an item in the Sunday notebook that is not original. I just don't believe in it. I would be appalled if the *Times* felt it had to run something like that in the Sunday notebook.

"Sandy Alderson, when he was president of the Oakland A's, called me one day when he was calling around the country correcting something in writers' notebooks. It had multiplied. The readers are not served. I don't know how solid the information is."

Chass said Bill Madden, a fellow multidecade veteran with the *New York Daily News*, writes his own Sunday material.

Mike Klis was another advocate of obtaining his own material, one-on-one if possible, while on the baseball beat. That's the good old days compared to his most recent assignment in the choreographed, group-interview world of the NFL.

"A few years back, *Denver Post* editors refused to allow us to reprint quotes without attribution," Klis said. "Because I thought it made me look lazy if I centered a note around a quote from another paper, I stopped using them, deciding instead to get my own national stuff from the visiting locker room." Before he moved to football, Klis used the national notes network only as a guide for ideas.

But Paul Hagen, the respected national writer for the *Philadelphia Daily News*, said that going the Chass-Madden-Klis route is not entirely practical. "I have the same concerns," Hagen said. "While I have nothing but respect for Murray, he's almost always going to have his calls returned. That's partly because he's done a good job of developing sources over the years, but, let's face it, partly because he works for the *New York Times*."

But whether they grind it out on a daily basis or write fifteen hundred words, original or borrowed, for Sunday, the new century's baseball writers must often do so in hurry-up fashion. The continual money-saving tactics of newspapers have rolled back deadlines that once easily accommodated night games, but now cause a race to the finish to file a completed, though bare-bones, story in time to make home-delivered papers. If a morning-newspaper employee has a first deadline of 10:45 to 11:00 p.m., his or her lucky stars are thanked profusely.

Bill Ballou of the *Worcester Telegram and Gazette* must file his Red Sox game stories between thirty and forty-five minutes earlier than he did in the late 1980s when he began on the beat. He does not make West Coast road trips because the stories simply would not make any edition with the three-hour time difference. Other East and Midwest newspapers have not staffed West Coast trips, costliest on their schedule, for the same impossible-deadline reason.

Baseball iconoclast Charles O. Finley may have had the right idea in concept when he pushed for night World Series games that eventually began in 1971. But with the slower pace of games dictated by network TV, young fans in the East and Midwest end up not watching the late innings on school nights. Worse yet, with these deadline-busting game times, their parents won't get a quote-filled story in their home-delivered paper the next morning.

"All the trends point toward decreased access and an unfavorable environment for the print media," said San Diego's Tom Krasovic. "During the postseason, the games start late and they take forever. Deadlines are blown because of that. Being on the West Coast does help, but the overall situation hurts. It is not better for print media compared to the 1960s and 1970s."

I can attest to this stressful situation personally. On October 14, 2003, at Wrigley Field, I was writing the story for game six of the Cubs-Marlins National League Championship Series for the *Times of Northwest Indiana*. With about an hour left before my first deadline and the Cubs' Mark Prior seemingly on cruise control in the sixth inning, I asked my seatmates from the paper if I should go for it and start the story. I had been thinking about how I would write a kind of heartfelt "Cubs make the World Series" lead for a week while they wriggled through the playoffs against the Marlins and Braves. The boys said start writing.

The prose flowed out about the curse-originating billy goat being put out to pasture, the 1969 black cat running under the Shea Stadium stands for good, and the ghosts of Lou Brock, Rafael Palmeiro, and other summarily traded homegrown Cubs no longer dragging their balls and chains through fans' psyches. I was proud of the effort. Then Steve Bartman deflected a foul ball, Dusty Baker froze at his dugout post, Alex Gonzalez booted a possible inning-ending double play grounder, and all hell broke loose. The wonderful lead—so I thought—was put on ice for the next night and, of course, never used. But with the 10:30 p.m. first deadline ticking steadily away, I had to crank like never before. The game moved faster than most other postseason affairs, yet it was a struggle to make deadline even with a skeletal, quoteless story, let alone a detailed explanation of the Bartman fiasco.

The deadline-dodging was far worse during the 2005 postseason. Assigned to cover the White Sox's run by the *Times of Northwest Indiana*, I could not file a story with postgame quotes for the newspaper's first edition, which had close to a 10:30 p.m. central time deadline. With games beginning not much before 8:00 p.m. central and dragging on through commercial breaks and other stoppages to three hours, the deadline dash was almost impossible. Usually I had to resort to a "plugger," a short filler-type story with pregame quotes, for the first edition. I was lucky to get a play-by-play game story, again without quotes, for the second edition, put to bed shortly after 11:00 p.m. The dragged-out night games of the World Series meant quotes only for an 11:30 p.m. deadline—just barely. The record-tying fourteen-inning affair in game three blew away all the deadlines except the final, around 1:30 a.m.

Wrestling the deadlines in October is the annual culmination of travel, workload, and regular-season tight deadlines that instigate burnout. Thus the concept of business as usual in deploying baseball writers must change, the sooner the better. The burden is almost too much for one individual.

To some extent, people like Leon Carter, sports editor of the *New York Daily News*, are listening. "It's a very demanding beat," Carter said. "What has worked for us is we pick certain trips and one week in spring training for our backup guys to work. After we talk to our beat guys, the substitution works. Having strong backup guys on both of the teams has worked out quite well."

Some papers give their regular writers three-day weekends off during home stands. But Detroit's Tom Gage said a diligent writer never can make up via comp time all the extra hours put in on the job, during and after the season.

The *Miami Herald* developed a unique approach to the brutal beat writer workload. The paper in essence developed a platoon system, much the same as left- and right-handed hitters sharing the same position. Clark Spencer and Kevin Baxter divvied up the Marlins' beat to each man's satisfaction.

"We decide before the season," Spencer said. "I'm the primary guy. I take one hundred games, he takes sixty-two. It's a grind.

"I always make sure we each get one West Coast trip. We make sure one guy doesn't get stuck going to Philadelphia all three times. We give it variety, some spice. I'm not going to stick him with nonglamour cities—the Cincinnatis, the Milwaukees. Kevin also does national stuff.

"If you're covering a team out of the race, by July it gets tough. I'd rather have a fresh writer than a guy who was dog-tired by the end of the year. Still, I didn't have a day off the last six weeks of 2003."

Although the two-decade veterans somehow chug along, the baseball beat is not a veterans' game anymore. The likes of Jerome Holtzman and Joe Goddard of the *Chicago Sun-Times* putting in their time on high schools before being promoted to baseball writer in their thirties have almost been relegated to another era. Now, in a trend that is not all positive when broadcast assignments are factored in, journalists just a couple of years out of college are suddenly working what used to be the penultimate job.

"I'm not an editor," former Milwaukee sportswriter Drew Olson said, "but when you're asking someone to work close to eighty hours a week for about eight months of the year and to be on the road for extended periods of time, it just makes sense that it's easier for someone just starting out—who isn't tethered by family obligations—to do that."

The appointment of twenty-four-year-old Chris Snow, who had distinguished himself in a short time in Minneapolis, as Red Sox beat writer for the *Boston Globe* was almost as much a conversation starter in the 2004–5 off-season as Murray Chass's Cooperstown speech was months earlier. And some eyes rolled when Jeff Passan penned a feature that included mention of Cubs ace Kerry Wood's clubhouse flatulence in May 2004. Passan also was just twenty-four, charged with serving much of the role of the *Kansas City Star*'s national baseball writer.

"What struck me was the gap in writers' ages," Murray Chass said. "In a number of settings I was the only older guy there. Other guys from the [New York] *Times* . . . I could be old enough to be their father."

Maybe twentysomething writers can better get through to players of the same age cohort. Certainly some who are old enough to be the players' fathers aren't relating as well as before.

"The chasm gets bigger as the money gets bigger," said Dan Shaughnessy, sports columnist for the *Boston Globe*. "I get older and they get younger. We have very little in common. I don't think they care about any of us [even the perceived more glamorous broadcasters]."

FOUR

Celebrity Players or Upstanding Role Models?

Just when you think you've seen and heard everything in baseball, something new comes into your gaggle of experiences.

Breezing past a group of reporters early in the 2004 season, Cubs catcher Michael Barrett asked us, "Do you guys need to interview me?" The answer almost always to such a question would be "yes," but I never heard a player verbalize the obvious in a daily clubhouse routine.

Months later, Barrett explained himself at length. "My personal opinion is that bad publicity is better than no publicity at all," he said. "There have been articles in the paper I haven't enjoyed. But, hey, my name is in the paper. To me, it's an honor to have your name in the paper, good or bad.

"The perfect example was in 2000. I made two errors that cost us [the Expos] the game and I was booed out of the stadium. But even in one of the worst moments of my career, it's a cool feeling to know people care about what you're going through right now. If you're honest with the fans [through the media], they realize how much of a person you are and they can relate to you, and that's what makes baseball the game it is."

An addendum to such sentiments was offered by Jeff Bagwell, longtime centerpiece of the Houston Astros, whose clubhouse could have been rated for years as one of the most media friendly. "We always looked at it as the media has a job to do and we have a job to do," Bagwell said. "We have to work together. If you appease each other I think things work out in the long run. Both sides have to handle themselves. There's a big *if* there. It has to work both ways."

Amazingly, too many players don't get it. Today's Major Leaguers give off the image of aloofness, if not outward hostility, to the phalanx of media that provide them publicity their teams otherwise could not afford to purchase.

The best-paid players are being compensated like Hollywood celebrities, and they can live their lives as such. Tinseltown stars often throw a moat around themselves. Yet part of the age-old appeal of baseball is its accessibility, both in person to fans and through the media. If the mainstays of the sport ever become as distant as the stars of the big and small screen, something is lost forever. Baseball ceases to function in its traditional mold.

For all its faults in marketing and promotion, compared to the NFL and NBA, baseball remains the most media-accessible sport. For a 7:05 p.m. game, the home and visiting clubhouses typically open at 3:35 p.m. The media is shooed out of the home locker room during batting practice at around 4:20 p.m., but additional player-manager access is possible in the dugout and field while the visiting clubhouse remains open until around 5:30 p.m. Unless occasional team meetings interfere, the home clubhouse doors swing open again at that juncture for another forty-five minutes.

It may have been said amid a tense, angry, postgame, losing clubhouse back in August 1984, but there was more than a shred of truth in the comeback that Chicago radio reporter Bruce Levine directed at several New York Mets then. "Without us, you wouldn't have jobs," Levine said. Indeed if few came out to cover big league games, the crowds would not have followed and, in turn, the cash flow enabling players to achieve instant affluence would be absent.

But with frequent turnover on newspaper baseball beats, lack of ballpark presence by the majority of radio sports-talk-show hosts, and a sizeable number of newspaper columnists, pressure to get short sound bites by radio and TV reporters, and thrown-against-the-wall information by nascent Internet blogs, players have a sharply decreasing appetite for fulfilling what seems a necessary part of their jobs. Just when technological advances enable an explosion of information to be enjoyed by the average consumer, players in the most media-accessible professional sport are increasingly keeping their distance, increasingly watching what they say and when they say it, and withdrawing some of the trust that naturally should be present.

The end result is an ill-served public, which does not receive a wholly accurate picture of a favorite sport, overeager media spoiling the working conditions for more responsible colleagues, and players who can be unfairly portrayed as overpaid, insufferable jerks.

The latter is an image that can hardly be affixed to Pirates first baseman Sean Casey, a glib man who during his long tenure with the Reds understood one important role of players.

"I realize with the media, you guys have a job to do, too," Casey said. "You guys get a paycheck, support a family, pay the bills by what you write and what you can relay to the fans, and how they perceive athletes. I try to be as cooperative as I can. You have bills to pay as I do.

"I look at it as everyone does what they're passionate about. Some people do things they're not passionate about. They just show up at work every day. I never want to forget that. My dad instilled in me that nobody is more important than anyone else. Everyone in life has a job to do. You bring great joy in what you write. You bring different emotions to people by what you write."

Dealing with the media is part of a big leaguer's job, according to longtime left-hander Jamie Moyer, who first began talking to reporters as a Cub in 1986.

"There's a certain professionalism that goes along with everybody," Moyer said. "Not just media, but players also need to give that respect back to the media. I've been on some clubs where if things go well, players are standing in front of their locker with their chests out, smiling and happy, and willing to talk to anybody. But when things go bad, they don't want to talk to the media. That's wrong. You deal with the media and be upfront. If you say you don't want to talk, you'll get together tomorrow."

Cleveland Indians left-hander C. C. Sabathia believes you get more with sugar instead of vinegar. "You want to interact with these guys," he said. "For the most part, they're going to believe what Hoynsy [*Cleveland Plain Dealer* beat writer Paul Hoynes] writes. "They're in here [locker room] so much. I think if you are a good guy, it's a great career move to do as much stuff with the media as possible."

Completing a media-friendly lineup is reliever Ray King, who made a name for himself with the St. Louis Cardinals in 2003–5 before moving on to Colorado. There's a practical business reason for good diplomatic relations with the media and fans. "You never want to burn a bridge," King said. "This game is not forever. You never know where you'll be tomorrow. All of a sudden, there might be two or three media guys who are higher up in certain places where you want to get a job or get your foot in the door."

If the hubris of the past few decades was swept clean and all could start out fresh, the odds may favor players who are of the Barrett-Bagwell-Casey-Moyer-Sabathia-King mold. But cynicism, mixed with a healthy dash of realism, might counter such positive statements. The sense of mistrust works both ways. Just listen to veteran Chicago sportscaster Tom Shaer, who cut his teeth working in tough media market Boston.

"Players make so much money, they care so little about marketing the game," Shaer said. "They've been convinced by the players union and their agents that they don't need to care. They don't give a damn about selling tickets. They don't figure there's any percentage in doing media stuff. They do media stuff if they feel like being nice.

"The majority are not good guys. The majority are either indifferent or adversarial. It didn't used to be that way. The standard in players' contracts is that they are supposed to engage in reasonable efforts to promote the sport. No one has ever, ever enforced that. I blame the owners and players."

Shaer has some basis in his criticism. During gigs with several TV stations, he had to work clubhouses, dugouts, and batting cages to snare those ever-pesky sound bites. The players are not always available at the snap of a finger from a large broadcast media outlet. Although Shaer frequently was in attendance at ballparks, in contrast to many of his contemporaries, he may not have had the extra time to "work" players one-on-one, an absolute necessity in bridging the inherent eyebrow-lifting at media intentions.

I found a different Major Leaguer than Shaer did. Toiling in clubhouses for the better part of two decades, I discovered that Bagwell's analysis was no empty platitude. Building relationships and minimizing conflicts involved arriving early each day and talking to players person-to-person, in a noninterview setting. Not every communication with a big leaguer should be a media member needing an interview. The tape recorder, camera, or notebook should be sidelined at this point. More often than not, the successful bridging of the gap was accomplished by talking to the players about themselves as individuals even away from baseball, inquiring about their families, social and civic interests, and leavening the whole discourse with a little humor—basically treating them like the normal people that they'd be if they did not possess the singular skill to play baseball at the highest possible level.

" 'Hello, how ya doing?' goes a long ways with me," former, long-time slugging outfielder Ellis Burks said in 2004. "People acknowledge your name, not just put the microphone in your face and say, 'Answer this.' I like for a person to introduce themselves to me and I do the same thing before I answer questions. I want to know who you are. That way, when I see you the other time, it will be that much easier."

Some of the most animated, even entertaining conversations have been off-the-cuff all the way up to a publicity-hating fellow like Barry Bonds. Perhaps some information would be filtered into my written or broadcast work, but the original purpose is an effort to get to know the player and let them get to know you. If the end result is access when the interview going gets tough, so be it. That's also Journalism 101, practiced by reporters in any City Hall or cop shop in the country away from sports' toy factory. Familiarity does not breed contempt if you handle yourself the right way.

That all said, anyone working in baseball media is dealing with high-profile types enjoying a radically different pay scale and potential lifestyle than anyone else in the room. With a minimum salary of three hundred thousand dollars—compared to sixty-eight thousand in the late 1980s—the players can attain affluence available only to the top 1 percent of American wage earners. Their perspective cannot be the same as it was when they were struggling through the minors on fifteen hundred dollars a month.

And when salaries skyrocket toward the twenty-million-dollar mark, the ballplayers are now on a par with Hollywood celebrities, who by nature and necessity have to cast a moat around themselves to ward off intrusive media and overzealous fans, if not outright stalkers. It is in this classification, of whether they are near or at the top of celebrity rankings, and whether instant affluence changes them for the worse, that players are divided.

Longtime catcher Todd Pratt pointed me in one direction at midsummer 2004 when he told me that money does change, and spoil, many of his fellow big leaguers. Perhaps the sweaty, straining position behind the plate gives catchers an honest appraisal of life, because Michael Barrett believes the rise in earning power has an effect. "It's a little bit of that, a little bit of perception," he said. "It's the way people put some players on a pedestal. We're just like normal people who have been blessed with an opportunity to play at a Major League level and make a substantial amount of money. With that comes a great deal of responsibility.

"A lot of players aren't equipped to handle that as well. We don't make the best decisions a lot of times. We try to be good role models . . . If you ask the average person to live our lifestyle, it would be very difficult. It's not like a guy makes $15 million, $20 million for ten years and has time to adjust to that lifestyle. If he's making $10 million, it's one year, two years. To be able to adjust to that lifestyle, you have very little time to make that adjustment. You might come across as a guy who's changed. In reality, money does change people a lot. At the same time, I don't believe when you step on that field, the amount of money has anything to do with how you play the game. On the field, you're all playing the same game."

Another plain-speaking type, almost the Harry S Truman of baseball during his time, was Rod Beck, former Giants and Cubs closer. Beck was as down-to-earth a player as I ever met during his short Chicago tenure in 1998–99. "I came into life like that," Beck said. "I was taught by my parents and every coach I had to not pull any punches. I learned to talk about it in truth. If people don't like the truth, that's their own problem. I'm one of those guys if you don't want to hear the truth, don't ask me."

A true throwback, Beck would hold court in his locker in his skivvies, beer in hand, long after games, before repairing to Bernie's, a popular bar a block northwest of Wrigley Field, to mingle with fans. While rehabbing his arm at class-A Iowa in 2003, he invited fans to join him for libations after games at his trailer in the stadium parking lot.

"I'm not sure money is the root of all evil as much as stature," Beck said. "You become a celebrity when you become a superstar. Everybody wants a piece of you.

"A lot of it is putting up a guard. They don't want to be taken down from that stature. People who achieve fame at a high level wish to keep it. It's a survival instinct kicking in. The scary part is, why can't you keep it while being honest? Wouldn't that make it more so, solidifying your stature? But for some people, that's frightening. That's their defense mechanism kicking in—everyone keep away."

Offering the contrary view was lifetime Houston Astro Craig Biggio, still as dirty-uniformed a player on the cusp of forty as he was as a young catcher in the late 1980s. "I speak for myself, whether you have two dollars in the bank or twenty dollars in the bank, you treat people the way you want to be treated," he said. "It was the way you were raised. You just remember who you are. Money might change some people but for the most part it doesn't change everybody."

Meanwhile, money was not the push to Jamie Moyer, even though he had amassed a comfortable paycheck after twenty seasons and had high overhead at home with six children to support. "I can honestly say I wasn't looking for fame and fortune," Moyer said in 2004. "I played because I love the game and still do. I see a lot of players to whom money really doesn't matter. They live lives where it doesn't affect them. Others spend frivolously. If you live within your means, great. That's your personal side. As a family man, I have responsibilities."

But the players are able to spend like few others in the country. John Hickey, Mariners beat writer for the *Seattle Post-Intelligencer*, remembered pitcher Dave Stewart cataloguing a shopping trip in the clubhouse while Hickey covered the Oakland Athletics in the 1980s.

"He pulled out the receipt," Hickey recalled. "He said what the heck did I buy for eighteen hundred dollars? Two sweaters, eight hundred dollars each. Two pairs of socks, one hundred dollars each. Who needs a pair of one-hundred-dollar socks? They've moved into a nouveau riche class. They buy a house; they don't buy their furniture at Sears. They have a craftsman make 'em."

Then comes a telling Moyer statement that automatically creates at least a little gulf: "We are entertainers and we are in the entertainment business."

You won't get an argument from Cubs ace Mark Prior. "Obviously the money's great," he said. "We understand we are entertainers. With that brings a lot of responsibility in the public realm. On the flip side is your public and private life, where people try to dig in and merge them. I try to find a happy medium, what your public responsibility is and private responsibility is. Instead of going to movies, fans come out for three hours to watch a baseball game. I don't mind entertaining. But I also know who I report to—the twenty-four other guys on the team, the manager, and the coaches."

Problem is, as "entertainers," as celebrities, the ballplayers have lost their means for privacy. And in a scary age, previous restraints that governed social civility don't exist. The media is seen as a conveyance of private information the players do not want let out.

"That's where it gets scary," Prior said. "That's where you find where standoffish people are trying to be distant with the media. In this day and age, in the world we live in, you don't know who's out there. It's not back when Babe Ruth played, [not] even the 1980s. People follow you home, want to know where you live. That's where you get scared. You don't know if they're fans or have a malicious intent. We're probably the only professional athletes where people know our schedule, when we're home and not home, and they know exactly how much we make."

Prior and fellow Cubs pitcher Kerry Wood found their privacy invaded when their home addresses became a matter of public record. Property transfers—the sale of homes—are available to the general public. Newspapers have now started regularly publishing celebrities' home purchases, sometimes with an accompanying photo. Prior's Chicago residence was listed. In addition to one fan following him home on the interstate from a game in Milwaukee, the right-hander was awakened by others calling his name outside his bedroom window at 2:00 a.m.

"Maybe one out of a thousand people know how to use that," Prior said of the property transfer process. "But you don't have to put it on the front page of the section. That's where you have a lot of trouble. That's why guys get away, try to bolt out of town, and don't live in the cities where they play."

Wood was even more blunt. "In my opinion, if it's public record and the public really wants to find out about it, let them dig it up and find it," he said. "Don't print it in the fuckin' paper you sell to millions of people. What kind of shit is that? People found their way to my house just from a photo of a restaurant right next to it."

Wood's anger was even more white-hot when the subject of Fox Sports was brought up. While he mowed down the Braves in Atlanta during two victories in the 2003 National League Division Series, the angle-hungry Fox production crew kept focusing on the reactions of Wood's wife, Sarah. Ballplayers feel they are macho enough to protect themselves, but they don't want members of their families exposed to an uncertain public.

"The first time they had Sarah on TV the whole game, I told them I didn't want her on," Wood said. "Not because I'm trying to be a dick, but it's a security issue. She gets recognized without me. She's not a public figure. I told Fox to keep her off TV. Sharon [Pannozzo, Cubs media relations director] talked to them. But they put her on TV the next game. They wanted to put me on after the game. They asked me three times. I said I wasn't going to do it. I'm not going to honor their request to talk. I gave them a chance.

"At some point I've got to look out for the safety of my family. They don't care. Was it really necessary to have a split-screen of me and my family in the postseason, or were they trying to make it a drama because she gets excited in the game? If just having a playoff baseball game on your station isn't enough, then maybe you shouldn't have playoff baseball on."

The Woods love taking their pug and Jack Russell terrier out and about, including to a Chicago neighborhood dog park called "Wiggly Field," but found it almost impossible during the 2003 NLCS. The pitcher was mobbed. They have to attend movies at 2:00 p.m. on weekdays. He also reported the couple was the object of aggressive fan adulation while out to dinner.

"At times it becomes frustrating," Wood said. "We were out for Sarah's birthday. The table across from us, they called someone on their cell phone. Fifteen minutes later, people in Cubs gear sit down and stare at us. You're eating dinner in a fishbowl.

"I want to live a normal life, but I don't have a normal job. Before I got into the big leagues, I never recognized celebrities. I would have recognized Nolan Ryan [a childhood hero], but I wouldn't have said a word to him. I would have been way too intimidated."

Even a normal-guy manager like the Twins' Ron Gardenhire finds that he's recognized more, and more is desired from him, as he moves about off the field. "Kirby Puckett, to be a normal, everyday guy, he couldn't do it," he said. "He couldn't go anywhere without someone wanting something. I've had to change the way I do things. People see me, recognize me. I'm honored, but I don't want to be disruptive in any way. It's flattering. It does changes your life. You have to make adjustments."

Seattle writer John Hickey said many players have even withdrawn from public contact on the road, instead using the ballpark as a home away from home. "Players didn't spend as much time in the clubhouse as they do now," Hickey said. "Eddie Guardado gets to the clubhouse at noon for a 7:00 p.m. game. He plays cards, talks on the phone, reads. The clubhouse becomes your home. When you're on the road, a lot of players choose to spend time in the hotel room and clubhouse. Players don't embrace the city they're in. Chicago, they'd go to the Art Institute. San Diego, to the beach. But this doesn't really happen anymore."

Given that their private lives are anything but, given such fan reaction and the prying media, the ability of players to function as role models and allow their fans to know more about them through the media is increasingly compromised. So is their ability to offer candid appraisals of their own and their teams' performances. Assuming the hero's mantle for their young fans is hard when segments of the media and public are alternately criticizing and stalking them.

The purist's definition of a role model is one's parents or teachers. Iconoclast relief pitcher Mike Marshall said in 1974 he would not sign an autograph for young fans unless they also showed him the autograph of a truly significant role model, such as a teacher.

"As far as being a role model, we shouldn't have to be," Rod Beck said just before his career ended in 2004. "But we are whether we like it or not. You shouldn't have to divulge your personal life, unless you choose to reveal it. As far as how you affect the game, things that pertain to the sports world, there is some obligation [to the fans]."

Reliever Ray King believes that players have an obligation to the fans. "The media is kind of like our bridge [to the fans]," he said. "You feel good, the fans feel good, and the media feels kind of good. You scratch my back, I'll scratch yours to where we can both make each other feel good. The more people read your articles, the better you're going to feel."

King's former Cardinals teammate Jim Edmonds agrees. "I definitely think the fans are why you're out there," Edmonds said. "It's okay for the people to understand who you are and where you're coming from. The biggest problem is that the information doesn't get out where it's supposed to be. The obligation is to get the story right, not a story just to fill the void."

Yet even if the flow of information is not cut off by more suspicious baseball celebrities, they are more guarded in their comments. Cleveland Indians outfielder Casey Blake confirmed that he and others think about what they'll say after games when the media horde is admitted. So many players and managers feel they've been burned after on- or off-the-record comments that they tend toward the bland when they open their mouths.

"I do that myself," Jeff Bagwell said. "I stay away from controversy. I always have to think about what I say—otherwise there will be problems with the media."

Jamie Moyer said that the editing process in print and broadcast skews the true meaning of what players really say. "You watch some of these shows take part of the interview out and embarrass the player," he said. "It's all looked upon as being funny. That's horrible, personally. I really try to pick and choose who I talk to and what I say, and that's unfortunate."

The Cubs rarely, if ever, give their "A" material for public consumption when being interviewed. "To be perfectly honest, I've been that way since day one," Mark Prior said. "I know what I believe and I know what I think. Not all what I think needs to be said. 'B' material? Maybe my 'C' material. They say I'm nonchalant in my press conferences. Literally every starting pitcher on this staff can write on a piece of paper the answers before they're asked. It's the same questions: 'How did you feel? If there was a certain pitch that changed the course of a game, what were you thinking with that?'"

"We're all aware things get twisted in the paper and nothing gets done about it," Kerry Wood said. "You try to be as careful as you can talking to people and give them no chance to twist anything. You've got reporters coming up the next day and asking about what you said, and it's totally opposite of what you said. You've got one reporter who printed it and ten more standing there who printed it a different way. That's what gets guys frustrated.

"Understand our jobs. You've got guys getting down on you. Obviously it would be boring if you wrote everything we said. I've been saying the same shit for five years. I mix it up every now and then, but it's mostly the same shit. It makes your job tougher than it should be, but we're guarded for a reason. It's pretty bland answers, to be honest with you."

But if players and other baseball types who grew up talking plain English weigh their words carefully, imagine the turmoil endured by Spanish-speaking players who struggle to add English as a second language. The huge influx of Latin players over the past twenty years has made media-player communication that much more difficult.

These big leaguers' audio comments often are not used by radio stations because their English is so broken or garbled. With TV, the visual element can somewhat cover the audio problems. Print reporters can try to clean up the broken English.

The majority of big league teams have invested heavily in their Caribbean development programs, so they have added English classes for their imports. Some players take to the language well, while others haven't. At least the situation is improved compared to the 1950s, when Orlando Cepeda felt almost all alone coming into the Giants system from Puerto Rico.

"It was very hard," Hall of Famer Cepeda, now a Giants instructor, said. "They didn't have too many Latin players [in the National League]. Maybe five—Tony Taylor, Roberto Clemente, Roman Mejias, Felix Mantilla, Juan Pizarro. You had to struggle to communicate.

"It was an unfair situation. Many times they [media] didn't want to know where we're coming from. It was a big difference coming from Puerto Rico to the States. The food, language, everything. It was very hard for us. Some of the coaches labeled us hothead, hot dog, lazy. We were just confused. It was tough being black and Latin in Virginia in 1955."

The situation had improved to a degree by the time Tony Pena broke in as a Pirates catcher in the 1980s. But even learning the language in shotgun fashion at the center of the action—first behind the plate, then as Kansas City Royals manager—Pena realizes the effort to communicate is sometimes a struggle. And thus media accounts of Hispanic players may not paint a true picture due to the language barrier.

"It was hard for me to put the words together," Pena said. "I have to do it every single day. You guys have a job to do like we do. I always spend time to give you as much information as I can. Still, Latin-American players have a fear to express themselves. Our culture is different. Latin-American people are very sensitive. We have a lot of pride. If we're afraid, we don't want to talk.

"We use a lot of shortcuts in our language. Try to use the same shortcut in English, it doesn't work."

Even a veteran player like outfielder Moises Alou, who grew up in a storied baseball family and attended junior college in the United States, struggles to use English correctly. "I learn a word or two every week," he said of the process continuing even after fifteen seasons in the majors.

Alou realized he would not get the same coverage in broadcast interviews because of his thick accent. "I don't [sound good], and for me as a Latin person, I totally understand that," he said. "I would like to do some TV work when I retire, but I know I won't be able to get a job on an English-speaking station because of my accent, and maybe there are some words I don't know. Spanish-language [TV] I can do if I want to."

The language barrier has caused some Hispanic players to withdraw within their ethnic group in the clubhouses, Alou said.

"There's a case of some players who don't want to learn the language," he said. "There're a lot of guys who don't want to do it. They isolate themselves hanging out with Spanish [speaking] players, listening to Spanish TV, radio, and music.

"Anyone who has been in the big leagues for awhile, if you are smart enough to play the game, you're smart enough to learn the language. They should be ashamed they don't learn the language."

The linguistics process should work only one way—media members needn't learn Spanish in their own country, both Pena and Alou agree. "I don't think you guys should learn Spanish," Pena said. "The players should make an effort to get better, to help the team." "I don't think you should make an effort to learn the language," Alou said. "You should make a better effort to understand the guy. For me, there are a lot of people who don't think I'm a nice guy because I'm moody. I'm a guy who wants to have my time, read about my horses, play cards. They misread me. Not because of the language, but overall. It makes it a little more difficult to understand the player. You should appreciate the effort a Latin player is making to do an interview."

The gulf within a gulf—Hispanic players versus the media—is worsened when only a handful of Hispanic Americans, who can more easily understand the language and culture, work in mainstream media. The Spanish-speaking writers and broadcasters have gravitated to Spanish-language media outlets. TV stations have boosted their hiring of Hispanic-surnamed on-air talent, but those reporters and anchors have tended to move over to the news side, not sports.

In any language, there are ways to narrow the gulf and minimize conflicts. Hall-of-Famer-to-be Roger Clemens, for one, learned to deal with all kinds of coverage over two decades. By his definition, his chroniclers needed to just be fair.

"The only time when I was taken aback was when it was below the belt," Clemens said. "I can deal with it, but my family doesn't want to deal with it. One hand flips the other. For me to have the privilege, wearing a uniform, I get to go to the Middle East and talk to the troops. I get to go do that to raise people's spirits.

"But yet, I know there's going to be a chance where I'm going to be unfairly judged in another way. You have to deal with the good and the bad. Things get blown out of proportion because someone didn't do their homework."

Ray King said the players and media can easily cooperate to create a semblance of trust and a relationship. "Spring training is the best time to get to know players," he said of putting down notebooks and tape recorders and just chatting informally. "You introduce yourself, get insight. If they want to interview you, they should ask in advance how much time you need. Do you need to ice down? After the game, some guys are in their own space. Some guys are ready to talk to the media right away. Some guys like to do certain things before they talk. You can get to know that person on a personal level instead of being the starting pitcher tonight."

Craig Biggio believes players need thick skins to play in the majors. King said players must accept negative news because that's simply the flow of the game. "It comes with the territory," he said. "You could go ten games without giving up anything. Next game after that you're going to lose the game. You're going to be one of the first guys to be interviewed. You've got to stand up and say, 'They beat me.' You can't get mad at the media if the headline says, 'King blew the game for Cards.' Because that's what you've done. Read it, accept it. You can't get mad. I can't fault another person because I didn't do my job."

C. C. Sabathia also understands the politics of player-media relationships. "Always try to put a positive spin on it and make things work to your advantage," Sabathia said. "You can't let a guy sitting behind a desk at a newspaper affect what you're doing on the field. It never has and never will affect me."

Basic human relationships mean a lot to Mark Prior. "My biggest thing, and it has nothing to do with baseball, is more respect," he said. "Respecting what I need to do on a given day. On the flip side, I understand the media people have a job to do, too. If they have a specific question on my performance or what I need to do, I'll talk to them or have someone come get me."

Prior's definition of media fundamentals? "You're writing the truth, writing the facts, not manipulating statements and quotes," he said. "Not being sneaky with reporting. Not eavesdropping on private conversations. Not building you up to tear you down."

The tough part is to get both players and those who need their insight to follow the guidebook to a more harmonious working life.

FIVE

Not Baseball's Golden Children

My battle plan for "working" Barry Bonds was two-fold. Considered the National League's best all-around player in 1996, but with the concept of a seventy-three-homer or even sixty-homer season still virtually science fiction, Bonds was a prime quarry for an interview for my *Diamond Gems* radio show and my weekly National League column in the *Times of Northwest Indiana*. Having developed at least a talking relationship with the normally media-averse Bonds, I figured I'd try to set him up for a future interview in the Giants' first season trip to Wrigley Field from April 18 to 21, 1996.

First, I'd pitch Bonds on the idea of the multimedia interview at a later date. I wouldn't rush him to do the interview during the April trip. Each day I'd informally converse with him without a notebook or tape recorder. Second, I figured I'd make a further impression on the moody slugger by giving his father Bobby, the Giants' hitting coach, a dub of vintage videotape from the 1981 season. The elder Bonds had finished his career with the Cubs in '81, so I had clips of the pair of two-homer games he had authored in his swan song. The video, recorded by a neighbor off an old top-loading vcr, probably wouldn't have otherwise been available to the Bonds family.

The tactic worked. Barry Bonds agreed to an interview during the Giants' other two-game stop in Chicago at midsummer. So on July 30, 1996, Bonds and I sat down in the visitors' dugout before a game. I started rolling tape on my brand-new Marantz cassette recorder.

My first question dealt with why Bonds kept a distance between himself and the media—and, in turn, the fans who might otherwise have embraced his five-tool game. I got more than I bargained for in the superstar's quirky stream of consciousness.

"I wasn't the 'Golden Child,' so I wasn't picked to be," Bonds said. "And not too many famous children of famous people are. The marketable people, the ones loved in society, are the unknown names. They're the ones who shock people by surprise.

"You check the stats. How many [famous] fathers' children have become the marketable stars, the public figures? You can't think of them, except Ken Griffey Jr., and his father [Ken, Sr.] wasn't the main guy on the Big Red Machine. Johnny Bench, Pete Rose, Joe Morgan overshadowed him.

"We of famous parents aren't the 'Golden Children.' Michael Jordan, Magic Johnson, Shaquille O'Neal, Joe Montana, Muhammad Ali, they're the unknowns. They take the world by surprise."

Bonds admitted he "rebelled" against the media. He then recounted his family connections. Godfather, Willie Mays. Cousins, Reggie Jackson and Reggie Smith.

"You're a young kid trying to make it. You're going through situations [where comments are directed at you like], 'Can you be Mr. October like your cousin?' or 'Can you be as great as your godfather?' or 'Will you ever do 30-30 like your father?'

"Then people in the media come up to you and say, 'Oh, Bobby... oops, Barry I mean.' The media never grasped Barry Bonds. That's where our misunderstanding came in, that's where the tangles came in, that's where the battle came in.

"As much as I wanted to mingle when I first started my career in the minors, when I was so accessible, they never embraced Barry Bonds. They always embraced the son of a great family. So I rebelled against them.

"That was my own mistake. But you can't tell a young child at the time he's making a mistake. You're not mature enough to understand it or see it. The only thing you want is for people to embrace you as a human being. I never was embraced by the media for what I was doing."

In a moment there were comparisons with the athletic royalty of the day. I detected a hint of an inferiority complex.

"When Michael Jordan makes a great move, it's 'Oh, Michael.' When Dennis Rodman makes a great move, it's 'Oh, Dennis.' When Barry Bonds does something, it's 'Bobby... oops, I mean Barry. He does things just like his godfather, but he hasn't been able to come through in the playoffs like his cousin Reggie yet.'

"No one's ever been able to embrace me, so I haven't been able to give them the time back," he said. "I tried to in the beginning, but now I refuse to, because I think it's their turn."

A couple of minutes later, after a few more questions, I finally stopped the tape. I had enough grist for two radio interviews, two columns, maybe even a magazine story. Bonds's train of thought astounded me. What kind of "embracing" did he need? Didn't he get more than enough acclaim and credit for his feats to cancel out any perceived naysayers?

Bonds was glib, good looking, and robotically productive. He seemed to be throwing away a possible role as baseball's spokesman, not to mention a huge supplement to his growing fortune. The ultimate role model worked a few miles away from Wrigley Field at the United Center.

So I put the question to him man-to-man while we still sat in repose in the dugout: "Why can't you be like Mike? Jordan has been decent to the media most of his career. There's millions of dollars to be made [in endorsements] if you're just nice to those who talk to you."

Bonds had no response. He looked at me impassively without even a shrug. The question seemed to wash over him like a gentle wave. The concept of being a good guy, looking interviewers squarely in the eye like Jordan, and reaching out to the fans just did not connect. You could not graft Jordan's persona onto Bonds. Yet common sense seemed to dictate that a smart guy like Bonds would grab the millions in extra income when he could. It simply made smart business sense to be a nice guy to one and all he touched.

Bonds was the most up-close-and-personal example I had encountered of standoffish, star baseball players offering up an explanation of their behavior. I had long heard of the legends of Ted Williams, spitting in the direction of the press box in the 1950s; Steve Carlton clamming up through most of his work as the best post–Sandy Koufax left-hander; Dave Kingman's borderline antisocial behavior, despite terrific acclaim in his Chicago hometown; and Albert Belle's aggressive antipathy toward media who tried to get too close to his personal space. Much more recently, left-handers such as Randy Johnson and Kenny Rogers came out of left field to accost TV camera operators they perceived as getting too close and personal.

I could never figure out why these brilliant examples of baseball prowess, obviously intelligent enough to reach a high level of performance, would intentionally trash their status as heroes, throw away surefire additional endorsement income, and wreck whatever potential they possessed to promote the very sport that provided their base livelihood.

The media itself, considered a pain in the collective posterior to many millennium-era baseball figures, was not really the provocateur for such standoffish-to-hostile behavior. In the majority of the cases the players themselves instigated their problems with the media and, in turn, ruined any chance they had to become heroes with a fandom that only wanted to embrace them.

Ah, there's that word again. If Bonds felt he wasn't "embraced" at the start of his career, he seemed to change his tune when I sat down with him one-on-one at the Giants' spring training camp in Scottsdale, Arizona, in 2002 to discuss the impact of his seventy-three-homer season. Once again, the interview was earmarked for a special *Diamond Gems* program on the slugging feat, with accompanying print-media transcription offshoots.

"All I ever wanted to do was enjoy the game like I was in Little League and your parents came out to the game," Bonds said. "Whether you did bad or good, everyone always cheered for you. It's taken me nine years in San Francisco where I was embraced by baseball, I was embraced by the media, and I was embraced by the fans. I finally had my dream come true. I finally got to enjoy playing the game of baseball. Everyone around me enjoyed it, too. It was the best feeling in the world. It took seventy-three homers to be embraced by that, but better late than never.

"I don't feel less of a person because I play baseball and I don't have a Chevy commercial or something like that. There are a lot of people who are homeless or have little in their lives, and I have an opportunity to make millions of dollars playing baseball. I have nothing to complain about."

But the good feeling engendered by the record-breaking season soon dissipated. The clouds of steroid accusations began to form in 2003. They coalesced into a storm by the off-season of 2004–5 when, among other horror stories, Bonds's own grand-jury admission of steroid use—claiming he did not know the true nature of the juice—tainted him and his accomplishments.

Any media honeymoon that existed in 2001 had long since dissipated by the time Bonds faced the press, inquiring about his reaction to the flurry of steroid stories, on February 22, 2004.

"All of you have lied," he shot back at reporters assembled at the Giants spring-training camp. "Should you have an asterisk behind your names? All of you have dirt. When your closet is clean, come clean someone else's. Right now, baseball needs to go forward. You guys need to turn the page, let us play the game. We will fix it. Don't turn it into a spectacle because you have the freedom to come into our office and snoop and make up stories."

None of the pre-Bonds, media-fan antagonists had a brush with scandal in this manner. For whatever internal psychological reasons, they simply decided to keep their distance and shut off the public from whatever special feeling fueled their talents.

Steve Carlton was the biggest name of the zipped-lip crowd in the 1970s and early 1980s. Prior to that period, nontalking athletes were not a problem, with little premium put on quotes or in-depth interviews. Ted Williams's sporadic hostility did not disrupt the game-oriented coverage of Boston writers. Besides, the Splendid Splinter could be as animated and glib as they come when in the right mood.

But as print journalism expanded into the verbal flow of the clubhouse with broadcast purveyors on their tail, the ballplayer who shunned quotes stood out like a sore thumb. His silence became an ongoing issue unto itself.

Carlton, always high-strung and edgy, was not particularly distant from the media during his early Cardinals years. But once he said the wrong thing at the wrong time, which the late announcer Harry Caray theorized was the start of his distancing himself from the public. The day after Carlton struck out nineteen Mets, but lost 4–3 on a pair of two-run Ron Swoboda homers in September 1969, Caray interviewed him on the St. Louis radio pregame show. Caray recalled he asked where one of the home-run pitches to Swoboda had entered his hitting zone. The answer, according to Caray: "It was cock-high." Without any five-second delay, the utterance went out live to ruffle the sensibilities of Middle America listening in on the Cardinals' far-flung radio network.

Spun out of St. Louis before the 1972 season by a ridiculous salary dispute begun by autocratic owner Gussie Busch, Carlton got immediate revenge with a twenty-seven-victory season for the Phillies team that won just fifty-nine overall in '72. He was still on speaking terms until he was buffeted by typical City of Brotherly Love criticism of his slump to twenty losses in 1973.

The loss of Carlton's voice robbed the public of a fascinating look at a disciplined athlete. The pitcher's training methods, such as immersing his arm in a bucket of rice, were ahead of their time. The explanation of how he could break off his biting slider was kept in the clubhouse. Carlton could not publicly express joy in how he helped lead the Phillies from bottom-feeder to contender status, and eventually to their first World Series title, as the 1970s progressed. Fans never really knew what made "Lefty" tick through the bulk of his 346 victories.

"Lefty never let anybody know what was going on his world," said former Phillies pitcher Dickie Noles. "He was a very reserved person. He kept his distance. It was almost hysterical to see a press person go over to his locker, then Lefty would come over to shoo him away."

Carlton tried to persuade the likes of Noles and other young players just coming up also to boycott the media. His already legendary status was a powerful lure for the kids to play follow the leader.

"If Lefty ain't going to talk to them, we weren't going to talk to them," Noles said.

Noles eventually began conversing with reporters as he shed his own considerable immaturity, a holdover from a troubled childhood. And Carlton began talking long after his career was over—the old "they start to say hello when it's time to say good-bye." Sure enough, Carlton got in trouble with his mouth, being rebuked for statements that at the turn of the millennium made him out to be some kind of right-wing loon.

Silence was golden to Carlton. Much more verbal was the Tigers' Kirk Gibson, who extended some of his combativeness to the media. Sometimes glib, sometimes surly, Gibson could still shoo you away long after his career was over, when he was a Detroit broadcaster.

Reporters covering Detroit had to work for their time with Gibson, a certified tough guy as a former standout Michigan State football player. The *Detroit News*'s Tom Gage, on the beat then and now, remembers Gibson grudgingly giving respect to reporters who stood up to him.

"He used to run over shortstops and second basemen, so he would also steamroll the media if he could," Gage said. "If you thought you were right, you just had to dig in and go toe-to-toe with him. There were a couple of times I did. That's something he respected."

In his distant replay, a bit mellower Gibson, who became Tigers bench coach, realizes he could have toned down his responses.

"I'm not going to say I wasn't moody or brash at times," he said. "There were times where I had situations if I had to go it over again, I'd do it differently. I am who I am. I honestly can tell you I was overwhelmed when I came out of Michigan State as the next Mickey Mantle, thanks to Sparky [Anderson's hype], going back to my hometown. A lot was expected of me."

Gibson's status as the local-boy-making-good made him the center of media attention, a status he probably could have done without.

"You could talk to me," he said. "There were games where things would happen and I'd say I don't think it's a very good time to talk. There were people who felt that was an opportunity to get something foolish out of me. Those type of people I have a problem with."

Gage seconded Gibson's notion.

"He has changed a lot," he said. "He would admit even then he was difficult. I think he finally understood we had a job to do. We weren't trying to irritate him on purpose."

Gibson said prying interviews broke up his game-preparation system. As an athlete coming up through the regimentation of big-time college football, he was a creature of habit.

"My routine started at 2:30, 3:00 p.m. in the batting cage," he said. "Once I started, I was here to do that. Some of my problems with the media were with guys who didn't respect that. People came up to me and said they had a deadline. There's an old saying, 'A lack of preparation on your part doesn't constitute an emergency on mine.'"

Gibson figured many interviewers had already made up their minds about him.

"I don't like prewritten stories where people have the context of the stories already made and they cut your comments up," he said. "I don't like people who infringe on private matters. I got burned big-time early in my career. I invited a guy out and he burned me bad. Anything pertinent to the game, fine."

Gibson also claimed he took it for his team with the media, pulling off a kind of misdirection play. "There were several times I did foolish things to put the spotlight on me so they wouldn't put it on others. I could handle it. They'd come to me instead of them. It was part of who I was as part of the team. I didn't care. I felt I was resilient enough to take it.

"I stuck up for my teammates. To this day, I don't like hit-and-run guys. Guys who come in and maybe write something controversial, then not show up."

One reporter who did show up, but still earned Gibson's rebuke, was the *Detroit Free Press*'s Mike Downey. With media still traveling on the team plane in the mid-1980s, Downey's sartorial style did not meet with Gibson's approval. The tension between the two spilled over into another century.

"Mike Downey hates me over one incident," Gibson said. "We had a dress code [on the plane]. He came on with a pair of jeans and a crappy old ugly shirt. I just confronted him and said you have to adhere to the dress code. From that day on he hated me. He should have said, 'You're right.' "

Gibson still won't get that out of Downey two decades later. In fact, he gets a response with compounded interest.

"Kirk Gibson is as insincere as Madonna saying 'Ouch!' on her wedding night [I stole that line from Joey Bishop, the last of the Rat Pack]," said Downey, most recently a *Chicago Tribune* sports columnist. "Do not believe a word Kirk Gibson says. He might even believe this completely made-up story he told you, but it's just one more example of what a rude, crude creature he was, is, and always shall be."

At least Carlton and Gibson did not get menacing in the manner of Dave Kingman and Albert Belle, two poster children for the worst kind of media relations.

Kingman threw away acclaim in his hometown of Chicago like a fisherman tosses his catch back into the water. Handsome and possessed of a good speaking voice, Kingman should have been the toast of the town when he enjoyed his best Cubs season with forty-eight homers, then the upper limit of slugging standards, in 1979. But the moody slugger wanted no part of celebrity.

In two separate interviews, in 1992 and 2004, Kingman tried to explain himself. "We're all different," he said. "We all put our pants on different, I guess. Everybody goes about their business in their own way. I probably wouldn't make too many changes if I had to go out and do it all over again. We all do our job the way we feel it's best for us.

"We all do things we enjoy doing and those [the trappings of celebrity] are things I probably wouldn't have felt comfortable with. There's other things I had more confidence in and could be comfortable with.

"Avoiding the press was the way that gave me peace away from baseball. I'm still a very private person, and that hasn't changed."

Kingman took umbrage at a humorous feature by the *Chicago Sun-Times*'s Joe Goddard in spring training 1979 that revealed he won his teammates' vote as the worst-dressed Cub. As a result, he declined most interviews throughout his dream power season.

Then, in spring training 1980, an unprovoked Kingman dumped ice water on the head of Don Friske, the beat writer for the Chicago suburban *Daily Herald*. Later in 1980, while on the disabled list, Kingman did not even attend his own T-shirt day at Wrigley Field. He reportedly was seen riding a jet-ski on Lake Michigan off Navy Pier, and he reportedly tossed a female TV producer into the lake from his boat. In 1981, after a disgusted Cubs management had traded Kingman to the Mets, he opened a short-lived ice cream parlor two miles west of Wrigley Field. The men's room was labeled "press room."

Kingman tried to top himself in 1986 after he had moved on to serve as a designated hitter for the Oakland Athletics. One day in the Oakland Coliseum press box, sportswriter Susan Fornoff opened a gift package. It contained a rat in a cage, courtesy of Kingman. Female journalists in clubhouses still were relatively new on the scene in the mid-1980s, a fact that Kingman apparently did not accept easily.

In his heart of hearts, he probably is repulsed by memories of such infantile behavior, that of a frat boy gone wild. The problem was that dealing with the media was part of his job description. And some questioned how dedicated the sometimes-clunky Kingman was to baseball. He'd rather go fishing, and often he did. Cubs manager Herman Franks recalled arriving at Wrigley Field to find Kingman asleep in the trainer's room. He had awoken before dawn to fish on the lake and needed to service his sleep deficit.

In dealing with any media, Kingman seemed to trust broadcasters a smidgeon more than writers.

"Sportscasters on radio and TV can tell it like it is," he said then. "They have no way of misinterpreting or inserting their feelings into their report. When they ask you a question, the public can make up its own mind.

"In print, a writer will interpret his feelings toward an individual. Sometimes it's unjust and unfair. The reader at times comes away with a tainted feeling toward an athlete. I wasn't out there trying to be in a popularity contest.

"I feel if you have a bad game between the white lines, you have a right to be criticized. If you lose a game, drop a last-inning fly ball, that's their option. I don't think sportswriters should get carried away with what happens outside the white lines."

Kingman claimed he actually respected some scribes during our 1992 interview.

"There are quite a few writers who I respect and enjoy reading and who have become close friends," he said. "But there are many, many bad writers out there who will write their columns, never venture into the clubhouse, and never make the effort to really get to know somebody before they write their articles. These are the people I don't have any time for."

At least Kingman was consistent from his high school days in the mid-1960s. Bob Frisk, then sports editor of the *Daily Herald*, described the youthful Kingman as "different," performing in front of an involved father whose schedule as a United Airlines executive permitted him to attend a lot of Kingman's baseball and basketball games.

"Dave never gave us any problems," said Frisk, now assistant managing editor at his paper. "Most of these high school athletes are so anxious to talk to media. At that age, they jump at the chance to see the media. I never had the idea that Dave really cared one way or another. He was kind of aloof. You usually don't see that in a high school kid."

Years later, at his Cubs peak, Lloyd Meyer, Kingman's American Legion coach, witnessed two moods of Kingman at different games at Wrigley Field.

"The first game, he comes into the dugout, and I reach around the corner, holler at him," Meyer said. "You knew he recognized my voice. He would not look up. I must have stood around for five minutes before he turned around and said, 'Hi.' At another game he asked me, 'Where have you been all season?' It was like Jekyll and Hyde. I've never tried to figure him out. I like him. I've had bad kids, and Dave was not a bad person."

Imagine what Downey would have thought of Albert Belle had he covered him as often as he did Gibson. Downey wouldn't have been able to crack a joke. Belle was the scariest right-handed hitter in baseball through much of the 1990s—and also the scariest Major Leaguer for media, public relations people, teammates, and even innocent fans to deal with.

By the time I crossed paths with Belle, his persona was so touchy that any reporter steered as far away as possible from his presence. About 9:50 a.m. one Sunday in 1998 at then new Comiskey Park, I arrived early to interview another White Sox player for a feature. Few players had arrived yet. Spying Belle by his locker, I stood as distant as clubhouse dimensions permitted. A TV set on the other side of the clubhouse was tuned to ESPN's *The Sports Reporters*, hosted by Dick Schaap. Somehow Belle had rabbit ears at this distance. He strode quickly across the room, changed channels, and pronounced to no one in particular, "We don't need this shit."

By then Belle had dished out much of the same to so many who had crossed his path, and crossed him. Almost a baseball scientist, a hitter passionate about his talent and naturally intelligent, Belle started drifting off-kilter early in his career with the Cleveland Indians and just got worse with each passing year.

"He was a strange dude," said longtime beat writer Paul Hoynes of the *Cleveland Plain Dealer*. "When he first came up, there were times you could talk to him. He could charm the birds off a tree. He was a great guy. He was good to talk to, with good points of view, points of view you didn't expect. But there were times he was an SOB."

Those times seemed to increase tenfold as the Indians revived from their daffy Major League days of the late 1980s to become an American League powerhouse by 1994.

Belle became baseball's bad boy with constant incidents. He corked his bat in 1994. Teammate Jason Grimsley heisted the incriminating evidence from the umpires' room at new Comiskey Park by crawling through a hole in the false ceiling. Belle verbally accosted NBC's Hannah Storm and other media members who got too close to him. Camera operators were menaced by him in tunnels leading from the field to the clubhouse. He used his own vehicle to chase some Halloween trick-or-treaters who got too mischievous with him. Teammates complained that he turned the clubhouse thermostat down to near meat-locker levels; and he rolled-blocked the Brewers' Fernando Vina at second base at old County Stadium in Milwaukee, touching off some bad blood between the Brewers and Indians.

"He was the worst guy I ever covered, just a pain in the ass," Hoynes said. "I think he was a little crazy, but I also think there was some calculation behind every move he made. He intimidated people, he tried to bully people. The people he did that to were those with no recourse—clubbies, clubhouse managers—just to get off on it. He would try to get rises from people for on reason.

"But if you stood up to him, if you told him to stick a thumb in his ear, he was okay with it. He just liked scaring people. After games, he would make it a point to sit in front of his locker, face the reporters, and glower at them. He'd dare you to go up and talk to him, and then he'd tell you to go fuck off."

Indians media relations chief Bart Swain became Belle's long-suffering handler, if you could call him that.

"For years I tried to get through to him," Swain said. "Every time he would try to improve his image, he would shoot himself in the foot. An example is when he came up with a candy bar and didn't show up for his press conference.

"He would use intimidation with media and people he considered beneath him. I've never met anyone like him and I've never had a bigger challenge. The challenge wasn't to get him to talk, the challenge was to keep him out of the news."

Swain sweated it out that Belle wouldn't be in the police blotter with the Indians defending lawsuits as a result of his actions.

"I had to make sure he didn't throw a ball at a photographer or push a writer," he said. "I've had incidents at old Cleveland Stadium from local TV cameramen he would cross paths with in the tunnel to the clubhouse. He slammed them against the wall. There were no witnesses, so he knew he could get away with it."

Belle wrecked a potentially glittering image of a baseball mastermind.

"He was a big student of the game," Swain said. "He charted every at bat on index cards. He was very intelligent and smart. But he was so intense with his pregame rituals. He was a slave to his routine and you couldn't approach him then. He was so much into his preparation that it affected what he did."

Swain had enough when Belle threatened Storm during the 1995 World Series. "He blamed me for having media in the dugout in the World Series," Swain said. "Media in the dugout in the World Series? Imagine that! After that World Series, we pretty much knew he wasn't coming back. He hasn't talked with me since he was fined in 1996 spring training, which we paid for."

Belle helped drag down the entire Indians' image, which is a cause for regret for Swain since Cleveland should have been one of baseball's feel-good stories at a time of horrific labor strife.

"In 1994–96, the image of our club was poor," he said. "After he left, the image began to improve as Jim Thome rose to the forefront. Jim became a popular player, the most accessible guy on the team."

Making life even more difficult for Hoynes and his colleagues were the likes of Eddie Murray and Kenny Lofton.

"Eddie just didn't like dealing with the media, but was nice about it," Swain said. "I noticed that Kenny liked talking about anything but baseball. And his locker was next to Albert's. When he didn't talk, everyone went to Kenny. Other than Albert, I enjoyed being around these guys."

"It was a tough clubhouse in 1995," Hoynes said. "Dennis Martinez, Orel Hershiser, Eddie Murray, Lofton, Albert. Orel was at one end. He was working it. Dennis Martinez was worth a story a day. He was always pissed off at somebody. Once Albert left, it was like the whole clubhouse breathed a sigh of relief. It was always Albert Belle and the Cleveland Indians. They were compared to the Oakland Raiders and he was the Darth Vader of baseball.

"It kind of took the appeal of the club away. It should have been the best baseball story in a decade after the Indians had forty years of doing nothing."

Belle moved on to the White Sox for the 1997 season. Amazingly he began to open up ever so slightly for the traveling beat writers.

One night the *Chicago Sun-Times*'s Joe Goddard had a voice-mail message in his hotel room. Belle had called him, desiring to talk. Sure enough, the pair conversed. At other times Belle chatted in groups. But the master batsman was the last guy the Sox needed to play catch-up ball in their public-relations battle with the crosstown Cubs.

Belle faded from view after a few more injury-plagued seasons in Baltimore. He simply threw away a good thing.

"He wouldn't open himself up to the media and public," Swain said. "He could have owned Cleveland. His leaving Cleveland was met with so much disdain because he never opened himself to the public."

Somehow Milton Bradley took over where Belle left off in Cleveland. A talented but emotional outfielder, Bradley wore out his welcome at Jacobs Field in 2004. He landed with the Dodgers in midseason 2004. The change of scenery at first seemed to help.

"When he was acquired from Cleveland, Milton already had some history," then Dodgers bench coach Jim Riggleman said. "He had problems with the manager. But he was a pretty good citizen for us. He was not a problem in the clubhouse and got along with his teammates."

Bradley was susceptible to fits of anger, though. He threw a bag of baseballs onto the field after an ejection and was suspended for four games. "We made the point with him that we need you on the field," Riggleman said. "We handled it very professionally and privately."

But during a late-season game against Colorado at Dodger Stadium, Bradley fought fire with fire after a fan threw a plastic bottle at him shortly after he made an error that permitted two runs to score. Bradley took the bottle and slammed it into the first row of stands down the right-field line, just missing a fan, then went wild on the field before being shooed into the clubhouse.

"That was so flagrant that Trace [Dodgers manager Jim Tracy] had a long talk with him and said you need to get some help," Riggleman recalled. "This is something that's beyond our expertise. There were a lot of conversations privately with Trace to keep him on board." Bradley soon apologized for the bottle incident and said he would seek help with anger management.

But the outfielder kept compounding his problems after he returned from the suspension over the bottle incident for the Dodgers-Cardinals National League Division Series. After an off-day workout at Busch Stadium in St. Louis, Bradley talked to the media, including *Los Angeles Times* beat writer Jason Reid. Cardinals fans had booed Bradley in game one of the series, so Reid asked Bradley about the catcalls.

Irritated again, Bradley called Reid, who also was African American, an "Uncle Tom." "You're a sellout." Angered, Reid began yelling at Bradley.

A Fox Sports Net TV crew recorded the incident. But they caved in—without calling their office—and erased the tape upon the demand of Dodgers public relations official John Olguin.

Bradley later told Los Angeles KCBS-TV that Reid kept pushing on him.

"He was just one of those guys who wants to keep harping on it," Bradley claimed. "I told him what I felt about the situation and I told him how I felt about how he was choosing to handle it." Reid, he added, "took offense to that and . . . started getting physical with me." The player claimed he began walking away "to leave the situation alone."

Riggleman sided with Reid.

"He just said the magic words to Jason," he said. "Jason was infuriated and was coming after him. To me it was over the edge. He's telling Jason he should [as a writer] be taking better care of him.

"I think Milton had just fair relations with the media in L.A. T. J. Simers [*Los Angeles Times* columnist] was very sarcastic at the start, but by the end of the season was getting along with him."

Bradley had more problems in L.A. in 2005, verbally tussling with second baseman Jeff Kent. His Dodger Stadium tenure was mercifully ended with a trade to lower-key Oakland late in 2005.

Project ahead ten years. How many fans will have fond memories of Milton Bradley? Perhaps he'll mellow in the manner of Kingman and Gibson. Kingman has attended a number of midwinter Cubs Conventions since 1992, willingly signing hundreds of autographs, posing for fans' photos and, yes, even doing interviews. Gibson was part of manager Alan Trammell's staff in the Herculean effort to revive the Tigers; hey, don't all coaches this side of Rod Carew chew the fat with media? Gibby was quite animated when I spoke to him in Trammell's office for half an hour in 2004.

But sometimes the old defiance shows through. Gibson declined to chat about another subject in 2005. Bonds has said he'd simply like to go off to a remote island and disappear after his career. Few have heard from Belle or even want to after he called it quits.

The fans lose out due to their silence or petulance. In the end, baseball's non–golden children have lost even more.

SIX

LaTroy and Carl as Jekyll and Hyde

When they're at the apogee of their verbal skills, LaTroy Hawkins and Carl Everett could be among baseball's leaders in the lively art of conversation.

But that high point is unpredictable in the lives of these two emotional big leaguers who played on opposite sides of Chicago during 2004 and 2005, before Hawkins was traded from the Cubs to the San Francisco Giants and while Everett served as an outfielder and designated hitter for the White Sox. You could sit down and debate in long form the issues of the world with Hawkins and Everett. Or they could dismiss you just as easily.

Both veterans of highly charged confrontations with umpires, Hawkins and Everett sat down separately in midsummer 2004 to describe what makes them turn on and off their accessibility to the media and, in turn, the baseball consuming public.

What emerged from the jawboning sessions are players thrust into celebrity status who want none of the trappings of the same. Hawkins and Everett may be more sharp-edged in their public relations stance than most of their fellow Major Leaguers. But their explanations show a basic tenet: Athletes in many cases simply desire to play their favorite sports, but not to have to deal with all the ancillary duties that come with their new-found high profiles.

Hawkins and Everett also reveal a misunderstanding of the working style and motivations of the media that is prevalent among athletes. It's regrettable that they've sometimes thrown up barriers between themselves and the media. Yet their words, tinged with suspicion, can enlighten those baseball officials who truly care that their highly paid charges properly represent their teams and their sport.

Hawkins beat me to the Wrigley Field dugout at 3:00 p.m. one day, four hours before game time. I sent word into the still-closed Cubs clubhouse that I had arrived, then ran around to the bench. Hawkins already was sitting there. "I'm a punctual man," he explained.

Eight miles south, Everett declined to talk pregame, as was his custom upon arrival for his second tour of duty with the White Sox. He would moderate that stance in 2005—and got himself in trouble for controversial comments on social issues as a result of his expanded access. For our chat, we finally decided on an emptying U.S. Cellular Field locker room after a rare Saturday day game. As the last of his teammates filed out of the locker room to enjoy an uncommon night on the town, Everett sat down and held court without the hint of a two-minute offense to wrap up the conversation. He had been described as a good one-on-one talker by those who knew him during his Houston Astros days. But his tenures in big markets like New York and Boston were something entirely different.

I wondered why each man couldn't bottle such peaceful moments. Hawkins was described by a fellow Cub as a "great teammate." Despite a string of controversies dating back to his Mets days, Everett always is gainfully employed due to his switch-hitting skills.

The same question I had posed to Barry Bonds in 1996 was put to Everett. If you're like Michael Jordan, who was decent to the media with a pleasing public image much of his career, you'd make so much more money, right?

"Be like Mike?" Everett answered a question with a question. "Money doesn't float everybody's boat. You have your greedy players who want that attention.

"The people that are in contact with me know me. The rest of it, it doesn't matter to me. A lot of other guys who want that media attention can't go to the mall. I want to go outside and have people leave me alone. My deal is I have the right to say no. If I don't want to sign your autograph, I'm not going to sign it. That's what people don't understand.

"I've got a skill you don't have. Don't try to punish me because you can't do it. My time right now, I want to myself, I'm not giving it to you. When I leave here, I don't have to answer to nobody. I'm not a ballplayer once I leave this ballpark. I'm only a ballplayer at the ballpark. When I leave here, I'm a human being. When I leave this game, I don't care if you remember me or not. Those guys I compete against, they know who I am. I socialize with my small group. I don't care what they [the public] think about it."

Both men feel they're honest to a fault, a quality not possessed by other players.

"I'm not a politician," Hawkins said. "We have enough politicians in the game. Believe me, we have enough. We have enough people who candy-coat everything they say, make it look hunky-dory when things aren't hunky-dory. I don't want to be one of those people."

Everett never has applied sugar where he ended up using vinegar. In a 2005 magazine interview, he took a religious fundamentalist stance, criticizing gay lifestyles while proclaiming that dinosaurs could not have existed, since they were not mentioned in the Bible.

"Guys are always worried about their image," Everett said. "Then they say things they shouldn't say. Then they end up having to eat their words. I've seen guys say things they shouldn't have said to the media, that they should have only said to their teammates, and know their teammates are saying, 'I don't really want to play with this guy, because he doesn't want me as a teammate.' A lot of guys they say are great guys, they're terrible guys. The majority of guys they say are bad guys are awesome guys, guys you want to hang with."

Oddly enough, the kind of imagery Everett offered about the ballplayer possessing a skill beyond the media person's capability ended up being chewed over in print and on TV and radio when Hawkins uttered something similar during a bizarre June 7, 2004, Wrigley Field news conference. On that day, Hawkins tried to sum himself up when he was anointed Cubs closer after incumbent Joe Borowski went down with a shoulder injury. The unusual train of thought permanently damaged Hawkins's relations with Chicago media while ending up as grist for sports talk-show and column satire. Much the same as Everett's past style, it was a textbook example of how not to handle yourself in public.

"I can do what you do," Hawkins told the assembled, and astonished, media. "You can't do what I do."

In the same breath, Hawkins announced he would not talk to the media anymore—later amended to selective comments at his own discretion.

"That's why I did this," he said at the press conference. "I'm completely done. Don't hover around my locker. I'm not going to be the guy to talk every day like Joe [Borowski]. I just want to do my job and go home."

Then Hawkins seemed to expect a response from the gathered media. "All right?" he said. "I can't hear you. All right?"

No one answered Hawkins. The press conference ended. Hawkins exited stage left. Weeks later, he had calmed down when we chatted in the dugout.

"I talk when I feel like talking," he said. "The more you talk to the media, the more chance you have to be taken out of context. They switch little words around and make it seem like you're happy, make it seem totally in a different way than you said it.

"I'm my own person. I handle things totally different than a lot of other people. It was the way I was raised. I pretty much am similar to my mom in a lot of the ways she handled things. She was reserved, but she said what was on her mind. Good or bad, she was going to say it. But she said she doesn't bother anybody. I'm the same way. I don't bother nobody. I don't want you bothering me. Just let me do my job and let me go home to my family."

Hawkins, a native of Gary, Indiana, came home when he signed with the Cubs, who play thirty-five miles up the road. He knew he'd jumped up far in class from middle-market Minneapolis–St. Paul to world-class Chicago. But he did not want to shout for joy when he saved his first game as a Cub earlier in 2004, claiming he would call those friends and relatives who needed to know rather than sit for an interview.

"You've got to take the good with the bad as a celebrity," he said. "I don't want to be a celebrity. But I have to come to the conclusion that since I came to Chicago I'm sorta, kind of, am a celebrity. I don't like it. It doesn't matter what position you are with the Cubs, you're a Cub. In Minnesota, you can hover up under the radar. Here you can't hover up under the radar. Everything you do is above the radar. That comes with the territory. I'm slowly learning to deal with it."

Ballplayers cannot deny they are celebrities, Everett said.

"That's what we are," he said. "We are entertainers. We entertain our audience. We have skills others don't have. That's another thing fans don't understand. You don't boo guys who can't play, because they're not going to do anything anyway. If a movie sucks, you don't see it. If a player sucks, you don't see him. If a guy can't play, don't pay him no mind."

But whether they play in Chicago, Boston, or smaller markets such as Tampa Bay or Kansas City, players like Hawkins and Everett will end up with unwelcome notoriety, leading off the highlights on *SportsCenter*, should they stumble into controversy.

Everett's career was perhaps the most stormy of any active big leaguer. A calm, measured man during our interview, his temper has gotten the best of him too many times.

His two children were temporarily removed from his custody, amid charges of child abuse, while he was a Met in 1994. Everett engaged in shouting matches with triple-A manager Sal Rende, Red Sox manager Jimy Williams, and pitching coach Joe Kerrigan, Red Sox teammate Darren Lewis, and *Boston Globe* columnist Dan Shaughnessy. He went into the stands after fans once and got upset on a commercial plane flight.

Everett was lucky he didn't draw long suspensions after run-ins with umpires. He made an obscene gesture at Larry Poncino. His most famous duel was with Ron Kulpa in 2000. Kulpa accused Everett's foot of being illegally outside the batter's box. Everett appeared to head-butt Kulpa. A year later, Mariners pitcher Jamie Moyer also complained of the positioning of Everett's feet in the batter's box. Moyer hit Everett with a pitch, prompting the outfielder to holler at Moyer and point twice to the Fenway Park bleachers. Two at bats later, Everett homered off Moyer. As he rounded the bases, Everett grabbed his crotch and spit in the direction of the mound.

The incidents are a matter of public record that Everett cannot deny. That said, he insists he was inflamed even further by what he claims is the only "unfair" media market in which he has played.

"It's unfair for the entire team for what that particular media is trying to do," Everett said. "They don't want that team to win. They always want a division in the clubhouse. I didn't talk to the media, but I had quotes every day. They made them up. Nobody cares when it's a guy they're trying to bring down."

Life has been calmer for Everett once Red Sox GM Dan Duquette dispatched him from Boston, the most intense media town in the majors. He was rightly roasted for his actions. No doubt he has matured since then, helped out by the spotlight being off him in such low-key media markets as Chicago's South Side with the White Sox, Dallas–Fort Worth, and Montreal. But he still has a hard line toward those who cover him.

"People would not buy the paper if they just wrote what went on in the game," he said. "You guys come in here, ask a question to a guy who hit a home run. What were you thinking when you were at the plate? Well, same thing I'm always thinking. I was trying to make solid contact.

"Criticism is different than lying. No one has to explain if you've messed up in a game. This game is tough. Someone who hasn't played can't be critical in that area [hitting fundamentals] because they have no idea what they're talking about. Guys go into a slump because of that or that, how would you know? You never played, you never swung a bat, you never faced a ninety-five-mile-per-hour fastball."

Hawkins was far more low-key until the afternoon of July 21, 2004. Only minutes after serving up two ninth-inning Cardinals homers, including Albert Pujols's third of the game and twenty-sixth this season, Hawkins began jawing with plate umpire Tim Tschida over two disputed pitches that were called inside. The conversation got more heated, so Hawkins was ejected. The reliever started to lunge at Tschida while Cubs manager Dusty Baker tried to hold him back. Baker was not successful. Four of Baker's coaches joined in and barely prevented the straining Hawkins from getting to Tschida. The five-on-one struggle was a draw for a few seconds before Hawkins finally was wrestled back to the dugout and into the clubhouse runway.

Hawkins had no media boycott afterward. He calmly described what he believed was an affront from Tschida from an August 16, 2002, incident at the Metrodome, when the umpire supposedly told Hawkins to move his bullpen chair into foul territory.

"He doesn't like me, plain and simple," Hawkins said at the time. "I didn't curse at him or nothing. He threw me out of the game."

Hawkins said his blowup had nothing to do with being charged with the loss after serving up the homers to Pujols with a man on and to Reggie Sanders in the three-run Cardinals inning.

"The damage was already done," he said. "They hit two home runs. Fine. I've always said you can hit me and beat me. I've got no problem with that. Not when I was throwing the ball, two pitches down the middle."

Tschida denied holding a grudge against Hawkins.

"I would say his imagination is a little fertile," Tschida said.

Hawkins should have been able to fight through such negatives. He wanted to sign with the Cubs, for whom he rooted growing up in Gary. He took a salary concession to come to Wrigley Field. But Hawkins almost proved that you cannot come home again in 2004.

"Coming home to play definitely was one of those moments in my life that I'm very proud of," he said. "My family was very excited about it. I grew up a Cubs fan. Being a fan, I've been through all the ups and downs with the players and organization."

But Hawkins did not like the questions posed during his introductory press conference as a Cub.

"When I got here, the first day I came into controversy," he said. "Me coming over here as a setup man and [Joe] Borowski was the closer. Word got out that I had in my contract [additional] money for games finished. The first question they asked in the news conference was about me coming to be the closer and taking Joe Borowski's job.

"I told them I'm not coming to take the closer's job, I'm coming here to set up Joe and help the team win, to make Borowski's job easier. I felt from day one they were trying to drive a wedge between Borowski and myself, and we were determined not to let that happen. They kept trying, and it got to the point where I thought I should tell them how I thought about them, period. Because they were wrong, totally wrong, in what they were trying to do. What they were trying to do was sell newspapers.

"That was the straw that broke the camel's back, from the start. They kept prying at it. It was total disrespect to Joe. He was trying to pitch through the pain."

Hawkins's homecoming truly turned nightmarish down the 2004 stretch. Up two games in the loss column with nine games to go in the National League's wild-card race, the Cubs simply stopped hitting, losing seven of those games and being eliminated from the postseason on the next to last day of the season. Hawkins compounded the misery by blowing saves in two of the losses, to the Mets and Reds. Immediately after the season, in an analysis of the roster, *Chicago Tribune* beat writer Paul Sullivan, never a Hawkins favorite, termed the reliever a "serial clubhouse killer."

Hawkins, though, already had taken shots at those he deemed irresponsible.

"Some guys are just lowdown, dirty snakes-in-the-grass," he said. "They're never writing things that pertain to baseball or good things about the team. They're always looking for the negative things. You see guys every day, you have to figure they'd write something positive about somebody. Or something that's true. You can't always write bad stuff.

"I'm a good judge of character. I do a lot of observing. I go out to the places people go and I people-watch. I check out my surroundings, I observe people."

Hawkins apparently did not do a good enough job observing media covering him. Only a minority were out to do any character assassination. But his suspicious nature got the best of him when he decided to zip his lips the majority of media-access time.

Despite his stormy Boston past, Everett had a slightly more moderate view of the media. However, his definition of "fair" might be different than those who cover him.

"All media aren't bad, all aren't out to write a bad story and make a name for themselves," Everett said. "My thing is I'll talk to anyone who is fair. Once you lie, once you make something up, I have nothing to talk to you about. That's all the Boston media has ever done.

"The media doesn't stop my performance. A lot of stuff about athletes and entertainers is made up. We as a public society have always been brainwashed [by media]. We believe everything we read and everything we see."

Hawkins's claim that he could do the reporters' job, but they couldn't pitch, was based on a Web site to which he occasionally contributed. Oddly enough, he said he might work the same way the reporters he criticized did if he could put himself in their shoes.

"If I was in your guys' position," he said, "and I had a boss and deadlines and what the people want to hear about, I'd be like 50 percent of all of you—screw the players. Everybody's under orders, everyone has a boss, unless you own your own company.

"I got a job to do. They're [the media] not going to pay my salary. But you have to know there are repercussions. You might not get the access to all the other guys in the clubhouse. You've got to take the good with the bad. You all got a job to do. Remember, if you never say anything positive, it will be tough to get interviews, very tough."

Everett does not necessarily believe the theory that without the media he would not have the high profile and affluence he enjoys.

"It works both ways," he said. "Without us, they wouldn't have their jobs. When you talk about needing each other, you may need each other to a degree. At the same time, Manny Ramirez never talks to the media. Manny's one of the top players in the game. His performance on the field continues to get him a job. He's shown the world, 'I don't need you, I can play.'"

But the media isn't going away anytime soon. Hawkins realizes that fact. Any good image he enjoys with the fans is media driven.

"They [media] play a big role," he said. "People read the papers, they listen to the radio. They don't know you personally, so they go by what they read. They may have a misconception of you way off the charts. Or they can wait till they meet you. Usually they go by what the media writes about you."

Understanding that fact is the first step. But achieving peace and harmony for 162 games often is a challenge for Hawkins, Everett, and other wary types akin to making the jump from triple-A to the Major Leagues.

SEVEN

A Lot Less Chewin' the Fat with Managers

The manager's office was the last cracker-barrel outpost in baseball. Now the cracker barrels are going the way of the one-dollar bleacher ticket. Instead, it's the interview room or a Tokyo–subway-style packed dugout session.

Before managers' communications with the outside world became ritually stage-managed, they talked to their public in little alcoves tucked underneath the stands at ballparks, where the homilies of the game would be dispensed. Half-dressed, mouths full of chaw, baseball's skippers, or pilots, or whatever the convenient nickname for manager was, held court one-on-one, or in intimate groups, to give at least the semi-inside tales of their teams and opponents. Storytelling was part of the package for the most adept conversationalists.

Part of a manager's daily routine was to deal with the media and, in turn, the fans. He usually was the front man for his franchise. Even a people-politics-challenged chap like former Cubs general manager Larry Himes said media relations was one of his three top requirements for a manager.

Before the days of the onslaught of broadcasting crews with their equipment, managers gabbed with writers as informally as possible. If not in their offices, they'd lean back in the dugout to hold court. Or they'd lean against the cage during batting practice for shorter bursts of jabber. It was a time-honored tradition for this conduit of information and opinion. The daily relationship of baseball employee to media messenger to fan depended upon it.

Some were masters at this game. Sparky Anderson could talk all day if someone would let him in his incarnations as Reds and Tigers manager. The inquiring media mind could get Sparky in a group, or one-on-one, and walk away with more quotes and insight than he could use.

Don Zimmer was another favorite in such circumstances. "Popeye" was a rougher version of Anderson. Get him agitated, and his eyes would bulge like some kind of 1950s American International sci-fi flick fiend. But several sessions with Zimmer produced some surprising material. In a 1990 one-on-one in his Wrigley Field office, Zimmer said he did not have a metal plate in his head as commonly perceived. Instead Zimmer said he had a set of metal "buttons" that had held an old skull injury together from a 1953 beaning. Furthermore Zimmer said, when he awoke from being stunned, he thought it was the next day. His wife, Soot, told him it was an entire week. Zimmer displayed his human, almost softer side here. Amazing how nine years later, spying my radio microphone near the right side of his face in the U.S. Cellular Field's visitors' dugout, he suddenly bellowed, "I've been telling you to stay the hell away from me for the last fifteen years!" Whatever I had done to peeve Zimmer in the ensuing years must have been incredibly subtle. If that was the case for me, how could it not have been for him, too?

Such outbursts notwithstanding, chewin' the fat with managers was one of the most pleasurable aspects of covering baseball, which included drawbacks like rain delays, extra-inning marathons, ninety-five-degree days in underventilated, non-air-conditioned press boxes and tiny interview rooms, and the end of free bratwursts with their secret stadium sauce at Miller Park in Milwaukee. And the ability to get up close and personal with the managers, getting to know them on a first-name basis, was crucial to understanding the psyche of a team, and why it won or lost.

The example that stood head and shoulders above the rest was Jim Riggleman, who had a five-year run as Cubs manager following his three seasons running the Padres. Riggleman would dutifully do his group interviews during batting practice and after the game. But the one-on-one sessions with him about once a month in his office provided a comfort zone when I was not a traveling writer (who receive the prime access available in a caste-conscious sport).

Riggleman provided such a good analysis of the Cubs that I did not have to agitate myself trying to pry information out of semi-communicative general manager Ed Lynch. But he did not give away the entire store. I did not know for several months that he verbally jumped both outfielder Lance Johnson and catcher Benito Santiago, both of whom Riggleman believed were jaking it during a massive midsummer collapse in 1999. Accused of being soft, almost milquetoast by columnists and sports-talk-show gabbers, Riggleman was quietly tough—and rightly kept conflicts private.

"Sometimes things have to get real bad before things straighten out," he said.

Riggleman's relations with the media were so good that when he first returned to Chicago as a Cleveland Indians coach in 2000, after being fired the previous fall as Cubs manager, he spent a full ninety minutes receiving print and broadcast well-wishers in the visitors dugout at U.S. Cellular Field.

"All of those writers who spent time with me meant a lot to me," he said. "I left on good terms with [Cubs management] and the writers.

"There were a couple of things I was taught when I started managing [in the Cardinals farm system in the early 1980s]. George Kissell said something to me that always stuck with me: Treat people the way you want to be treated. George was referring to players. I realized that everyone there is a piece of the machinery that makes it go. People like ticket takers and the grounds crew. Everyone has a job to do.

"I treat people with respect. You don't be rude. I like talking baseball. I did not feel offended when anyone brought up a baseball question. The thing I liked was the stuff I would not only do in my office but also on the field. It has as much to do with common courtesy as anything. You learn to deal with increasing numbers of media as you move up. In the minors, there's one writer in your office after the game. Quite often there's nobody in there. You do want to talk about your club, so you're not irritated when you make it to the majors. It's a gradual process that's an accepted part of the job coming up through the minor leagues.

"In today's world, the issue of the media comes up. They're thought of by some as sob's. It's immediately assumed it's an adversarial relationship—a lot by managers. But you guys are not coming to the ballpark thinking you're going to rip people."

Amazingly, Terry Francona had possessed some of the same thoughts even after going through the dual media grinders of managing the Philadelphia Phillies and Boston Red Sox.

"You try to treat people right and you hope they treat you right in return," Francona said. "Everybody has a job to do. I don't wake up in the morning and run to the newspaper to see what they said about me. I just do my job. I show up early, prepare as best as I can, and live with the results. If I let things on the periphery skew my thinking, then I'm probably in the wrong job.

"I don't have a problem with writers or media asking questions. That's their job. If I don't have a good answer, then I'm not doing my job. The more the [media] onslaught, that means there's interest. That's good. It's my responsibility to handle it and move on."

Almost all managers' stances are in the same ballpark. However, the chewin'-the-fat era is giving way quickly to a more homogenized system in which the manager is only available in large group settings. Sensitive or tough questions—best asked one-on-one so as to not offend sensibilities or put someone truly on the spot—now have to be risked for his larger audience. All the while, a media-relations official usually monitors the proceedings. If the manager does not answer these queries or even shuts down the mass talkfest, another flow of information that has been present in the game for ages is cut off from the baseball consumers.

Perhaps Riggleman spoiled me. Witnessing what followed him both in Chicago and in the game overall, I realized he probably was the exception instead of the rule.

Don Baylor turned out to be the anti-Riggleman as his successor. Personally a decent man, Baylor did not encourage long sessions with the media or one-on-one confabs in his office or around the batting cage.

Baylor seemed to be leaning to exit, stage left, during his pregame sessions in front of the Cubs dugout. One time I asked him all three questions during a media talk, which were usually scheduled early before batting practice, as if to get them out of the way. After one Sunday game in 2000, I asked Baylor—then standing on the steps leading to his office—the first question: Why did he leave wild lefty reliever Daniel Garibay in to walk in the winning run during the tenth inning? The answer was what I thought it would be—his bullpen had been worn out and Baylor had no choice but to keep going with Garibay. But then I kept silent, as a courtesy, to wait for a follow-up question from the collection of young TV producers who had gathered around me with their camera operators. None was forthcoming, so Baylor started to turn around to walk back to his office before several other writers arrived to pull him back.

Usually managers announce big news at the start of a media session, pre- or postgame. Halfway through a postgame conference in August 2001, I asked Baylor if consideration was being given to putting pitcher Kerry Wood on the disabled list. He replied in the affirmative—Wood was being disabled immediately. But would he have made the announcement on his own?

One or two brief encounters in the manager's office revealed that Baylor wasn't all that enamored with top management. But I could not get the true measure of the man, like Riggleman. Keeping with their style, none of the traveling Cubs writers tried to cultivate a one-on-one relationship even given their additional exposure on the road, where they did not have to compete with electronic media for Baylor's time. The night before he was fired in July 2002, Baylor finally confessed to an Associated Press reporter in Atlanta that he felt undercut by the lack of support he received the previous October, when he fired pitching coach Oscar Acosta. He made no such statement a few minutes previously in his pregame group interview with the traveling writers.

Wondering why Baylor appeared standoffish when he broke in to the majors under old-school manager Earl Weaver in Baltimore, he had an interesting response. He later played for manager Dave Garcia in Anaheim, "who spent more time with the media than his players, and the players resented him for that."

Riggleman saw both sides. "The Garcia comment was good," he said. "Players can't feel you're spending so much time in the office with the press. But you can do both. You can spend time with the press and be out with the players. If you start giving short, curt answers, they'll [media] resent it."

If access to Baylor was fettered, it diminished further when Dusty Baker took over as manager in 2003. Possessor of the top Chicago celebrity manager's ranking since Leo Durocher, Baker had one group media session before the game, either in the dugout or the cramped interview room just inside from the dugout. Media interrogators had to throw any hardballs and feature material in this mix along with the garden-variety questions.

Baker, who was glibber than Baylor, used a verbal technique to fend off some questions. He'd respond with another question, personally directed at the reporter, even trying to put the latter on the spot. The old Marine reservist possessed a disarming technique.

Some of the questions were best asked one-on-one in private, but Baker afforded little such access. So before one night game in midseason 2004, I asked the manager if his team, which was running the bases like a bunch of drunken sailors, needed a "remedial" course in base running. Baker objected to the use of the word "remedial," apparently believing it was the equivalent of the old dunce cap or being sent to the corner in school. Hours later, Corey Patterson and Aramis Ramirez then went out to commit base-running blunders in the same inning. The next morning, I prepared to ask a follow-up question on base running. Baker sensed the subject and launched a preemptive strike. "You're not going to bring up that remedial stuff?" he said. Not being a Johnny Carson–style ad-libber, I bumbled a response. "What should I call it, Little League?" I said. "Now you're out of line," Baker said. The exchange was deemed entertaining enough be rerun numerous times the next three days on all-sports WSCR-Radio.

During spring training 2005, I slipped into Baker's office at Fitch Park in Mesa to suggest that such questions best be asked away from the group setting. Baker understood the concept, but made no promises. I wasn't the only one who could not hang around the manager's office, the furnishings of which had been upgraded since Riggleman's day with photos of luminaries ranging from Hank Aaron to John Lee Hooker. Still, the very concept of one-on-one with the manager had worked well on a limited basis with Baker. Around the batting cage before game seven of the 2003 National League Championship Series, with very little pregame access for any reporter other than staged press conferences, Baker admitted that he had shortened his battered and increasingly injured bullpen. In the same location, more than a month after the 2004 "remedial" tiff, he shed some important light on the quietly deteriorating Sammy Sosa situation before it mushroomed into a full-blown issue.

If trying to get in Baker's head was a challenge, imagine the labors of New York Yankees beat writers, who were under the gun to produce scoops even though they could only talk to manager Joe Torre in one big pregame scrum. Torre's pregame movements around ballparks were minded so closely by Yankees officials that no media person could steal time with him without being questioned or preempted.

Given the restricted access to Baker, Torre, and other managers, the continued presence of Bobby Cox and Jack McKeon in the game in 2005 was refreshing. These two managers were both old-school and media savvy. McKeon, in fact, mingled with the media into the wee hours at the postgame parties outside Pro Player Stadium during the 2003 NLCS. He even ascended the bandstand to try out his singing voice.

"I talk to anybody," said McKeon, who would depart the Marlins job after 2005. "I think it's my job to visit with you guys and give you some time. If I can help you do your job, I feel good about it.

"I'm different. I like to be with the writers, tell stories, talk baseball. That's the way it should be. But today we don't have that mentality. You want to protect guys. But you also want to sell [baseball]. We're salesmen. They [the team] don't stop me. I do what I want to do [with the media]. I take a lot of stuff on my own."

Cox is found lounging on the bench before most Braves games, and not just for a few minutes. He's open for business.

"It's easier that way rather than getting into a room with fifty or sixty people at one time, and then it turns into a real news conference," Cox said. "I like the informal, BS a little bit, go off-the-record a little bit, tell a few stories, laugh. When you have those big things in those closed rooms, it's not as much fun for either the writers or the managers.

"It's fun. Writers are good people. They're like umpires. Sometimes you disagree with them, but they're good people."

Cox said his style is easier to achieve in a smaller market. "It's easy for managers [in a big market] to do it all at one time," he said. "In a smaller market, you make yourself available on the bench anytime you want."

An open manager often translates into an open clubhouse. The Braves have been one of the best locker rooms in the game while Cox ran the show, since 1990.

"You'd prefer that," he said. "You try to do your research. That's kept a lot of players off a lot of teams, to be honest. You might be a good player but a bad apple. Maybe he doesn't fit on our team, he'll fit somewhere else. We'll try to make it as happy as we can and as enjoyable for a player.

"You want to let players have a voice and be themselves. But you have the last say. Everybody has a job to do, and we need to make ourselves as accessible as possible. It's free advertising for the game of baseball. It's part of our job."

A manager who values character on an equal plane as talent is the Twins' Ron Gardenhire.

"If it's questionable makeup, we'll pass on a guy because it doesn't fit our clubhouse," he said. "We want our players to understand other people have a job to do, too.

"People want to know what you're like. We have an obligation to let you do your job. As long as you don't overstep the boundaries, do your job as much as you want to do. I think personal life is off-limits unless the player volunteers [information]. Their privacy should be respected. But we are in the limelight."

Another media-friendly manager is the Astros' Phil Garner. Known as "Scrap Iron" for his hustling style as a 1970s infielder before he went on to manage the Brewers and Tigers before his Houston gig, Garner understands that unfavorable stories sometimes have to be authored about him or his ball club.

"One of the first things I learned in managing is that if some stories are painful and critical, if the story is documented and the reporter worked to get the truth, then I have to deal with it," he said. "It's not something you get angry about. One of the reasons I have a good relationship with Tom Haudricourt [of the *Milwaukee Journal Sentinel*] is he wrote some tough stories, but they were well-rounded. He never wrote anything that was hearsay and threw it out there to see if there was anything to it. I may not like that, but I respect it."

Garner understands that the print media is held to a higher standard because its representatives face the players on a daily basis. "You better have backup," he said. "You better corroborate your story."

He also realizes the pressure that other outlets face in building ratings or readership. That will be as much a managerial headache as his closer failing in a save situation.

"What I've seen from different media outlets is they want the in-your-face style of reporting, to push the envelope a little bit," Garner said. "What is controversial or creates controversy. Go back to the twenties or thirties, media was part of the marketing arm of clubs. Since then we've gone from one extreme to another extreme. Some media might be on a mission to destroy what might be good about some things. That's what I see—taking something and twisting it a little bit."

A lot of the twisting would be done during crisis times, when managers are especially tested on and off the field. A total of 119 losses and an old-line franchise in free fall must have been galling to Alan Trammell as a rookie Detroit Tigers manager in 2003—and former team leader of Detroit's 1984 World Series champions. Then there was the media to face before and after each disaster.

"I handled it to the best of my ability," Trammell said. "Whatever profession, anybody just came to you and only wanted to talk to you about bad things, negative things, it gets old. I knew that was part of the deal. What were they going to talk about?"

At least Trammel had good training.

"I think I was brought up well, taught by the best—Sparky Anderson," he said. "Sparky taught us to not duck the media. If you don't want to talk to them, tell them and then leave. Don't run and hide or leave early. Thankfully, I listened."

While there are still some cracker-barrel adherents among the rampant choreographing of managers, Larry Bowa made life more difficult for the always-inquisitive Philadelphia media in his four seasons as Phillies manager that ended in 2004. Although he played under old-school managers like Paul Owens, Danny Ozark, and Dallas Green, Bowa's bantam-rooster personality and built-in paranoia created conflict with those who covered him.

"I think early on he tried," said Paul Hagen, ace national baseball writer for the *Philadelphia Daily News*. "But, remember, this is a guy who on the day he was hired proudly announced several times, 'I will lie to the media.' That's not exactly the best way to get a relationship started. And since the perception that [predecessor Terry] Francona had been too cozy with the writers, he went to the opposite extreme.

At the beginning of his first spring training, we weren't even allowed into his office to do our daily morning updates. We had to stand outside the clubhouse, even when it was raining. So I think he drew a line in the sand early."

Bowa, who worked as an ESPN baseball analyst after his firing, before latching on as Yankees bench coach, responded that the media often comes to work with an agenda or in search of conflict.

"If you just give the details of the game, it's boring," he said. "They'd much rather have a player and manager not getting along with each other, a pitcher and pitching coach not getting along with each other. It's a shame. All over baseball, you always had one or two guys not liking the manager or pitching coach, and nobody made a big deal of it.

"I know how it [media] works. One thing I really dislike is the 'unidentified source' or 'unnamed player.' I'm not one. If I have something to say, I'll say it. Anybody can put that on any article."

Bowa claimed that today's baseball journalists do not seek out one-on-one relationships with managers or players.

"I don't think they want that relationship," he said, "because if they have a chance to take a shot, they'll take a shot. If you have a close relationship, they might back off. I'm not going to do that [work with the manager] and get beat by two other writers. I'm not going to give them 'A' material, controversy."

Standing in while taking media fire is the mark of a stout-hearted manager, Riggleman said.

"Jim Tracy is unbelievable," he said of his former boss on the Dodgers, now the Pirates manager. "T. J. Simers [*Los Angeles Times* columnist] went out of his way to make smart-ass comments about Tracy. His schtick is sarcasm. But Jim handled it tremendously. He's a brilliant guy. He'll be guarded, but he'll give you the time."

And in the end, that's all the messengers to the public want. Enough time to pick a manager's brain and then judge his heart and soul. Press conferences with sharp-eyed and -eared minders don't accomplish this task. Baseball can't reverse the hands of time. But it ought to try, because cracker barrels are pretty cozy, and conversation pieces to boot.

EIGHT

All the News That's Not Fit to Print

"**N**umber twenty-one is the biggest asshole in baseball."

That evaluation from a source inside the Cubs clubhouse at midsummer 2004 did it for me. I had to write a lengthy feature about the increasingly fractious relationship between slugger Sammy Sosa and manager Dusty Baker and his coaching staff. I had remembered a former Cub, known as a good citizen in baseball, remarking a year before that Sosa "was the worst teammate you could possibly have."

I approached another Cubs source, who confirmed my suspicions that the slumping Sosa did not want to be moved down in the batting order and resisted moving closer to the plate. He described Sosa as "sensitive and selfish." A catcher with another National League team then confirmed that he no longer had to "bust Sosa inside" and instead called for pitches off the outside corner, which Sosa could scarcely reach from his outer-limits batting stance.

The end result, displayed on the front sports page of the *Times of Northwest Indiana*, featured only one on-the-record comment—from Sosa himself. The subject was such a lightning rod—the fall of Chicago's greatest modern-day baseball idol—that anonymity had to be guaranteed to get the information needed. A week later, the Sosa issue blew up publicly and raged through his eventual trade to the Baltimore Orioles the following February.

The manner in which the Sosa story was assembled tapped into the accepted manner in which "inside-baseball" tales are now crafted by the media in far greater quantity than during the mid–twentieth century. The basic tenet is there's no such thing as a free lunch in obtaining such information.

An intricate web of relationships, quid pro quos, understanding sensibilities, and off-the-record stances bring advance word of trades and free-agent signings; private opinions about players, managers, and owners; updates on injuries; and salary information that used to be guesswork prior to the free-agent era.

If the truth be known, get twenty-five players, six managers and coaches, and a bevy of front-office executives together, and the majority will talk on- or off-the-record. It's human nature, despite would-be modern-day "plumbers" like Cubs manager Dusty Baker seeking to stem leaks.

"Part of it is there's too many snitches," Baker said in the spring of 2005. "That's where the problem comes in to me. You're going to print it, and I can't blame you for that. But snitches in the clubhouse? Too much stuff got out that shouldn't have got out and got exaggerated once it gets out. There's a snitch everywhere. If I catch who the snitches are, now we got a problem."

But snitches, as Baker defines them, are in every corner of a ballpark. "Deep Throat" was not invented for Watergate; his cousins stalked stadiums decades previously. Whether sportswriters used their information depended on the standards of the time.

Then and now, the media must protect these sources, or whatever the polite or impolite term for them might be. In the process of such masking and filtering, a number of stories, comments, and opinions never make print or broadcast. They are so inflammatory, offensive, or sensitive that the originator of the information would be burned badly if publicized—and the media messenger also would be singed in the process.

A sign affixed in a clubhouse for decades exhorts baseball folks to keep their lips zipped about private goings-on in their inner sanctum. In essence, the sign said what goes on in the clubhouse stays in the clubhouse. Of course, signs such as these are like speed-limit postings—a guidepost, but never the absolute in practice.

The media partially adheres to that policy. To maintain relationships and protect conduits for future stories, not all the potential news and notes they witness or hear is fit to print or broadcast.

A basic adherence to the law of the press—prohibiting libel and slander—is the first set of checks and balances. Anything written or spoken that is either reckless disregard for the truth, or besmirches an individual's character, is potential grist for a lawsuit. Although libel and slander suits are difficult to win, the ones that are successfully pursued cost media outlets millions of dollars in court-mandated settlements. It is a gray area into which those who cover baseball regularly tread lightly.

But even if libel per se is not involved, the access to the originators of information among the players, managers, coaches, and executive ranks cannot be risked if confidence or anonymity is betrayed or stories that have to be sat upon out of necessity are made public. Access is everything in the game. Without it, you might as well buy a twenty-five-dollar ticket to get in and bring a lot more for inflated concession prices.

Baseball types are willing to help the media in which they have trust. In national politics or security issues, a "high-level administration source" on a national political or security story could mean a presidential press secretary, chief of staff, or cabinet member. Similarly a baseball source, or "so-and-so told friends," more than likely is a key player, executive, or agent willing to provide background information without risking any kind of public offense to the parties involved.

The media person must cover the team regularly, show a willingness to handle information accurately and not publish a source's name if anonymity is requested before he can tap into the huge wellspring of baseball information.

"If I give you something without attribution, it's for you to use [in your own words]," Seattle Mariners general manager Bill Bavasi said. "I trust you. I want to help. You've got mouths to feed and a job to do. I think it's good for you to talk about it [in the media person's own words]. But for me to talk about it, makes no sense.

"My concern is ripping players for other people. I won't give that. If I have to give you something off-the-record and without attribution at all, then it's something sensitive. If it can help you, great. If it's something that can hurt people, I won't even do that.

"I'm pretty tight-lipped and usually try to go on-the-record. I don't do a whole lot of off-the-record stuff. I especially don't comment on somebody else's club or the job somebody else does, and go off-the-record. That's just chicken shit. When I read that, I really get angry."

Off-the-record is not plain-speaking Minnesota Twins general manager Terry Ryan's style. The majority of material the longtime scouting master divulges is for publication.

"I'm careful in confiding," Ryan said. "With a question, there's a reasonable answer to give without having to go off-the-record all the time. When I talk to people, certainly on the radio, I try to be up-front and honest. Instead of going off-the-record, there are ways around it. I've had my share of gaffes when I've said something I shouldn't have. But I've always had good rapport with the media."

Ryan has learned to trust the regular writers traveling with the Twins.

"We have a certain loyalty to each other and they know what they can or might not use," he said. "We don't have that much difficulty up in Minnesota."

Emulating Ryan is Cubs general manager Jim Hendry. The broadcast journalism major at Spring Hill College in Alabama has been one of the more open and accessible general managers in the game since he took over what he classified as his dream job in mid-2002. Although Hendry never gives away the store when he's cooking up a deal, he'll often provide reporters just enough to write their stories, provided they've earned his confidence with the way they handle information.

"If you give the media their respect, then in return they'll understand there are a lot of things you can't go into," Hendry said. "I think it's a matter of understanding clearly you have a job to do. I'm not here to say my job is more important than anyone else's. I give mutual respect and I think in return I've gotten that respect back from your peers.

"It's an acquired trust. I give more background information than off-the-record. I was here in a lot of capacities before I was general manager, and I had the advantage of a relationship with a lot of media before I became GM. I certainly understand what our goals are, and I don't want the media to write anything but the facts. If we're not doing the job, if we're not winning enough, then I understand there's also constructive criticism."

Some general managers try to manipulate events and opinions through the media. So then are they politicians in the purest sense?

"Oh, please," Bavasi said. "Of course. I have no idea if it's good or bad for the game. Everybody's got to put their head on the pillow every night and get a sound sleep. Their level of ethics isn't as high as others. They're not promoting the club; they're promoting themselves."

Talk about money predominates baseball coverage. Players' multimillion-dollar salaries are nearly an obsession. So is the payroll level of each team. Executives are more likely to reveal salaries (which are disseminated by the Associated Press as soon as a signing becomes official). But they are much more circumspect when discussing their own overall budgets, on- or off-the-record.

"Does the fact you talk about it bother me? No," Bavasi said. "I don't know that any GM is expected to explain that. You operate within the parameters of a budget. You make deals, free-agent signings. Questions you have to answer relate to the free-agent signings, trades, minor leagues. Any GM who answers questions about payroll budget is making a foolish move.

"From my point of opinion, fans want to hear about talent. Most people want to talk about baseball. The three clubs I've been with, every dime of available payroll was spent on players. I was in Anaheim, and in my years we never made any money. The only time we were close to breaking even was when they prepared to sell out. In L.A. Fox was dedicated to trying to win. We were losing tens of millions of dollars a year. Here in Seattle, this organization was not making money. The money goes right back into the ball club. The budget depends on how much we draw. Nobody's walking away with money in baseball. There might have been one owner making money, and I don't think he is anymore."

Requests not to use information come all the time from players, managers, and executives. And the fear of cutting one's self off from a vital source curbs the dissemination of much information. Jim O'Donnell noted this fear in a 1989 suburban *Chicago Daily Herald* column. O'Donnell chided reporters covering the Chicago Bulls for not taking Michael Jordan to task for fathering his first child, Michael Jeffrey, out of wedlock, before he married wife Juanita. The reasoning: If Jordan cuts you off, you can't cover him and the Bulls.

Sometimes even the commissioner of baseball requested a red light on the information flow. The late Rick Talley, sports columnist for *Chicago Today*, an afternoon daily owned by the Tribune Company, was asked by Bowie Kuhn in the winter of 1969–70 to sit on a story about Major League Baseball's investigation of Cubs manager Leo Durocher. Kuhn and his lieutenants feared they might have a second Black Sox Scandal on their hands. The commissioner feared confirmation of reports that Durocher won sixty thousand dollars betting against his own team in a September 9, 1969, game against the Mets in Shea Stadium. Durocher had started ace Fergie Jenkins on two days' rest, then let him bat in the top of the fifth with the Mets up 6–1.

Talley complied with Kuhn's request to protect baseball. Durocher also was investigated by the Internal Revenue Service and several Chicago newspaper investigative reporters. The *Today's* Bob Glass later claimed that Cubs owner Phil Wrigley paid off "thousands" in Durocher's gambling debts in Las Vegas to clean his slate. Lynn Walker Durocher, The Lip's wife at the time, said several investigative types showed up at their doorstep in search of the truth. Talley was fortunate not to print the story of the investigation. No entity found anything to pin on Durocher. He could have sued Talley and others for one whopping libel accusation if they had written stories. However the media would not have been so sanguine even two decades later. The Pete Rose saga dragged on for months before a final ruling by commissioner Bart Giamatti. Now, the mere fact that Major League Baseball was investigating its most controversial characters would be hyped to the heavens.

Durocher and Rose were linked to gambling, baseball's top capital crime. Most recently, the subject that most reporters needed to use care in disseminating was the steroid issue. Many fans and even media pundits wondered why the baseball press did not jump all over the issue when it was apparent players were injecting themselves with steroids of all kinds as far back as the mid-1990s.

One of the harshest critics was Charles Yesalis, professor of Health Policy and Administration and Exercise and Sport Science at Penn State. Yesalis had researched the nonmedical use of steroids and related supplements for nearly three decades, writing books and testifying before Congress.

"This baseball scandal is by far the biggest drug and cheating scandal I've ever seen in sports, including on an international level. It eclipses even the [1998] Tour de France blood-doping scandal,"

Yesalis said in Barry Rozner's March 15, 2005, sports column in the suburban *Chicago Daily Herald*. "There're a lot of people embarrassed that they made these baseball players out to be heroes when they were cheating.

"Part of it is too many sycophant sports journalists who are not seekers of the truth. They couldn't make a living in journalism behaving that way, except in sports, where you look the other way.

"Now they can either look the fool and protect the sport or all of a sudden you come on board and write the mea culpa."

One simple answer suffices: libel laws. A public figure simply can't be accused of illegal drug use unless absolute proof exists of such actions. The truth is the media's defense in libel or slander. But if a reporter does not have the truth nailed down, he simply can't run with an accusatory story about the use of steroids or other illegal drugs. That's why the cocaine scandal in baseball in the 1980s did not hit print until the famous Pittsburgh drug trial involving several big leaguers.

The steroid clues abounded, but concrete proof was not easily available. The media types could not get into the private bathrooms of clubhouses where Jose Canseco supposedly injected steroids into the buttocks of himself and others. Steroids were no doubt employed off-site from baseball stadiums, away from the prying eye of media, team officials, and law-enforcement personnel. If no players admitted it, and executives such as San Diego Padres general manager Kevin Towers kept their suspicions to themselves, then the accurate sourcing of the scandal was largely cut off at the pass.

Steroids had insidiously crept into baseball early on in the process. Former Phillies pitcher Dickie Noles said possible steroid use was a conversation piece as early as the 1980s. Whispers about Canseco's linkage with the drugs began when he burst on the scene as a "Bash Brother" with Mark McGwire in the closing years of the 1980s. *Washington Post* columnist Thomas Boswell accused Canseco of steroid use on a CBS TV broadcast in 1988. Yet until Associated Press reporter Steve Wilstein noticed a bottle of andro in McGwire's locker during the 1998 season, no media representative ever caught a player in the act or elicited an admission of use.

Media outlets "should have set the investigative forces on stampede," ESPN.com's Jayson Stark said in a *Chicago Tribune* article on

February 25, 2005. "We should have been more aggressive. But I don't know how we would have proved it. And if you can't prove it, how would you write it?"

The *New York Times* interviewed twenty-five Major League players, executives, and strength coaches in an October 2000 exposé that detailed how steroid abuse had become rampant. In 2002 the late Ken Caminiti admitted to *Sports Illustrated* he had used steroids while winning the 1996 National League's Most Valuable Player Award. The same year a just-retired Canseco finally spoke out on the subject, claiming 85 percent of players used steroids—a grossly exaggerated figure, but at least an admission of a problem.

The 2002 season was my first brush with steroids, on June 18 while covering the Cubs–Texas Rangers night interleague game at Wrigley Field. Earlier that day, Rangers manager Jerry Narron said on WSCR-AM (670) that Chicago fans are knowledgeable enough to know which players seem to be employing steroids. Producers at the all-sports station believed the statements were curious enough to replay a half hour later.

I tracked down Narron in the visiting manager's office at Wrigley Field before the game. I asked him why he made the on-air comments.

"Just a super regard for the fans in Chicago, what outstanding sports fans they are, how intelligent they are, and how well they follow their clubs," he said. "They're such intelligent, good baseball people."

I then took the tape of Narron's fresh comments across the field to Sosa, who from time to time had fielded questions about whether he used steroids to bulk up his physique since 1998. Sosa always denied the steroid suggestions, originally claiming he used "Flintstone vitamins" for energy during the '98 home-run race.

Sosa listened intently to the Narron comments for five minutes by his locker. "Ask him," he responded when queried why Narron would make such a statement.

The slugger then closed the subject without further comment once the tape had been turned off.

"I'm not in the mood for that," he said. "I'm here to play baseball."

I then asked Cubs president Andy MacPhail, at the time doubling as general manager, for his reaction. He refused to talk about steroids, claiming it was a subject of Basic Agreement bargaining sessions with the Major League Baseball Players Association in which he was participating as a management negotiator at the time. However, he was clearly upset by Narron's left-handed implications about alleged Chicago baseball steroid users.

Narron also said he had no specific knowledge of steroid users. He theorized that the number of juiced-up players is much less than the numbers claimed in comments by professed former users Ken Caminiti and Jose Canseco.

"There's no way it's anywhere close to the 50 percent or whatever," he said. "There's probably somebody in baseball using them, but it's probably a very, very small minority of players."

Steroids, along with other illegal drugs, cross the pale when they affect a player's performance. If a reporter can prove such use, restrictions on what he writes are thrown off. But other bits of baseball figures' personal lives, such as their marriages or other relationships, are usually regarded as out of the public eye if they don't impact their work. Rumors of sex scandals usually stay the subject of press-box chatter, sometimes elevating themselves to urban legend status when they spread word-of-mouth to the fans, simply because of that libel rule. My own rule of thumb is if a player or executive volunteers information, I'll use it. But I won't go prying.

Near the end of the 2002 season I discovered that one player's on-field problems could have been related to his marital woes. His wife told me that she and her husband were separated and had consistent conflicts over his most recent choice of teams. The wife was bringing the couple's brood of kids to the ballpark to see their father. I realized that the family was going through enough agony, so they did not need to see their problems offered up for public consumption.

Still another challenge is holding back on continued evidence of primordial racial and religious attitudes, which have reared their ugly heads in baseball since it went professional in 1869. Again the question of keeping good relations with sources and being able to prove private, derogatory comments are the top considerations in not sharing the information with the public.

During the 2004 season, Cubs manager Dusty Baker and relief pitcher LaTroy Hawkins received hate mail with the epithet "nigger" included. Hawkins even showed me a scrawled hand-written letter, seemingly penned by a seven-year-old. "My God, this shows that what Jackie Robinson and Henry Aaron went through is still going on in the twenty-first century," I told Baker. Although it was a legitimate story, neither Baker nor Hawkins wanted it used. "You won't change their minds, and you'll only make it worse," Baker said. I had to honor their wishes. The story was not published at the time. When Baker revealed the hate mail after Hawkins was traded in May 2005, I was able to use their names there. But a story isn't a story if the people involved won't confirm its facts and cooperate at the time. And if a reporter deals with these gentlemen on a regular basis, he cannot burn his bridges in a mad dash for a scoop.

"He said, she said" accusations also applied to a series of club-house statements that would be outrageously offensive if made public. And if they were not recorded as evidence, libel would be in play, let alone pariah status in the clubhouse for the reporter.

One prominent white player, raised in traditionally conservative areas of the country, referred to an African American player on another team as a "nigger." On another occasion, he asked me if I "knew those guys with the long beards . . . can they do a rain dance?" With rain closing in on Wrigley Field, the player obviously meant Orthodox Jewish rabbis. I replied that I did not and that no faction of Judaism engages in such mystic, tribal behavior. And on a third occasion, the player said that Reds owner Marge Schott was being piled on after her ignorant comments about Hitler doing a good job for the German people, but ending up going too far. I rebuked such thinking, but could do nothing with such comments in print or on the air.

Such mistaken interpretations weren't confined to the clubhouse. One time, a baseball executive, chewing over current events and history, wondered why so much trouble in the Middle East resulted from the state of Israel's existence. "Why couldn't they settle the [Holocaust] refugees in Arizona and New Mexico?" he wondered. Obviously this honcho did not do well in his American history classes, since Harry S Truman would have been impeached, or worse, had he opened the doors to millions of displaced persons in 1946–47. Such an opinion might have been on a par with Al Campanis's statement about African Americans not possessing the "necessities" for management. But it was said one-on-one, off-the-cuff, with no recording devices whirring.

Sometimes a personality being interviewed does not even know the ethnicity of his questioner. A controversial former baseball personality railed against the "Jewish owner [Jerry Reinsdorf] of the Bulls" and the "Jewish general manager" [Jerry Krause] while I talked to him at his home. Without missing a beat, I asked him "if he minded being interviewed by a Jewish reporter?" He was taken aback. "Oh, no, I don't mind," he blurted out. "Some of my best friends are Jewish . . . Back then [the 1950s], Jewish girls were the only ones who would give you blow jobs."

This last statement was an extension of the sexual-scatological subculture of the clubhouse. If everything witnessed among the scratchin' and spittin' crowd was made available for public consumption, the end product would be a combination of *Hustler* magazine and *Animal House*. Most experienced media just figure a baseball team is a boys' club and leave it at that.

Some of the sounds and sights are hilarious in recounting idle press-box moments. Back in the mid-1980s, I witnessed a prominent Cubs pitcher call out to his buddy across the clubhouse: "Hey, faggot, come here and blow me. Give me some head." It was not what he said but the way he said it, and no offense meant to homosexuals. No publicity, either. Winding the clock forward ten years, I was running my radio tape recorder for an interview with the glib Tony Gwynn in the San Diego Padres clubhouse. Across the way, some kind of flatulence noises were emanating from a grinning Ken Caminiti. I had no choice but to keep the tape rolling and hope the machine did not pick up the apparent expulsions. Turns out Caminiti had some kind of gag gizmo that produced the faux gas. That was Caminiti's public image of fun contrasting with his mounting private hell of steroid and other drug abuse that would culminate in his premature death.

But in the early years of the twenty-first century, the line, however shaky, that had kept most of the clubhouse high jinks and jawboning out of the public eye began to be crossed, further widening the gulf between baseball people and media. An advocate of realism without strict boundaries in sports journalism had taken root in quintessentially Middle American Kansas City, of all places.

Kansas City Star sports editor Mike Fannin dramatically improved his section, elevating it to an aggressive stance in a part of the country that does not really expect such coverage. Fannin believes in a cutting-edge approach in which the classic game story is "almost dead," with readers instead expecting "breaking news or analysis, something they can't get anywhere else."

"Beat writers get blinders on," Fannin continued. "They go into places and talk to people that readers can't. We should go where they can't go or can't see on TV or the Internet. They can allow readers to be part of the process. Don't we owe that to the fans?

"I don't think our readers pick up the paper to read baseball game stories. They want to know who likes who, who feuds with who."

Early in the 2004 season, Fannin commissioned twenty-four-year-old Jeff Passan, who had previously worked in Newark, Buffalo, and Washington DC, to craft a feature on the Chicago Cubs, then coming off preseason predictions of their first World Series berth since 1945. Passan hooked up with the Cubs during their first trip to St. Louis. His piece ran in the May 4, 2004, edition of the *Star*. Within days of its publication, he had the Cubs clubhouse in an uproar, their already edgy mood toward the media tilting downward as a result.

Passan first wrote of a conversation between Cubs general manager Jim Hendry and surgery-rehabbing pitcher Ryan Dempster:

"I gotta pay your bills to fly back and forth?" Hendry asked.

"Hey, I have to keep doing rehab," Dempster replied.

"Well, you better be going coach on the way back," Hendry said.

Players accused Passan of eavesdropping on a private conversation with that exchange. At first and second glance, that doesn't seem to be offensive, especially if one knows Hendry's sense of humor. But a few paragraphs further down really got the Cubs' ire up.

Passan described ace pitcher Kerry Wood arriving in the middle of the clubhouse, where teammates were watching TV or lounging.

"Wood didn't care what they were doing," Passan wrote. "He lifted his leg, expelled a stream of wind and sat down like nothing happened. 'I'm sorry,' Wood said. 'I felt it coming back there. I sprinted in here. Had to do it.' Teammates hiked up their shirts to shield their noses. Wood grinned devilishly."

The remainder of the story was a garden-variety clubhouse mood piece. But the Cubs were angry. Wood tried to call Fannin and missed connections. Fannin did not at first believe Wood's voice was the one on the message. Passan attempted to return the call through the Cubs and failed to reach the pitcher. Fannin again passed along a message to Wood after the season to call him. Eventually Wood just let it go, but said many others wouldn't have been as calm.

"If they had done it about somebody else and if that kid [Passan] came back in the clubhouse, there might have been a problem," Wood said. "You're talking about guys' personal stuff that obviously wasn't meant for the paper, and you printed it. That's going to piss some guys off."

Passan could not believe the fallout.

"I was definitely surprised with the reaction," he said. "It was a feature story to capture their [Cubs] personality. It was a story about why the Cubs were cool. When you deal with baseball players as a feature writer, access is limited. You try to capture the best you can in limited time. Kerry Wood is one of the faces of the Cubs."

Passan did not see the flatulence reference as making fun of Wood's personality. He also would have deleted it if asked by Fannin or his deputies.

"It was light-hearted enough to see it as a gauge of his personality," Passan said. "I come from a generation where you have different types of media, guys going crazy on *Around the Horn*. Our job is to give something different. I'm trying to go for a different angle."

Fannin said the story was humanizing players in a realistic manner consistent with the standards of the times.

"Readers like to read about people," Fannin said. "If you don't bring a certain level of humanity to storytelling, you lose out."

But was the reference to the expulsion of gas necessary, since most assume the boys' club of a locker room trends toward the scatological and cruder-than-crude anyway?

"The only complaint we got about that story was from Kerry Wood," Fannin said. "Barriers have been pushed back. We live in a real world where people die in Iraq. To put someone farted in the paper is not comparable to people dying in Iraq. People look in the sports pages for relief.

"Baseball writers have a long and undistinguished history about not writing about things. We should write what we see and write what we hear. Jeff was not eavesdropping. Jeff's job was to swoop in and write a story about the Cubs. It's about what's going on in the clubhouse, it's about camaraderie."

Fannin would have to push most writers to cross the barrier. Few would go as far as Passan in writing a no-holds-barred description of the boys' club.

"Guys pulling pranks or burping in the clubhouse, I don't think that's appropriate to put in the paper," said Bruce Miles, the suburban *Chicago Daily Herald* beat writer since 1998. "I don't see why the reader would care. The clubhouse is their domain and we're guests there for a limited amount of time. To me that's eavesdropping type of journalism.

"I read the Kansas City story. I can see both sides of it. If you let people in the clubhouse, technically I guess they're free to write about what they observe. On the other hand, if players get upset about private conversations being recorded in the paper or having personal habits and hygiene put in the paper, if you don't want that in the paper, don't let people in. But if you are let in, you have to respect people's privacy."

Miles claims he's his own self-censor.

"All the judgment has been mine. My rule has been the rule of players: Write what you want, but don't get personal. You can say a GM made a bad trade, but that doesn't make him a bad guy, a bad father, a bad husband. You can say the pitcher made a bad pitch, but that doesn't make him all the bad other things."

Curbs on profane or guttural language in the average newspaper also clamp down on capturing the true flavor of the clubhouse. George Carlin's old seven bad words are absolutely prohibited, so "bleep" or the first letter of the word, followed by a series of short dashes are used instead of an obscenity. Many newspapers even frown on the word "ass," so "butt" or some other substitute has to be used.

Even though Passan crossed the barrier at Fannin's direction, he is not without his own standards, despite being raised in Generation Y or whatever.

"The time when you write about somebody's personal life is when it starts affecting the way he performs on the field," he said. "If someone comes in hung over in the morning and has a good game,

I will not write about it. But if he consistently does it and it affects his play, and the general manager says so, that's when it becomes an issue."

Fannin's intentions may have been forthright and honest. But by breaking down a barrier about reporting boys-will-be-boys behavior, the aggressive editor may have closed a door where he intended to open one. The Passan story seemed like a fulcrum point at which the Cubs, whose players made up a pretty open clubhouse during their near-dream season in 2003, began withdrawing from the media.

Players increasingly populated a rump lounge with folding chairs amid the bare cinder-block walls of the equipment room, just to get away from the media, in a cramped clubhouse where the lounge, weight room, and trainer's room won't hold the entire team. "It's all concrete back there, under the stands, it's dark and nasty," Wood said. "It's just a place to sit in silence because you can't do it at your locker."

Meanwhile media members had to stand at one end of the Wrigley Field clubhouse to wait for players while TV cameras were banned pregame. Fewer players were available before and after games.

"Unfortunately the good writers and good reporters kind of got screwed by that, but it's guilt by association," Wood said.

The spiral continued downward toward season's end, with the twin rhubarbs of Sammy Sosa's unauthorized first-inning departure from the clubhouse on the final day and players' complaints against the TV broadcast team of Chip Caray and Steve Stone.

Entering the books was another example of the distancing between two parties who need each other to survive when all other pretense is stripped away. The delicate balancing acts and gentlemen's agreements to convey some stories while leaving others on the cutting-room floor still stood in media-baseball relations.

But the strong motivations to conduct business as usual were ebbing. The question yet to be answered is whether the public will end up knowing too much and turning away from whatever positive emotional attachment they have with baseball.

NINE

The Red and Blue States of
Baseball Journalism

Baseball commissioner Bud Selig and Rich Levin, his ever present public relations chief, may not be fully aware of a problem on their hands, having been smothered in a cocoon of national, big-newspaper and broadcast-outlet coverage that tails them wherever they go.

Their beloved game, which has long depended upon the printed word to spread its aura and legend, is actually suffering a rollback in original newspaper coverage in America's heartland—the "red states" as first defined in the 2000 election, then codified four years later.

Simply put, if you are a baseball fan in the wide swath of the world's breadbasket in between the mountain ranges, you'll be hard-pressed to enjoy a diversity of original, comprehensive media coverage of baseball unless you live in the actual big league markets.

Smaller dailies in the outer ring of fan-interest geographic areas, and even those within a short drive of big-league ballparks, have in many cases rolled back staff-originated baseball coverage, using nuts-and-bolts, down-the-middle Associated Press accounts. A combination of money-saving, profits-preserving management styles is the culprit, one that gathered the momentum of a hurricane with two thousand jobs lost in the newspaper industry during 2005. Added to that was an additional groping by management for a local "niche" that other outlets cannot supply in a hyper-competitive media world. In the place of baseball and other pro coverage is "narrowcasting" to the tenth degree: reams of high school sports and other community and amateur athletic copy that appeals to far fewer readers in aggregate, but also is much more economical to produce.

Contrast this with rabid rooters in the old-line baseball cities of the East Coast—certified "blue states." The population- and newspaper-heavy region offers fans a wide potpourri of media choices, extremely competitive coverage, and literally an all-you-can-eat flow of baseball information. The curse-purged Red Sox backer enjoys a minimum of two writers each from the *Boston Globe* and *Boston Herald* at all road ports of call, including faraway Seattle. When the Red Sox go to New York, the Boston papers will deploy a small army of writers and columnists. If he lives outside Boston, the Sox fan can read traveling writers from newspapers in Providence, Hartford, and Worcester, among others.

The complete definition of "blue states" also includes California, Oregon, and Washington. For many years, baseball coverage on the "Left Coast" mimicked its Atlantic-hailing cousins in quantity, if not always quality. But the turn of the millennium has shifted coverage, particularly in the three California big league markets. Concentration of ownership of newspapers in fewer companies in both the Los Angeles and San Francisco areas has dampened the total number of different newspapers originating coverage.

But crossing all geographic boundaries is what should be a disturbing trend for the likes of Selig, who grew up with two traveling writers covering the Braves in Milwaukee. The number of newspapers electing to travel full time with teams has declined since the economy, especially the advertising market, nosedived in 2001 and some advertising, such as help-wanted, shifted for good to the Internet. Travel is, after all, an optional expense. Wire services provide a cheaper alternative, even if the story angle focusing on the local team often is diffused. Baseball built what passes for its publicity machine on teams being covered by multiple traveling writers so players' feats from all over the country were personally conveyed to eager readers. The sharpest decline in travel was in the Los Angeles area. Baseball's power structure, including its elite writers association and media-relations departments, was slow to acknowledge the evolving trend.

At first it all sounds like some esoteric business practice that should be of little interest outside the media industry. But fans in Illinois, Iowa, Indiana, and western Michigan want to read and hear about the Cubs. Ditto with those red-garbed loyalists following the

Cardinals in Missouri, southern Illinois, Oklahoma, Arkansas, and other mid-South locales.

Some editors and publishers will simply bail out on the concept of a well-rounded newspaper. They'll concede pro coverage to the wire services, metropolitan daily newspapers, the Internet, TV, and sports-talk radio. But there's an inherent flaw in such thinking. In addition to writing down-the-middle game stories, the AP's game-notes package, also spread between the two participating teams, was cut in half in recent years, according to AP sportswriters. MLB.com, which covers every team, cannot present 100 percent unfettered coverage given its partial ownership by the baseball establishment. TV offers highlights and interview snippets, but nothing in-depth, informative, or illuminating. Sports-talk radio is nothing more than what its own management desires—entertainment, and if we can work a little journalism in, fine and dandy. National TV and radio do not focus on individual teams, except inflating everything concerning New York and Boston to far beyond even their legitimate importance.

As outmoded as they seem in their deadlines and delivery systems—compared to more immediate, more technologically advanced media—newspapers remain the most in-depth conveyors of news that exist today. Baseball was a newspaper sport through most of the twentieth century and remains so. For any baseball fans, the layout of stories, photos, and above all, box scores, is a morning ritual that can scarcely be duplicated by any other media. At the same time, a newspaper dispatching its own writer shows a commitment to go beyond the very basics. Even if some editors' intentions are more basic—keeping up with competitor papers' coverage or simply to feed a feeling of ego and prestige—the reader is better served when newspapers take their own baseball coverage seriously.

And that rating goes beyond the sports pages.

"Newspapers probably do a better job than any other media serving the public interest," said die-hard Cubs fan Mark Gibson, advertising manager of State Farm Insurance in Bloomington, Illinois, 130 miles southwest of Chicago.

Witnessing Chicago press boxes full of traveling writers from New York, Boston, Philadelphia, Los Angeles, and San Francisco when I started working baseball regularly at the end of the 1980s,

I wondered how sociological and economic factors were different on the two coasts. After all, Chicago was a sports–media-light town, with only two traveling writers from the metro papers covering the Cubs and White Sox from 1978 to 1988. The trend continued well into the present. For about half of spring training in recent seasons, just three Chicago writers plus an MLB.com writer were posted at the Cubs' spring training base in Mesa, Arizona. And I scratched my head about why such a baseball-crazed town like St. Louis could have one traveling writer for years in the *Post-Dispatch*'s Rick Hummel and successor Joe Strauss. In the first half of the 1990s, I could walk into Cards manager Joe Torre's office during his Chicago visits and chat one-on-one, a stark contrast with his latter-day New York Yankees duties.

Simply put, baseball fans on the East Coast *demand* competitive coverage.

"You'll get the real story here," said columnist Jackie MacMullan of the *Boston Globe*. "Guys [media] in New York are fearless, Philly is fearless. We're writing for fans who are more educated about their teams than we are."

"Readers are demanding," said sportswriter Michael Morrissey of the *New York Post*. "They're not going to waste time reading something that doesn't tell them anything. They're not going to waste time when life is so fast-paced, especially in the Northeast."

Even in a video- and Internet-saturated age, the heavy public transportation users in the big Eastern cities keep the newspaper habit relatively strong. The concentration of colleges in the New York, Boston, and Philadelphia areas also boosts literacy.

"Boston is one of the most literate cities," said Morrissey, a Boston native. "New York is up there. Reading newspapers, even though it's declining overall, is still part of their lifestyle."

So is winning. The forgiving nature of the heartland would never play within sniffing distance of the Atlantic.

"People in New York demand a winner, people in Boston demand a winner," Morrissey said. "Stuff that plays at U.S. Cellular Field and Wrigley Field would never play at Shea Stadium. The Mets alienated a lot of fans from 2001 to 2004."

You'd figure the Red Sox would have alienated all of New England after their myriad of stretch-drive and postseason pratfalls, along with the lifetime of humiliation administered by the Yankees that ended in the greatest postseason comeback ever in the 2004 American League Championship Series. But a collective, strange neurosis developed. Through the millennium, the aura of failure only increased Boston's popularity and the craving for microscopic coverage.

The *Worcester Telegram and Gazette*'s Bill Ballou, whose nineteen seasons on the beat ranked him in 2005 as the longest-serving traveling writer among the Boston press corps, said the Red Sox are the only team whose appeal was intimately tied to failure. The longer the BoSox fell short of their World Series title, the more their popularity grew.

"The Red Sox are the single biggest story in this city," MacMullan said. "The Red Sox are treated like a national treasure in this area."

Every move by every Red Sox personality is scrutinized and hyped.

"Johnny Damon got his hair cut in Lowell, so it's a huge photo on page 1 of our paper," *Lowell Sun* sportswriter Rob Bradford said. "One night, sitting in the office, we heard that Bronson Arroyo was sitting down at the White Castle bar. We were asked if we were going to send a photographer and reporter.

"We have the Lowell Spinners single-A team here. Pedro Martinez came to a game once, and it was crazy."

Meanwhile the explanation of New York coverage is simple. The Big Apple is the world's media capital. Competition is cutthroat.

But how Boston equaled New York in intensity of baseball coverage, ranking second in sheer numbers despite not rating top-five status as a metropolitan area, relates more to the collective neurosis involving the Red Sox and the sheer density of the population.

"The *Boston Globe* covers sports like the elections and Iraq," said MacMullan. "It's a very competitive market."

If Boston is "the Hub," cities large enough to sustain daily newspapers with heavy Red Sox coverage radiate out on the spokes of a wheel throughout New England.

"Worcester is a separate market with a separate paper, and it's only thirty-five miles from Boston," Ballou said. "Worcester is Massachusetts' second largest city. You go ninety miles west of Boston, and you're almost in New York."

The *Providence Journal* and *Hartford Courant*, which also travels with the Yankees, dip into the exchequer to go on the road with the Red Sox to keep their cities' readers from patronizing the Boston papers.

"Two days after the 2004 trade deadline, after scouting the Cape Cod League, I picked up the Providence paper," said longtime scout Gary Nickels, now working for the Dodgers. "It was like reading a Boston paper with its baseball coverage. Everything about the Red Sox was there."

Of course, many Red Sox players and executives will term the Boston media competition nasty, or worse. The sheer number of media squeezing into a tiny home clubhouse at Fenway Park creates tensions. Todd Walker, who played second for Boston in 2003, recalled how when one player started talking to one reporter at his locker, he was immediately swarmed by a media mob.

"We have developed a reputation as a tough media town," Mac-Mullan said. "People within our business have developed standards. We're not here to kiss guys' rear ends."

Ted Williams, the all-time Boston baseball icon, had no use for many aggressive, critical Boston writers and columnists. After a career spent spitting, sneering, and otherwise flipping off those who covered him, Williams stepped it up in spring training of 1961. Immediately after his retirement, new hitting instructor Williams had to be pulled away from trying to fight a visiting Boston writer when the former spotted him in Red Sox camp in Arizona.

Nomar Garciaparra, just after Williams among the group of all-time Red Sox favorites, departed for the Cubs in a July 31, 2004, trade amid months of media sniping. But the rest of the season spent in Chicago seemed such a contrast that on the season's final day, he thanked the local media for their "professionalism."

The only way for players to deal with the Boston media onslaught is straightforward, according to Tim Wakefield, the senior player on the 2004 Red Sox world champions.

"Honesty is the best way to deal with any kind of media," knuckleballer Wakefield said. "If you fail, I've always been a man who was taught to stand up. Be a man and accept responsibility for your actions. I've done that for the ten years I was here. Writers have a lot of respect for that. They don't like people who make excuses for anything that happens on the field. I've earned that respect from the writers.

Don't duck the Boston media, Wakefield advised. "You just open yourself up for more criticism if you do that," he said. "That's just the way I handle it personally. That's the advice I give a young player who comes here."

All-time Red Sox-turned-Yankee-then-Astro Roger Clemens has no publicly bad memories of his Boston days in spite of the attendant controversies and the stories he had heard of Ted Williams's and Carl Yastrzemski's media run-ins.

"For the most part I enjoyed it," he said. "Coming onto the scene, striking out twenty, kick-starting my career in that manner—baseball in the East to me is the ultimate. We had the tradition, the very high standard of winning at the University of Texas. The College World Series enabled me to handle Major League Baseball."

But throw race into the mix, and media-player relations in racial-harmony-challenged Boston got volatile. Somehow outfielder Ellis Burks, one of the game's gentlemen, learned how to survive and keep his sanity during two tours of duty with the Red Sox.

"It was a bit of a surprise to me the first few years," Burks said. "As a player in Boston, you got used to it. It's tough where there were a lot of times you got dragged into it [controversy, such as ones that enveloped Jim Rice and Dennis 'Oil Can' Boyd]. Things happen in a city that's had a lot of racial tension. As an African American player, you're the first one that questions are brought to. It's tough, you don't want to put your foot in your mouth. But when it comes down to it, I will tell you what's on my mind."

Burks would have had even more chroniclers in New York. Gotham is Boston, cubed, with the famed tabloids, the *Daily News* and *Post*, duking it out daily for a hard-fought piece of the ever-shrinking readership pie. Their back-page sports headlines, all in the spirit of the *Post*'s classic "Headless man in topless bar" style, vie for attention and are often reported in news dispatches across the country. The tabloids prod more sober competitors like the *New York Times* and a bevy of satellite-city and suburban dailies in three states to pant in the same pursuit of readers. With the Yankees establishing a latter-day dynasty and the Mets ranging wildly between contenders and expensive flops over the past decade, baseball is the main sales tool.

Stories circulated of supposed mandates to New York baseball writers to produce regular scoops or be booted off the beat, if not fired outright. The *Post*'s Michael Morrissey and *Daily News* sports editor Leon Carter did not disabuse me of this stereotype.

"The New York media is the toughest in baseball in the country," said Morrissey, who handled the Mets beat from 2001 to 2003. "There really is a mandate to break stories and keep ahead of the other tabloid. In Boston, it's not so much a circulation war. Boston's a pecking order. In New York, it's every man for himself.

"I just know there are certain expectations when you cover a beat in New York. Those expectations are that you'll break news regularly. It's pretty clear soon whether you're breaking news or not. It's not subjective."

Carter, like his cohorts at the helm of other New York sports sections, plays the big brother role for his writers. He's always watching and waiting for the next story to lure the readers away from the competition.

"They come into the job knowing that they have to break stories," Carter said. "No one says that you have to break a story seven days out of seven. You come into the job knowing you have to know what goes on, on your beat. When I read the other New York papers in the morning, when I see a story, I make that story known to that beat writer. I want to know what's going on in the beat."

Mimicking the game's year-round pace, Carter said New York baseball fans "eat up baseball now almost every day in the off-season. That was not always the case. In 1994 the Knicks were very good. The Knicks and football kept everyone warm [in the off-season]. But in 1996, when the Yankees won the World Series, baseball fever returned. That brought baseball back to an all-time high in New York. And when Alex Rodriguez came aboard, whatever level was there was taken up two levels. It's rare that starting with the last out of the World Series you can go two consecutive days with a Yankees or Mets five-hundred-word story. That was not the case in 1994."

Carter or his deputies will field calls from readers wondering about the status of the regular Yankees writer if his byline is absent for a period of time. The passion extends to cult sports. Long before the NHL went dark for the 2004–5 season, the *Daily News* would get letters or calls from fans in Long Island if the paper used an AP story on an Islanders road game.

The newspapers cannot afford to cut coverage even in losing seasons. "In the second half with the [losing] Mets, we would still keep the beat writer or backup on the road," Carter said. "That doesn't mean there won't be news. The worst feeling in the world is to compromise coverage."

With hyper-interest in the two New York NFL teams, newspapers like the *Daily News* came up with a creative way to divide the coverage baby on football Sundays in September and October in order not to anger readers. The tabloid had a special twenty-eight-page NFL section on Mondays starting in 2000, while the baseball teams still hold forth on the trademark back page. "We did not want football to take away from baseball, so we did that special section," Carter said.

The New York baseball reporter's job is even harder simply because the sheer number of on-site competitors cuts down on the one-on-one reporting encounters necessary for scoops. That taxes both the imagination and relationship-building talents.

"The number one technique is hard work," Morrissey said. "You have to develop relationships. Working hard and working smart go hand in hand. The way you develop a rapport [with sources] is being knowledgeable about the sport. You show yourself as hard-working. You have to ask the right questions.

"You can develop one-on-one relationships with guys. It's not the same as two generations ago when all reporters had good one-on-one deals with most players. If you're lucky, you'll have good interpersonal relationships with half the guys, if you're good. But every guy in New York worth his salt is a one-on-one operator."

The seven to eight traveling writers are supplemented by reporters covering the Mets and Yankees for all-sports WFAN-Radio. The fifty-thousand-watt giant, occupying the old WNBC-Radio 660 frequency, is the only station in the country besides KOMO in Seattle to send a reporter on the road full time.

"You just try to develop sources," veteran WFAN Mets reporter Ed Coleman said. "One advantage I have is I'm there every day. Maybe guys trust me more. When [Bobby] Valentine was there, something always was going on. Valentine had his select guys he leaked stuff to."

Amazingly, veterans of playing in New York recalled being able to manage their media experiences without going crazy.

"New York's a little different [than Boston] because of the [winning] track record," Hall-of-Fame-bound pitcher Roger Clemens said. "You better have that high of standards. I enjoyed it."

Outfielder Rondell White, a media-friendly chap, could have been fodder for constant criticism as a free-agent Yankee in 2002.

"I played terrible there," he said. "They didn't dog me out as much like they could have. The reporters there were great with me. Nobody ever said I couldn't play the game. It's what you make of it. If you go in with a negative attitude, it will be a negative situation."

Minnesota Twins manager Ron Gardenhire enjoyed a relatively forgiving Midwestern market first as a top aide to Tom Kelly, then as Kelly's successor. But he had a turn at handling the fishbowl in New York as a 1980s Mets infielder.

"You have two choices," he said. "You can either be at war with them and say, 'No comment,' or you can oblige them and let them do their job. If you let them do their job, there will be no problem. They will ask tough questions. A lot of those guys' jobs are to stir it up a little bit. Answer them as best as you can. If I screwed the game up with an error and they come in, I just tell them I blew it. No bullshit that the sun got in my eye. I just told them I missed the ball. It wasn't anybody's fault but mine. They really can't do much with that."

The extra space both New York and Boston media outlets can clear for such sensationalized, saturated baseball coverage happens because amateur sports do not have the standing in their markets that editors deem they have in the heartland.

"New York always was a strong pro town," Carter said. "It never was a strong college town."

"High schools are not predominant here," the *Lowell Sun*'s Bradford said. "On our front page, if we have a Red Sox story, that'll almost always lead the paper."

The lack of distraction by lower-interest sports enables media talent to build up their political cachet. Not only do they have a chance to gain attention with breaking stories, but they also have a prime opportunity to get noticed by national media. Since most major news organizations are headquartered in New York, with ESPN not far up the road in Bristol, Connecticut, the aggressive, enterprising—and more important, politically astute—baseball scribe or broadcaster can break out onto an even bigger stage. That's one important reason much of the slant of national coverage is New York- or Boston-oriented.

ESPN's lead reporter Peter Gammons made his reputation with his groundbreaking Sunday notes columns in the *Boston Globe*. Gammons may seem an extension of the Red Sox at times and throw a lot of rumors against the wall that don't stick, but he's overall "still good for the industry," said Seattle Mariners general manager Bill Bavasi. Buster Olney's good work on the Yankees for a few years at the *New York Times* also netted a prime ESPN gig. Jayson Stark, formerly a *Philadelphia Inquirer* baseball mainstay, made an easy transition to ESPN.com. The formula is simple. If national media management sometimes appear in the East Coast ballparks, they'll befriend and hire the local talent. In comparison, the top Kansas City, Minneapolis, or Cleveland baseball writer only has a ghost of a chance to go national.

"Sure, you do it subconsciously," said Steve Friedman, former executive producer of *The Today Show* and CBS's *The Early Show*. Even though he was a Chicago native who also worked in Los Angeles, Friedman fell into the pattern of hiring those who crossed his path at his New York base.

"You see them, and whoever comes to mind [gets the job]. You see [baseball] through their prism. The center of the baseball universe is Boston and New York. It's also easier to get to Bristol [for ESPN studio appearances] from Philly than it is from Houston."

But there's far more to baseball than just the Eastern corridor, a fact that rankled discerning fans when Ken Burns's memorable PBS *Baseball* series aired during the early months of the strike in 1994. At the time, it seemed Burns extended all the old Yankees, Red Sox, and Brooklyn Dodgers legends to fill the majority of the series while teams west of the Appalachians were given short shrift. The careers of Stan Musial, Ernie Banks, and a host of others were downplayed compared to the already heavily publicized legends who were lucky enough to draw a New York or Boston team paycheck. Burns's work continued the trend of churning out books romanticizing the 1920s to 1950s era of the Dodgers and Yankees, and preceded a blizzard of books celebrating the Red Sox's 2004 feats.

Richard Lindberg, author and semi-official White Sox historian, called Burns's work "The ESPN Fly-Over Zone." That was a reference to "the great expanse of land stretching from the Ohio Valley to the western edge of the Rockies—*Baseball* was a disappointing and futile exercise of East Coast elitism, shutting out the cluster of teams situated in the heartland. Lindberg called historian Doris Kearns Goodwin's nostalgia for her youthful Brooklyn Dodgers "dewy-eyed." There was no similar storyteller for the Cubs, Cardinals, or Reds, three teams in business for more than a century at the time of the documentary.

Lindberg claimed that the program had "very little to say beyond thirty-second sound bites about the Tigers, Reds, Twins, Brewers, White Sox, Cubs, Indians, Cardinals, and Royals. Given the fabled Cubs-Cardinals rivalry, the great Tigers teams of the past, and a White Sox tragedy extending beyond the border of the 1919 Black Sox Scandal, Midwestern fans were badly shortchanged.

"Admittedly, the cinematic presentation and the visual imagery of *Baseball* was a stunning triumph," Lindberg said, "but the editorial content reflected strong regional bias and was exploitive and offense to the baseball purists living in the center of the country."

Lindberg also criticized a perceived East Coast–orientation to the format of ESPN-Radio, the highest-profile national sports radio network. "Do the underserved sports fans exiled west of the Hudson River–New England axis really care to listen to Red Sox manager Terry Francona spouting off to Dan Patrick and Rob Dibble about congratulatory calls [on a December 24, 2004, show]?" he wrote.

ESPN actually televised a mock-trial show in 2004 to judge whether the worst "curse" had afflicted either the Cubs or Red Sox. Harvard-based, legal-eagle Alan Dershowitz, a Red Sox fan, argued Boston's case—and even quoted from my 2000 book *The Million to One Team: Why the Chicago Cubs Haven't Won a Pennant since 1945* to argue his case. Despite the Red Sox's history of pennant contention compared to the Cubs' constant dwelling in the National League's nether world, the Eastern-oriented "jury" voted Boston as the most cursed of the two franchises.

At times fans in the middle of the country may get more news on the Yankees, Mets, and Red Sox than their own teams. While New York and Boston newspapers have been prompted to increase their already-sumptuous diet of baseball coverage, some of their counterparts throughout the Midwest have been moving in the other direction. The logical prompts of the home-run race of 1998 plus contending Cardinals and Cubs teams have not had the desired effect in boosting original baseball content.

The direction in the heartland is status quo, if not a rollback, in baseball coverage, where media outlets are already far from the big-league ballparks. Instead of the crunched-up cities of the Northeast all within cozy, traffic-clogged distances of stadiums, the Midwest, Southern, and Great Plains outlying cites are hard, long drives at high-speeds distance. The economics of dispatching reporters, paying hefty mileage totals and even overnight lodging, combined with supervising editors' cravings for a "niche" for their papers with local sports has relegated baseball to more encapsulated coverage.

Thus Cardinals fans spread out all over the Midwest and further south can access just one newspaper—the *St. Louis Post-Dispatch*—that follows the team home and on the road during the course of a season. The far-flung Redbird rooters just have one version of the ebb and flow of the long season. Meanwhile, on Friday, August 27, 2004, during a crucial series at Wrigley Field between the Cubs and Astros, only five daily newspapers manned the game. The day corresponded with the first night of high school football. One regularly covering suburban newspaper, the *Northwest Herald*, had to skip the game to borrow its Cubs writer for prep coverage in an all-men-on-deck stance. And even though the Cubs were squarely in the National League wild-card race—in fact were leading by one and a half games with one week to go—in 2004, only one outlying newspaper, the *Grand Rapids Press*, beefed up its coverage. The Cubs threatened to reach the postseason two years in a row for the first time since antiquity, but it was not enough to join the bandwagon.

Such a trend has not gone unnoticed by baseball officials who keep track of who staffs their games.

"I found it surprising the Peoria paper rarely comes up here," said Cubs media relations director Sharon Pannozzo. "Granted, geography here is much further away. In the East, big cities are close by [teams] with big papers. Major papers are in cities just an hour's drive away. Still, it's surprising the [outlying] papers weren't here [in a pennant race]. Rockford, Springfield [Illinois], a lot of small papers in Iowa, they don't cover us. They cover college football, high schools, sports within their communities."

The rollback is surprising in that Cubs interest has been ingrained in the multistate area around Chicago for a century. In 1967, WGN-TV finally satisfied a clamoring that had come for many years from TV stations throughout Illinois, Indiana, and Iowa. The video outlets wanted at least a partial schedule of Cubs telecasts to satisfy viewer demand in this pre-cable era. For several years prior to 1970, when big league baseball returned to Milwaukee after a five-year absence, Cubs telecasts were aired in Milwaukee, Madison, and Green Bay, Wisconsin. In the ensuing decades, as both Wrigley Field attendance and TV ratings could testify, interest in the Cubs had mushroomed from the already high level noted in '67.

Somehow, that trend was not picked up on by Midwestern supervising editors, many of whom would not classify themselves as avid sports fans. Only a partial explanation comes directly from sports editors who determine day-to-day coverage. Just as surprisingly, some of those who have elected to cover high schools over Major League Baseball count themselves big baseball fans.

"The Midwest traditionally is a more laid-back area," said David Schwartz, sports editor of the *Northwest Herald*, who grew up a dyed-in-the-wool Cardinals fan in west St. Louis County. "The Midwest is so much more forgiving. The economy isn't what it was five years ago. There's a very real trend in nonmajor metro markets to a real push toward community journalism. It's a push to cover the big [high school or college] football game while still having AP coverage that you're already paying for.

"High school sports is so much more of an event than on the East Coast. Even so, there are differences in interest. Lacrosse is big on the East Coast, we scratch our heads about it here. If we have one reporter left between covering Crystal Lake South versus Central and covering the Cubs, we'll cover the high school game."

The rise of the Internet starting in the mid-1990s "freaked out newspaper editors," Schwartz said. "They asked, 'What can we provide that they don't?'"

Despite such a philosophy, Schwartz will ramp up baseball coverage when he can. He and editor Chris Krug salted away travel money at the start of each year to be used in case a local pro or college team wins. Although the *Northwest Herald* used AP to cover the Cubs and White Sox on the first two prep Fridays of 2004, the paper traveled with the Cubs on their final long road trip of the season later in September of that year. To compensate, Schwartz cut out staff coverage of the sagging University of Illinois football team.

But other newspapers retreated from original baseball coverage in 2004. The *Rockford Register Star* rolled back coverage more than most. Going into the 1990s, the Gannett-owned daily deployed a staff person based in the Chicago area to cover the Cubs, White Sox, and other sports. In even earlier decades, according to sports editor Randy Ruef, the paper operated its own airplane, which would ferry its sportswriters to all the Big Ten football games on Saturday mornings.

Obviously, economics changed as corporate ownership and adherence to the highest stock prices governed news decisions. Eventually, the Chicago-based sportswriting position was pulled back into the downtown Rockford office, ninety miles northwest of Chicago. Through the 2003 season, the *Register Star* would staff occasional Cubs and White Sox games, meriting a reserved seat in the press boxes. In 2003, writer Andre Smith covered the Cubs for selected Wrigley Field games, then traveled with the team during the postseason.

Yet after Smith left to join an Iowa paper early in the 2004 season, Rockford elected not to staff Chicago baseball games. "We really backed down on travel with all the Internet and cable TV coverage," said Ruef. "When the Cubs do well, everyone shows up and there are plenty of choices of coverage we can take.

"Where my problems lie is that when people get stuff from a lot of sources on a national basis, they want more local news from us. To cover one game, you'd probably count twelve to thirteen hours of time for our reporter. Was that twelve hours worth the column? If he stayed in Rockford, he could do two, three local stories in that time."

Ruef's analysis of readers' desires thus was radically different from that of Eastern sports editors.

"Unless you're a well-known columnist, I don't think people care about bylines," Ruef said. "The public wants more [coverage], but also wants justification. We run a wire story [on baseball], blow up a photo, and it's a nice package. They want volume and size. I can make it look like we really went nuts over a team that we didn't staff. Even if we want to do more, we can't give the readers the same as the *Tribune* and *Sun-Times*. I don't want to sacrifice local coverage."

Although Smith and Ruef were prepared to cover the Cubs all the way through the 2003 World Series had not the fateful game six of the NLCS interfered, Ruef opted not to put in requests for postseason credentials for 2004. "We would have covered them from home," Ruef said.

Mike Nadel's Chicago-based sports column sufficed as occasional, original baseball news for the *Peoria Journal Star* and *Springfield State Journal-Register*. Previously, longtime Chicago columnist Bill Gleason authored a Chicago-based column for both the *South Bend Tribune* and *Daily Southtown*, the latter a southwest suburban Chicago daily that staffed road games of Chicago baseball teams. But when Gleason retired, the South Bend paper did not replace the Chicago coverage.

Cubs and Cardinals fans enjoy summers-full of argument and debate all throughout central and southern Illinois. So where would these passionate rooters turn for baseball coverage if the sparse AP coverage and agate box scores were not enough in their local dailies, and they did not read the *St. Louis Post-Dispatch*, *Chicago Tribune*, or *Chicago Sun-Times*, or access some online operation?

"You're not well-served by coverage around here if you don't go online," said Bloomington adman Mark Gibson. "For a lot of people, no matter if the information is credible, they turn on The Score [WSCR-AM, the all-sports radio station in Chicago]. My own radio never leaves 720 [WGN-Radio's frequency]."

A similar situation existed for Cardinals fans in Columbia, Missouri, two hours west of St. Louis. "People are really into the Cardinals here," said Joe Walljasper, sports editor of the *Columbia Tribune*. Operating in a smaller market, the Redbirds depend on drawing from a multistate region to have regularly filled Busch Stadium over the decades.

But even with the intense baseball interest at hand, Walljasper said his paper "hasn't covered a Cardinals game in years."

Economics is the main factor. "If you do it seriously, cover eighty home games, that's two hours each way with mileage and everything else," Walljasper said. "Figure $100 times eighty-one for the per-game expenses. If we're not going to do it full bore, what we could provide ourselves isn't that much different than AP provides. If I had my druthers, we would go there and have regular features."

Walljasper said Columbia-area residents have alternatives in the *St. Louis Post-Dispatch* and Internet providers such as MLB.com if they want wall-to-wall Cardinals coverage. However, that's a hazardous philosophy. An editor should never suggest his readers go elsewhere for vital information. He risks losing the readers permanently. Promoting such reader defections can be the result of forgoing staff coverage for nuts-and-bolts AP game stories and truncated notes packages.

Like the *Register Star* with Chicago baseball coverage, the *Topeka Capital Journal* once covered the Kansas City Royals much more comprehensively. Just after the franchise was founded in 1969, the newspaper had a full-time beat writer work the Royals' home and road games. That frequency was cut back to home games only in the 1990s. By 2002 the home games would still be covered until football season began, prompting the *Capital Journal* to bail out. Then in 2003 the paper began using AP for a number of home games.

"We did get some [negative] feedback," sports editor Eric Turner said of fans' reaction to AP coverage. "If Bartolo Colon pitched a one-hitter against the Royals, there would be thirteen inches of that, and one on the Royals. I would love to know for sure [how much reader dissatisfaction existed]. I'd like some data. We might have lost people to the *Kansas City Star*. I'm a huge baseball fan, and I was reading the *Star*.

"It absolutely can be a risk [to lose readers if staff coverage is cut]."

When the Royals had a mini-surge at midseason 2003, the *Capital Journal* resumed sending staffers to home games. Then the paper ramped it up, restoring earlier coverage levels in 2004. A Kansas City–based staffer now worked both the Royals and the NFL Chiefs.

Some August and September home games might go uncovered if there was a conflict with Chiefs games and practices. The KC-based coverage now was fed to other Morris Communications newspapers in suburban Kansas City, Dodge City, and Pittsburg, Kansas.

Even if the Missouri or Kansas reader forgoes his local paper to pick up the *Post-Dispatch* or *Star*, that's the limit of comprehensive baseball coverage in the region. The trend of one-newspaper, Major League markets is underrated in judging the competitive and diverse nature of baseball reporting. No suburban dailies have developed to provide traveling competition for the papers in St. Louis, Kansas City, Milwaukee, Houston, and San Diego. Even Chicago, the third-largest market in the country, only has three traveling newspapers wire-to-wire during the entire Cubs season, fewer than New York, Boston, Philadelphia, and Los Angeles.

Wouldn't the lack of competition, with the exception of MLB. com, which has some restrictions on its total scope of coverage, be bad for both sports journalists and their readers?

"In theory it could hurt," said Bob Dutton, Royals beat writer for the *Star*. "But in addition to MLB.com, we have sports-talk radio. In Kansas City we have fifteen radio reporters running around at all times. More choices are better. It's now not just newspaper-to-newspaper. I wish there were more newspapers; there'd be more jobs."

Dutton's boss, *Star* sports editor Mike Fannin, believes the one-newspaper markets have their "benefits and downsides. It's both good and bad."

"On a road trip the only people with [Dutton] are those working for the Royals radio network," he said. "The downside is it's not as urgent as you always need to be. But the upside is you can develop a story. If Bob hears at 10:00 p.m. there's some juicy tidbit that has to develop out, he is not forced to put it in the paper [on final deadline]. He can come back the next day and still deliver a scoop."

But a one-newspaper market can leave a gaping hole in reporting unless someone else steps in to fill it. Usually, a TV person can't fill that role with the pressure to get quick, fast-paced sound bites and with less than three minutes of total airtime on an evening-news sportscast.

One outlying heartland newspaper that doesn't dare cut coverage is the *Dayton Daily News*. The paper has long promoted legendary beat writer Hal McCoy's home-and-road Reds reporting—for a very good reason. "Surveys have shown that 30 percent of Reds fans are in the Dayton area," McCoy said.

But the Dayton and Topeka examples are exceptions to the rule of local-first philosophy, even though baseball in its darkest days had far more widespread readership than high school sports.

I experienced two rollbacks from pros to preps first-hand—commanded by editors who were baseball fans. In 2001, I persuaded Dave Marran, the longtime sports editor of the *Kenosha News*, circulating in the southeastern corner of Wisconsin, to let me author a weekly Cubs column. Kenosha is fifty-five miles from Chicago, thirty-five miles from Milwaukee, and is home to avid fans of teams in both cities.

Marran, himself a Cubs fan, had briefly run a Cubs-oriented Web site in his spare time. The column, averaging a thousand words, was packaged every Sunday with a similar piece on the Brewers by Milwaukee-based Greg Hoffman, who had covered the Brewers anyway for years for the *News*. Marran liked my production, and he said higher-up editors also were pleased.

Then 9/11 imploded media outlets' bottom lines, already sagging from a severe advertising recession that began in late 2000. I didn't figure the Cubs column would return for 2002, and Marran confirmed it. At the time, he said even though upper management classified themselves as avid sports fans, they ordered a focus on only local events within Kenosha County, where the *News* circulated. Late in 2004, Marran added that the decision was financially driven more than philosophically based.

The Cubs and Brewers coverage weren't the only coverage rollbacks for the *News*. Marran said that in the 1990s the paper had staffed almost all games played by the Green Bay Packers, by far the most popular pro team in their area, along with the entire state of Wisconsin, of course. The *News* even had published an instant book on the Packers' Super Bowl XXXI triumph. Also dropped were staff coverage of University of Wisconsin football and basketball, Marquette basketball, and some Chicago Bears games.

The Cubs and Brewers coverage were a "substantial financial and space commitment in a county that has eight high schools, two colleges, thirty-eight pages a week, and a staff of only six to handle it all," Marran said. "Because of our space and the growing demands for local coverage we were only able to fit in the nuts and bolts [of pro and major college coverage], which is what the AP was also giving us . . . I am better served putting that thousand dollars [spent on the Cubs column] into local coverage. I would be derelict in my duties as sports editor of the *Kenosha News* if I did not."

Also going by the wayside, in January 2005, was my weekly Lerner Newspapers Cubs-oriented column that I had fought so hard to convert away from low-interest high school sports fifteen years earlier.

New management from the suburban-based *Pioneer Press* absorbed Lerner into their operation. Chicago bureau chief Kathy Catrambone applied *Pioneer*'s intensely local suburban model to editions circulating in Chicago, even though the city and suburbs had different readership interests and standards. Catrambone informed me, without any knowledge of my background of breaking stories not seen in the big metro papers, that the downtown dailies could cover the Cubs so much better than *Pioneer*/Lerner. I was free to continue to write my column if it focused on high school sports—even though the newspapers continued to circulate in the neighborhood around Wrigley Field. When Catrambone made the announcement to me, she added she was planning to attend her eighth Cubs Convention in a few days—continuing a strange trend of professed Cubs rooters cutting coverage of the team while working as editors. I had to go along with the mandate, despite past struggles with the late Lou Lerner over the same issue, because of personal finances. Oddly enough, five months later Catrambone was laid off.

Obviously, Cubs fans are not as rabid as their Red Sox and Yankees counterparts, either in demanding in-depth coverage as readers or listeners, or in crafting the same as media managers.

To this day, I still cannot understand the thirst for narrowcasting in sports by editors. Unless they lived in isolated areas hundreds of miles from the nearest pro team—Odessa, Texas, site of *Friday Night Lights* comes to mind—the majority of sports fans would not logically have any intense readership interest in high school athletics unless their children participated.

"You have to be in a small town to have [widespread] interest in high school sports," Kansas City sports editor Mike Fannin said. "There's an old adage that every kid's name in the paper is [worth] a subscriber. I don't know if that's true."

A contrary view was offered by Bill Wolverton. A former sports columnist and Bears writer for the *Rockford Register Star*, Wolverton once said that extensive prep coverage at the expense of the pros was justified in his area. "We have a lot of prep junkies," he said of fans who had no apparent family links to participating high school athletes. But whether such boosters existed in any abundance, they were still far outnumbered by Rockford-area baseball fans who were originally made happy when NBC affiliate WTVO-TV began picking up that ad-hoc WGN network of Cubs telecasts back in 1967.

An example of the true economic impact, or lack thereof, for high school coverage for media outlets is the Marion-Carbondale market in far southern Illinois. Paxton Guy, the operations manager for the Clear Channel–owned local cluster of radio stations, said early in 2005 he had trouble selling his high school sports package. The reason was that a number of businesses had moved into the area in recent years, importing workers who had no ties to the local high schools. They did not listen to the broadcasts.

Are the editors' decisions about tipping their coverage heavily toward high schools not well-informed? Much evidence suggests yes.

"What's changed is people want more stories about *me, my kids*," Rockford sports editor Randy Ruef said. But in the same breath, he suggested such coverage is limited in his total circulation, depending upon whether readers' children are actually participating in youth or high school programs.

"Most complaints here come from women," Ruef added. They are defined as mothers who generally did not care about sports until their children began playing in high school and wanted to build up their scrapbooks. Throughout the newspaper industry, these mothers are figured to be temporary readers.

The parents' calls and complaints end up as the main impetus for overcoverage of preps. Often angrily demanding coverage of their child, and feeling a sense of entitlement from their local newspaper, the parents often direct their opinions at managing editors or executive editors, who wrongly misinterpret a groundswell of interest in local sports. As a result, even minor activities such as cross-country, tennis, and golf get coverage far out of proportion to their overall appeal and interest level.

In contrast, the baseball fan tends not to call up the paper unless the box scores, statistics, or standings are screwed up or omitted. Or, in the Chicago area, if the White Sox are given lesser play than the Cubs.

Ed Bannon, former Lerner Newspapers editor and general manager, kept a concisely local focus in his chain before he was replaced by Catrambone in 2004. But Bannon, a Chicago native and baseball fan, also believed there was a place for Cubs coverage even though the paper came out weekly. Although high schools were the main focus of Lerner's sports coverage, Bannon claimed that preps had a limited audience in an urban area.

"The only people who are prep fans are the parents, close family members, and possibly alumni who played the sport," he said. "I don't think there's as much loyalty even as I once thought. If one of those schools went downstate [to state championship tournaments], maybe they'd take notice.

"It's a rural mentality. A smaller town rallies around its team more than an urban area. The population is so mobile in an urban area, so you don't have people who went to high school in the area. And there are also people who went to the high schools who didn't get involved in sports. Editors who mandate it feel like it's an obvious connection—if people live there, since they cover village board, they should cover local high school team. With high school sports, it's so diffused with the number of sports, both genders, three or four levels of play, so many teams. Unless you do it comprehensively, every score for every team, it does not work great."

Sportswriters and copy-desk editors offered an inside-out look at preps versus pro coverage when they posted their opinions on SportsJournalists.com. They offered a differing view than their bosses on what is known in the newspaper business as the "scrapbook beat"—the scrapbooks of clippings collected by parents of high school athletes.

"Our readership surveys tell us that about 20 percent of our readers care about high school sports, far below the numbers of NFL, NASCAR, NBA, MLB, etcetera," was a typical response of one November

2004 poster. "Yet we cover the crap out of high school stuff, when it's obvious that not many care because there are fifty to seventy-six people at the games, because somebody writes a letter or bitches that little Johnny won't get a scholarship if the paper doesn't document what he's done."

Another SJ.com poster was even more blunt.

"This is not about 'embracing local,' " he wrote. "There's one reason and one reason only for this unhealthy obsession with preps: money. Newspaper editors want Johnnie and Jayne's mom and dad to buy a paper they normally wouldn't buy if their kids weren't in it . . . Actual editorial judgment be damned . . . The simplistic reaction is: Concede that [non-local] coverage and those sports while blowing out prep coverage to the extreme . . . A good small, medium, or large newspaper will contain a mixed bag of sports stories, with the biggest story of the day—be it local, regional, or national—as the lead story."

Preps versus pros was never an issue on the newspaper-rich West Coast, previously the other part of baseball journalism's "blue states." But the actual identifying color of the region had turned somewhat murky as the zeroes decade progressed. Straight, stark economics is causing severe rollbacks in baseball coverage in the Los Angeles and San Francisco areas, long known for big cadres of traveling beat writers.

The largest cut took place going into the 2005 season. The *San Jose Mercury News*, one of the region's best dailies, is owned by the Knight-Ridder chain, which also runs the *Contra Costa Times*, a smaller daily circulating in the East Bay part of the San Francisco–Oakland area. Rather than duplicating beat coverage of Bay Area teams while under the same corporate umbrella, each paper dropped its entire beat coverage of one Major League team. The *Mercury News* dropped its Oakland Athletics beat, shifting over to Giants reporter Chris Haft, who had been hired just before the 2004 season from Cincinnati to cover the A's. The *Times* ended its original Giants coverage, moving longtime beat man Joe Roderick over to the Athletics. Under the new arrangement, the *Mercury News* would provide Giants coverage to the *Times*, which in turn would originate Athletics stories for the *Mercury News*.

The baseball teams weren't the only franchises affected. The *Mer-*

cury News, which already had picked up coverage of the NBA's Golden State Warriors and University of California (Berkeley) sports from the *Times*, also ceded coverage of the NFL's Raiders to the smaller daily. In turn, the *Times* would pick up the San Jose paper's reportage of the NFL's 49ers.

Executives estimated that the savings would total fifty thousand dollars a year in travel costs. The silver lining was that no staffers were laid off—at that point. The newspaper, though, joined in the industry-wide epidemic of job cuts later in 2005.

"It would be fair to say that we don't relish making these moves," *Mercury News* executive editor Susan Goldberg wrote in a memo to her staff. "However, given the financial realities [of the shaky Bay Area economy], this is a way to save a considerable amount of money while having a minimal impact on readers."

But Goldberg's fiat made the *Mercury News* the largest daily in the country that did not fold or merge with another paper to drop daily coverage of a Major League baseball team in its area. In an interview, Goldberg said her paper's hands were forced.

"This was totally a cost move," she said, citing the concept of two writers from "sister papers a couple of dozen miles apart" both making an expensive trip to Detroit and points further east.

"This will be an invisible move to readers. We do still have access to beat coverage. A lot of people took this decision hard in the sports department. We don't consider travel costs covering sports teams to be discretionary. But we don't want to duplicate the effort and costs."

Often the quality and scope of sports coverage depends on the top editor's own passion for the subject.

"I'm not a huge sports fan, but I know it's important to a lot of people," Goldberg said. "Sports is not a game, it's entertainment coverage. It's what readers spend their time talking about around the water coolers. We put a lot of sports on the front page. Sports stories are good stories."

Other Bay Area newspapers made coverage cuts. In spring training 2005, both the *Sacramento Bee* and *Oakland Tribune* slashed travel and lodging expenses to where only one writer could be in Arizona at one time to cover either the Giants or Athletics.

The *Bee* cut even further to start the 2006 season. After having long traveled with the Giants and Athletics, using Bay Area–based staffers, the *Bee* pulled out of road coverage for both teams. Sports editor Bill Bradley said that enterprise features on baseball would take the place of the road games. The cost savings was estimated at seventy thousand dollars per team.

Denver fans also had fewer coverage choices. When the Colorado Rockies franchise began in 1993, the *Boulder Daily Camera* and *Colorado Springs Gazette* both joined the two major Denver papers in traveling full time. But both papers ceased traveling regularly by 2001 as both the economy and Rockies fortunes tumbled.

Similarly, the *Arizona Daily Star* in Tucson traveled wire-to-wire with Phoenix-based writer Jack Magruder starting in 1998, when the Arizona Diamondbacks began play. But, amazingly, the travel was cut out in 2001, just in time for the D-Backs' startling World Series victory. As the *Star* further cut its baseball coverage in 2005, Magruder left for the *East Valley Tribune*, based in Mesa, to take over its D-Backs beat.

All the while, the Los Angeles area bled original baseball coverage like helium rushing from a burst balloon.

In the wake of the Kirk Gibson– and Orel Hershiser–fueled Dodgers World Series victory in 1988, some eleven Los Angeles–area papers traveled through all or part of the team's road schedule.

In addition to the *Los Angeles Times*, the dying *Los Angeles Herald Examiner* was still on the road with reporter Ken Gurnick. The San Fernando Valley–based *Los Angeles Daily News* was along for the ride. The long roster of suburban and outlying papers on the road included the *Orange County Register*, *Long Beach Press-Telegram*, the *Daily Breeze* (Torrance), *Riverside Press-Enterprise*, *San Bernardino Sun*, *Pasadena Star-News*, *San Gabriel Valley Newspapers*, *Ventura County Star* and *La Opinion*, Los Angeles's Spanish-language daily. In addition, the *Inland Daily Bulletin* in suburban Ontario made the occasional San Diego and San Francisco trip along with a spring training jaunt.

"The competition in L.A. was intense," then Dodgers media-relations director Jay Lucas recalled. "Players would complain about it, that eight or nine guys were waiting around for them. That's how Ken Gurnick got his nickname, 'Mouse.' They worked sources downstairs and worked sources upstairs."

But the once bountiful Tinseltown newspaper market began to shrivel or consolidate. The *Herald Examiner* folded. By the mid-1990s, a number of the papers stopped traveling, including Long Beach, sidelining ace baseball scribe Gordon Verrell. By the turn of the century, the Dodgers' traveling crew shrunk to no more than four writers.

Worse yet, home games witnessed a cut in original coverage. The William Dean Singleton newspaper chain, based at the *Daily News*, assumed ownership of the San Bernardino, San Gabriel, Pasadena, and Ontario papers. Singleton also tried, but failed, to buy the *Orange County Register* and *Riverside Press-Enterprise*. Dodgers coverage was originated by the *Daily News*, while San Gabriel handled the Angels. Those stories were fed throughout the area chain.

"I think it hurts from a club standpoint," Lucas, now an Astros media-relations executive, said. "As a publicist, more of anything helps. With the total coverage of a team, the newspaper guys would have the notes, the inside-the-clubhouse information. That kind of information is still there, but it's not like it used to be. Fewer writers are covering baseball. In-depth coverage has changed."

"You'd only get four or five versions where we used to get eight or nine different versions," said Jim Gazzolo, former sports editor of the *Inland Daily Bulletin* and the *Times of Northwest Indiana*. "There were feature stories cut back on. Staff was cut so much you don't have off-day stories, and you don't have backup guys doing stories. More competition made the *L.A. Times* better."

Gazzolo remembers much more crowded press boxes in Los Angeles and Anaheim. "At a home game, you would fight for a seat at Dodger Stadium through the mid-1990s," he said. "Now you can walk right in and sit wherever you want. It got where [Angels owner Arte] Moreno built a private box and cut off part of the press box. It didn't matter, because there was less coverage and people anyway."

Further down the coast in San Diego, the *Union-Tribune*'s Tom Krasovic has some lonely trips to the East Coast and Midwest. He's the only full-time traveling writer with the Padres. He could remember when the *Union* and *Tribune* were separate newspapers while the team was also covered by the since-defunct San Diego edition of the *Los Angeles Times*.

If baseball fans want more and more of the same versions of stories about their favorite teams, they'll accept the rollback of baseball coverage with nary a whimper. They lose, and the game loses, if that trend continues.

"The main thing editors are asking more than ever is will they see the difference between our staff byline or an AP byline?" Kansas City sports editor Mike Higgins said. "That's where writers have to step up and prove they're better than the wire service, better than the nuts and bolts of play-by-play. If not, it's harder to make the case [for staff coverage]."

Bud Selig made a pastime of holding court in the old County Stadium press box while serving as Milwaukee Brewers owner. Now, if he'd visit other press boxes throughout the country, he wouldn't have as many writers with whom to gab. He might find a few reassigned to the local high school cross-country meet. Something a sport's commissioner should be concerned about, don't you think?

TEN

The Politics Of Baseball Media

Life imitates art in sports journalism—with one important exception. A talent can hit .350 in the minors in baseball, and he's almost always called up. There's no ignoring production. Whether he succeeds in the majors is a different story, but the top bush-league hitters and pitchers will usually get the summons.

But if a writer or broadcaster hits the equivalent of .350 below the Major League level of media, he or she may never hit the big time, through no fault of the individual. They may not be "wired" into the right person. Or the ivory-tower management may not even be aware of the talent.

Reaching the major leagues of sports media requires plugging in to an old boys' network—women are still in a tiny minority in management. More than any other aspect of media, sports journalism is almost akin to entertainment and is managed accordingly. Relationships and reputations count as much as, and sometimes more than, natural ability.

Such a trend was apparent when media observers discussed the lack of African American sports editors for an *Editor and Publisher* article by Allan Wolper on March 7, 2005.

"White editors are often like the coaches they cover," said Keith Woods, dean of the Poynter Institute for Media Studies. "They have an 'old boy' network and they take care of their friends."

"Any time there is a closed hiring process, you have an ethical problem," said Richard E. Lapchick, director of the Institute for Diversity and Ethics in Sport at the University of Central Florida. "The situation is similar to the time when there weren't any black quarterbacks."

Yet it wasn't just talent of color that had trouble getting a break. Talent of all kinds was locked out, partially by an overwhelming demand for only a few positions open at any time, but also the general tendency for media managers to hire those they know or formerly worked with. Just like coaches moving their assistants around the country with them, a media management person would move to a new job in a new city, summoning his most trusted and best-liked coworkers to join him.

Such a trend, of course, is workplace politics at its most basic. And the political system would expand to envelop almost all aspects of sports media. But that's not surprising, because the entertainment business per se operates in such a manner. Sports media is entertainment, no matter that the purists insist otherwise.

The hiring and assigning decisions in this kind of business will have an affect on how the consuming public views baseball and other sports. Who covers baseball, how knowledgeable they are, and how they relate to athletes who are increasingly suspicious of media means everything in accurately conveying the game to the fans forming its financial base.

"Nobody wants to admit this, but the media world is an extension of show business," said Chicago sportscaster Tom Shaer. "Sports media is entertainment. It shouldn't be that way.

"Your job is to get people to read, sell papers, and make money. Get people to watch and listen to broadcasts, build ratings, and sell commercials, too. You're in an entertainment-based business, you're dealing with performers. Media people don't like to see themselves as performers, but that's what they are.

"Every performer has an ego. Why else would you be willing to do it on a public stage? You have to have an ego to do this job. There are varying degrees of egos. People who are crazy enough to put their job out for public evaluation have to have some sort of mechanism that allows them to overcome fear of failure. That mechanism is ego."

When athletes complain that they make mistakes just like any other worker, only it's for public consumption, the same applies to those who cover them.

"If an insurance man screws up someone's policy, who knows about it?" Shaer asked. "The insurance man, the insured person, the home office. If you write a bad article, ninety thousand readers know you screwed up. If I get on the air and stumble around, four hundred thousand people in a week know I screw up. We all make mistakes. We're human.

"Why am I willing to keep myself out in the public eye? Because I've got an ego. Michael Jordan used to say he was not afraid of failure. I used to think it was a bullshit comment. Then I realized what he meant. The guy hit twenty-three game-winning buzzer-beaters in his career. He also missed about thirty of them. Missed thirty times! Yet he was willing to come back and try again. He had this colossal ego. He had the biggest ego I've ever covered. It's not a normal person who is willing to put himself in the public arena. Ego brings about strange behavior, but you can't work in the public area without some ego. The key is for all performers to control their egos."

Whether it's to rub shoulders with athletes or expose their work for public consumption or the pure joy of writing or broadcasting, applicants possessing at least a degree of ego flood media outlets with résumés, e-mails, and phone calls. They desperately work press boxes, the areas around dugouts and batting cages, media conventions, and bars trying to network their way into coveted jobs. Without a real meritocracy that rewards talent and performance as in the athletic arena, the scramble for the top often brings out the worst in people.

So many apply, few are considered, and even fewer are chosen. Everyone wants to be published or broadcast. In contrast, many radio stations actually run on-air spots for advertising salesmen, an often thankless job. The outlets have trouble finding candidates to beat the bush and get rejected fifteen of sixteen times in selling an intangible—airtime—to usually reluctant clients. Even if the salesman can handle daily turndowns and get momentum with some regular clients, the gig is far less glamorous than working on the air.

Governing the industry is an oligarchy of management, often "insiders" who have risen to their positions of authority and who have purposefully jumped aboard the management track. Be they copyeditors in newspapers or producers or editors in broadcast, management ranks will more often than not be stocked by those who have not been the upfront stars of the business. The best talent stays in the front lines, penning award-winning prose or fronting top-rated programming.

The most stark example in my memory is the late Mike Royko, the Babe Ruth of general columnists, never leaving his opinion post to take over as a top editor of the three Chicago papers for which he worked.

"I've often wondered if one of the problems ailing our industry is just this dynamic," Cotter Martin posted on SportsJournalists.com in March 2005. "Once upon a time, the majority of the smartest and most talented and best people in the newspaper business put in their time as reporters, then maybe as columnists before grabbing the reins as managers and executives. I don't see that happening much anymore. Management is supplied by the Peter Principle now. Maybe not everywhere. Maybe not in every case. But I'd argue it's the rule and not the exception that the least among us in newsrooms are climbing management ladders because the best among us don't want to.

"And that, if you ask me, is the overlooked variable for why newspapers are hurting in so many ways."

Many of the management types move from market to market in search of the better job, further diluting their media outlets' relationship to the community and knowledge of its traditions and nuances. Moving up in the business almost demands this rootless, vagabond existence that may look good on the résumé, but often is hell on both family life and ability to relate to each community.

"If I'm in New York and offered a job in Los Angeles, I'm not just going there to cover the Dodgers and Angels; you have to understand the community," said Reds announcer George Grande, who always has kept his home in Connecticut.

Rather than stick to a favorite job in a preferred market, "Most people in our business want to rise to the highest level," Grande added.

"I think people feel they can get a bigger and better opportunity elsewhere," said Susan Goldberg, executive editor of the *San Jose Mercury News*. "The only way to get that next step is to change your newspaper. I've been here two different times. I went to *USA Today* for ten years. Some journalists have itchy feet.

"For a top editing job, I like to promote from within. I like institutional knowledge. It makes us a smarter newspaper. For a sportswriter, having that home-team knowledge is helpful."

Even with such apparently open-minded stances like Goldberg's, the best ideas are often nurtured only from within, not without. And those who know the people with the power of the purse have the edge. Nobody has the time or inclination to sift through every résumé or audition tape.

"It's a business with so few openings," said Greg Rakestraw, program director of all-sports WXLW-AM in Indianapolis. "There's such a limited amount of accredited news organizations and sports organizations. A lot of it is a time crunch [on management]. As pressures for profit margins increase, more responsibilities are put on one individual. You're hurt for time. You look at an opening and you figure, 'I know this guy. I know his work.'"

Sports positions, even at the smallest outlets, are the most coveted in both print and broadcast. Turnover is the lowest among any department, except in the poorly paid, entry-level jobs. In contrast, copyeditors wishing to move from one publication to another don't have a difficult task; there's no thundering herd beating the door down for their inside, largely night-shift positions.

"We had an opening when [sometime baseball writer] Andre Smith left," said Randy Ruef, sports editor of the *Rockford Register Star*. "We were willing to take close to entry-level people. We had thirty-some applicants. Most other departments don't have nearly that much [applicants]. People out there like it. Everybody and their sister thinks they can be a sportswriter. It's hard to pick that [right] résumé. I feel comfortable if I know that person or he's been recommended to me by someone reputable. Even then, recommendations can be somewhat tainted."

New York is a world away from Rockford. The Big Apple is a "terminal market" for so many artists' careers. Once they've made it in New York, the talent doesn't want to live anywhere else, unless they can retire early to a tropical island. So in granting such career-plateau status, leading tabloid *Daily News* sports editor Leon Carter looks internally first when a baseball-writing position opens up.

"That's why having a strong backup guy is good," Carter said. "That person will get the first look. Then you look at who's doing a good job in the New York area. We have smaller, mid-sized papers in New Jersey. People move from paper to paper here. A person who is in New York has the edge over someone outside the area. Not everyone can work in New York. Not everyone can deal with the traffic, subways, culture."

Carter keeps a crate of résumés outside his office and catalogues those he would examine more closely.

"A lot of times, people who are trying to get to a major paper should update their clips," he said. "[Editors] will pay more attention to something that's only a few weeks old."

Carter won't have problems filling the baseball-writer job even with the inherent burnout factors and pressures to break stories that go along with it. But in even greater demand are sports-talk radio jobs. Preceding reputations and relationships do help, but hiring managers want to connect with the prospective talker before they do the same with the listeners.

"Hiring air personalities is like going on a date," said Marc Rayfield, general manager of all-sports WIP-Radio in Philadelphia. "You can't identify what you liked about a girl, but you just know you liked her. It's a chemistry."

"Hiring a host for The Fan in Denver is and always will be very challenging," said Tim Spence, program director of all-sports KKFN-AM in the Mile High City. "Why? Because the talent are the most important pieces of our puzzle. There is really no room for any mistakes. We go through extensive interviewing and reference checking. We most often test-drive the talent on the station just to see how it feels for them *and* for us. Over the years, all the program directors develop relationships with many other talent, [other] program directors, producers, and etcetera."

Rayfield said WIP receives about a half-dozen audition tapes per week. "Occasionally I'll listen to a tape or the program director will say, 'What do you think about this guy?'" he said.

No matter which media, the successful candidate to cover or pontificate about baseball often is much younger these days compared to the grizzled, sometimes boozing middle-aged scribe of the mid-twentieth century. Tender ages and resulting modest salaries, even more so than satisfying upper management's demand for diversity in race and gender in the employee ranks, has been the byword for profit-hungry media outlets in a new century. A generation ago, when I was matriculating from Northern Illinois University, the catchword was "five years experience"—decent-sized media outlets would only hire experienced writers and broadcasters and were willing to pay for it.

Sometimes youthful enthusiasm and energy needs some tempering. Otherwise, media outlets find themselves the center of attention rather than a conduit.

Jeff Passan took over the majority of the national baseball-writing duties at age twenty-four for the *Kansas City Star*, but he and sports editor Mike Fannin ended up in a hornet's nest with Passan's too-honest portrayal of the boys' club of the Cubs clubhouse in May 2004. Half a year later, tongues began clucking when Chris Snow, also just twenty-four, was tabbed from the *Minneapolis Star Tribune* for the all-important Red Sox beat for the esteemed *Boston Globe*.

"Instead of getting a wired, veteran reporter [more than a few of whom were approached and not interested], the *Globe* appears to be using the business model of putting youth on the beats and letting the vets handle the opinions," wrote David Scott of *Boston Sports Media*. "While it might be a cost-saving measure, it's a dangerous word-producing move. The columnists might bring you into the section, but the information guys are supposed to keep you there. He's [Snow] taking over the most pressure-filled reporter's position outside the White House and he's just twenty months removed from snapping late-night slices on M Street [Snow had been a *Globe* intern]."

But if putting twenty-something chaps on the beat raises some eyebrows, they are nothing compared to the wide-eyed, out-of-their-league interns sent by TV and radio stations into the clubhouse to wield microphones to snare sound bites. Not only are these kids ignorant of clubhouse decorum and even player identities, they also have cats catching their tongues when it comes time to asking questions.

My most profound encounter with an unprepared intern was a young woman from Fox-owned WFLD-TV in Chicago asking Cubs outfielder Doug Glanville in 1997 if he was Lance Johnson, another outfielder. Three years later, after I asked Cubs manager Don Baylor one Sunday afternoon why he allowed wild reliever Daniel Garibay to walk in the winning run late in the game, I waited respectfully for someone else to ask a follow-up question. Almost all the other media present were weekend-relief interns with their camera crews. Baylor was about to turn around to retreat into his office when other writers arrived like the cavalry to hold the manager in place.

"There were numerous times in the Bay Area where you had younger girls and guys put the mike in front of you and wait for other persons to ask questions, because they didn't know what to ask," Cardinals lefty Mark Mulder recalled of his Oakland days. "These people come in not knowing what to do."

"You ask, 'Why did they send this kid out without giving him some smaller work to get himself established before he came into the clubhouse?'" said reliever Ray King.

Former Phillies manager Larry Bowa, who knows how to stir the pot, witnessed numerous standoffs between the junior mike-wielders and more experienced writers while he conducted his post-game briefings.

"There's a whole lot of silence sometimes or they'll let the writers do it," said Bowa. "And the writers don't like that, so they won't ask questions. So you sit there with silence. It is sort of comical. The writers don't want to give them material."

The "kiddie" media become a headache for media relations officials.

"A lot of times they're getting questions from their [assignment] desks," said Cleveland Indians media relations director Bart Swain. "They've never even stepped foot in a locker room. They don't know where to go, they're hanging out near the shower, they're asking questions that are not relevant, they're hanging on writers' questions. It can be a problem. A lot of news desks are saying, 'Do this. Do that.' They're throwing people into the fire. They definitely stick out like a sore thumb."

Cubs media relations director Sharon Pannozzo even had to deal with a younger reporter taking a photo of a player's locker with a cell phone in 2004, an act that further alienated players from media, said pitcher Kerry Wood.

"They send interns with veterans as a learning experience," said Pannozzo. "They don't know how to conduct themselves. This isn't a training ground. You have to learn how to conduct yourself in the clubhouse and press box before you get here, like working college games. This isn't school here. I shouldn't be teaching you clubhouse etiquette. Veterans have to give young people some basic advice on basic conduct. I have to think their inexperience would show with their work performance. Unfortunately, if it's a legitimate media outlet, I have to credential them."

Sometimes experienced media who have no background in sports coverage, working for outlets that usually don't cover the game, find their way in. Or the rare appearance of a sports-talk-show host creates a scene. An example was an NBA playoff game in the late 1990s, where Chicago radio gabber Mike North's performance was a virtuoso. In gel-capped Pat Riley's postgame coach's session, North asked Riley whether he'd shave his head if he could be assured of beating the dynastic Bulls. North was ejected.

"There's questionable media at bigger events like the All-Star Game," said Pittsburgh Pirates media relations director Jim Trdinich. "We call them 'foofs,' 'foof media.' I don't know what they're doing there, but they work for legitimate, news-gathering sources. The foofs' parade has gotten a lot bigger. They apply for credentials. They may be from E Network or VH-1, usually nonbaseball outlets. They're looking for harebrained questions and come up with crazy answers."

Making matters worse is Major League Baseball's often overcredentialing of its big events while some legitimate media have trouble gaining access. In the Cubs' 1989 and 2003 National League Championship Series appearances, rows of seats in the auxiliary media section next to the Wrigley Field press box remained empty. These seats were assigned to a smorgasbord of foreign news organizations and even book publishing companies whose representatives did not show up.

Those who do show their faces often mass together in groups, or packs. Most prevalent in Chicago, the pack mentality is present throughout baseball. It is politics within politics in the game—media members hanging out for long stretches of time in the clubhouse or around the dugout. Almost as if they hung together for mutual self-protection, they often made no moves to interview players, coaches, or managers one-on-one, only acting when a scheduled manager's briefing brought all media together before the game.

The concept runs counter to every fundamental in journalism—do everything you can to get the information before the competition to beat them into print or on the air.

"Dick Young [legendary New York baseball writer] said to get something the other guy doesn't have," Reds voice George Grande said of helpful advice in his youthful days.

Although baseball was far from his number one sport, and even less so when a four-hour daily sports-talk radio show precluded a reasonable amount of in-person ballpark time, *Chicago Sun-Times* columnist Rick Telander called the group mentality "the clot . . . laziness . . . bizarre cowardliness."

Don't think that Major League players and managers haven't noticed. Mark Mulder remembered clumps of media gathered in and around the home clubhouse during his Oakland days.

"I don't understand lots of times why the media just hangs out in the clubhouse," Mulder said. "You also noticed them wandering around listening to conversations guys have. They're not coming up to ask questions. Not that it's bad, but I don't understand it. If you're in there, ask some questions. They hang out in a group. I see guys come in, hang out an hour before batting practice and don't ask anybody a single question. They didn't come up to me. They just hang out too much. Players talk about it. It's just the way it is with media."

Writers who were proud of adhering to basic reporting standards also noticed the groups moving about. They did not like what they witnessed.

"You've seen them sitting on the rail like railbirds at a track," said Bob Dvorchak, former Pirates beat writer for the *Pittsburgh Post-Gazette*. "You're not doing yourself any good just standing there talking to each other. Working the clubhouse, you get little nuggets of information readers ought to know, and journalists should be working to get that information.

"There might be a comfort zone [in a group], but you're not going to find information in the comfort zone. You've got to be on the front lines. I always got the best information one-on-one from a player. Over time, you can develop trust with a player, you can ask him something he won't say in a pack situation."

As with other problems in the business, the fault often is not the individuals assigned to cover games and athletes, but their editors' demand for action—or lack thereof. Some editors don't want to get beat. Others don't push their reporters hard enough to fulfill the Dick Young ideal of getting something fresh.

"It probably isn't good for the business," said former *Milwaukee Journal Sentinel* baseball writer Drew Olson, also a former president of the Baseball Writers Association of America. "I think editors play a role in this, also. The desire to have every morsel that the other guys have is very strong among many large-market editors. That leads to pressure to 'follow the pack' to avoid missing something and prevents independent reporting."

Olson cited Murray Chass's speech accepting the Spink Award in 2004. Chass added to that thought later.

"By doing that, they won't get beat on a story," he said of the groups. "Laziness is part of it. If you like your job at all, what's the fun of it if you just hang around with other [media] people?"

Sharing quotes from sources only available in group interviews or press conferences is considered reasonable. Sometimes a "pool" reporter is appointed to get information from an umpiring crew chief or another source who otherwise would not speak to a mass of reporters. However, many who are brought up in the old-school system of competition draw the line at regular cooperation between supposed rivals.

"I get the feeling sometimes that writers from opposing papers or Web sites work in conjunction with one another," said Bob Dutton, Royals beat writer for the *Kansas City Star*. "They're afraid of losing their jobs and getting bumped off the beat. It's a grind, but you've got to maintain your integrity and I've never made any deals with anybody to cooperate with them. I'd rather do it one-on-one."

The breakdown of pure competition is not just limited to baseball. Especially in the NFL, where media access is tightly controlled and choreographed, the practice might even be worse.

"In other sports in New York, the pack mentality still exists where sportswriters trade quotes with each other," said Michael Morrissey, former Mets beat writer for the *New York Post*.

Oddly enough, Dvorchak, also a veteran of the political beat and Gulf War coverage, said the pack mentality "is not indigenous to baseball."

"You see it in politics," he said. "I covered politics in the 1980s. Everybody moves in a herd and gets the same information. It's dangerous for journalists to move in packs and not go out and dig for information. It's essential to your own credibility as a journalist to break away from the pack and do as much work as possible on your own. You're actually doing your job as a professional. It's the only way to do it."

Clubhouse decorum sometimes breaks down when herds of reporters are formed. The most enterprising of a city's baseball media group could be talking one-on-one with a player, then suddenly find himself engulfed by the group feasting on the opening he has created. Hal McCoy may be a leader in his seniority of all beat writers covering the Cincinnati Reds for the *Dayton Daily News*, but he never desired to be a leader of a pack.

"I've noticed that," McCoy said. "I get followed around a lot. You talk to a player and pretty soon everybody's surrounding you. A lot has to do with TV camera guys and producers. Everybody wants the same thing, all the stories are the same, all the notes packages are the same."

Doesn't the reader want to hear more from the players, whose comments could be gleaned one-on-one, than heavy group coverage of the manager's pregame talk?

"No doubt about it," McCoy said. "I quote the manager as infrequently as possible unless he has something direct to say about a player. It's always better to go to the horse's mouth. Players make plays. Give them a chance to tell what happened."

Hanging together in the herd is not limited to the ballpark. While competing reporters certainly can be chummy away from the workplace, the extent to which that friendliness has developed was commented upon in a staff memo by *Los Angeles Times* sports editor Bill Dwyre, which was circulated online via SportsJournalists.com in April 2005.

Interestingly, Dwyre hinted that reporters should be "working" their sources a little better in the memo.

"Nobody takes a news source out to dinner anymore," he wrote. "We just take reporters from other papers. Nice we can help the bottom line of our competitors. Also, do we ever interview news sources or do we just gather in little clumps with other reporters at dinner and get our stories that way? Could this be a new phenomenon called Pack Journalism with Dinner? I think I might be the first to coin the phrase. Has a ring to it, doesn't it?"

Human nature to socialize while on the job combined with an underlying fear of developing relationships with celebrities will unfortunately continue. Dvorchak said at least the business training grounds should counsel against the practice.

"Journalism schools should preach this: Stay out of those packs as much as possible," he said.

The pack mentality is at least partially fueled by membership in the Baseball Writers Association of America, the oldest organized group of media in pro sports, and presently the only one operating in Major League Baseball. Until about three decades ago, the BBWAA had almost ironclad control over who was admitted to press boxes, even though the working areas were technically the property of the ball clubs or whichever entity operated the stadiums. In the ensuing years, such a grip has been loosened, but the BBWAA remains the best-treated group of media by baseball's establishment. Commissioner Bud Selig actually increased postgame clubhouse access for BBWAA members at one point.

With huge numbers of other media now credentialed to cover baseball, the advantages of BBWAA membership wouldn't appear to be huge. A card permits the bearer to be admitted to any Major League ballpark without clearance from the local team. Membership also is an insurance policy against mistreatment through denial of access. A lobbying group with baseball's ear is behind every cardholder.

BBWAA presidents and officers, selected from the ranks, insist the organization has pruned its membership to reflect only those newspaper reporters and columnists who regularly cover the game, along with their sports editors. But too many instances abound where members do not cover many games or have moved off the baseball beat, even out of the employment of daily newspapers.

In the meantime, other more regular baseball reporters for Internet sites cannot qualify for membership, by the strict interpretation of the national rules. Neither can reporters for newspapers or wire services, covering a full schedule of home games, and who are not full-time employees, qualify. I was not full time at the *Times of*

Northwest Indiana in 2004 when I covered eighty Cubs and twenty-two White Sox home games plus two weeks of spring training. I had maintained a similar schedule for a decade, but was repeatedly barred from membership while staffers who covered far fewer games were tendered BBWAA cards. Yet others who had moved on from the baseball beat retained membership due to a grandfathering clause.

In the early twenty-first century, BBWAA officials met to consider membership rules changes, but traditionalists among the ranks forestalled any liberalization. They forestalled others who believed change not only was good, but also necessary. An economic climate in which newspaper job cuts even affected several senior BBWAA members may have served as a wake-up call to those who previously felt smug and secure.

"It seems reasonable in this day and age with expertise on the Internet, with very good baseball writers, you have to bring them into the fold," said Tom Krasovic, longtime Padres beat writer for the *San Diego Union-Tribune*. "It's complicated, almost a slippery slope. It's like the Hall of Fame itself. There are people in there who probably don't belong and there are people who've never been admitted who should have been admitted."

One veteran scribe said political considerations affect membership ranks.

"The biggest reason for restricting membership is maintaining the integrity of postseason awards and Hall of Fame votes," said Mike Klis, Rockies beat writer and then national baseball writer for the *Denver Post* before he was shifted to the NFL's Broncos in 2005. "The onslaught of Web sites has only made the BBWAA more acutely aware of its membership guidelines.

"However, contrary to what many people might think, membership decisions are primarily enforced on a chapter-by-chapter basis. Liberal interpretations are needed in one-newspaper towns such as Atlanta, St. Louis, and San Diego if there are to be enough voters on awards.

"This means politics can become an issue when granting membership. And if, say, someone in a chapter doesn't like [a candidate with baseball-writing experience], he may not have a snowball's chance in the Coors humidor of getting in."

One example of one chapter admitting a writer turned down by another was Dave Reynolds, who covers Cardinals and Cubs games for the *Peoria Journal Star*. Reynolds was rejected for membership in the Chicago BBWAA chapter, but accepted in the much smaller, newspaper-poor St. Louis chapter.

If at first glance BBWAA membership policies would not be of interest to the baseball-consuming public, the issue of who votes for the Hall of Fame and postseason awards should change that. The annual vote for Cooperstown enshrinees almost always results in controversy, with deserving candidates kept out while some questionable choices gain entry. Writers/electors leave surefire candidates off their ballots entirely. The actual qualifications for voting thus are brought into question.

Seniority and service are paramount in BBWAA membership rules that govern voting rights.

"If somebody is a member for ten years and then leaves the beat or the newspaper business, he remains entitled to a vote," said *Philadelphia Daily News* national baseball writer Paul Hagen, a former president of the BBWAA.

Possessors of BBWAA "gold cards," signifying ten-year membership and grandfathered-in status, are given the full privileges of membership even if they don't still cover baseball, don't work for a daily newspaper anymore, or are not full-time employees.

That meant three *Chicago Tribune* writers who would not have qualified for BBWAA membership if they were first applying for membership based on their 2004 roles were allowed to vote for the Hall of Fame for the 2005 class. They were Olympics reporter Phil Hersh, who had not covered baseball regularly for more than twenty years; Bob Verdi, who wrote a Sunday column after working for nearly two decades as the newspaper's featured award-winning, full-time sports columnist; and nonstaffer Dave Van Dyck, who had built up two decades of service previously as a *Chicago Sun-Times* baseball writer before moving into Internet work for three years. Van Dyck was added to the newspaper's staff after the 2005 vote was completed.

In their published explanations of their 2005 vote, both Verdi and Hersh advocated the election of closers Bruce Sutter, Lee Smith, and Goose Gossage, while Van Dyck revealed his annual write-in vote for Pete Rose.

"When I feel I am far too removed from the game to vote with any authority, I will no longer do it," Hersh said. "I suspect that will happen sometime in the next ten years. After looking at the players eligible through 2008, I feel I can judge them fairly. I am still voting for people I saw play."

Verdi had left the *Tribune* late in 1997 to join the monthly *Golf Digest* and weekly *Golf World* as senior writer. He was not militant about continuing to be grandfathered in to vote.

"I've covered the guys on the ballots now, but that won't be the case in ten years," Verdi said. "If they called today and withdrew my right to vote if I wasn't covering baseball anymore, I won't take them to court. I try to stay on top of what's happening [in baseball], to not make a complete fool of myself."

Like others who believe BBWAA membership rules are skewed and political, Hersh suggests change might be for the best in Hall of Fame voting.

"Maybe there should be a cutoff point, like ten years after leaving the beat," he said. "Don't forget that players must wait five years, so even if you no longer are on the beat, you will have covered those for whom you are voting. As I recall, there is also a time period [ten years] that must be put in [as a BBWAA member] before a writer can vote."

But Hersh and *Tribune* media writer Ed Sherman both raised an even bigger question—whether media members should even vote for the Hall of Fame and annual sports awards at all, thereby making the news rather than just reporting it.

"The bigger issue is whether we should vote at all, given bonuses in contracts [for assorted achievements]," Hersh said.

"The writers, in essence, put money in the players' pockets," wrote Sherman in 2004. Explaining that he withdrew from voting for awards a few years back, he further advanced his logic: "Many writers will make their Hall of Fame votes and then turn around and write stories in which they were active participants. Maybe they could quote themselves. . . . Just keep the writers out of it. Let somebody else make the news."

Several newspapers, such as the *Los Angeles Times*, prohibit their writers from voting for awards.

Also taking part in balloting are female reporters, a situation that would have mortified the traditionalists just twenty-five years ago.

That's when the first wave of women journalists had to battle teams and leagues to gain access to locker rooms, then had to win over the cooperation of athletes almost person-by-person through the present day. Women work almost incident-free in baseball clubhouses in the twenty-first century. Near daily attendance, as with male journalists, breaks down barriers. Shannon Drayer, the pre- and postgame reporter for the Seattle Mariners' flagship radio station комо, is the only female riding the team airplane. Drayer, one of a half-dozen female reporters traveling with big league teams in 2005, reported she was welcome at all times.

"On the [airplane] intercom, they'll announce, 'Gentlemen and Shannon,'" Drayer said. "I was the only female trumpet player in [college] band. I'm comfortable around guys. Sometimes I think they like having a gal around. They'll open doors for me and put their best manners on."

Drayer will forever be grateful to catcher Ivan Rodriguez. As a radio rookie in 1999, she tried to ask a question in a group interview with Rodriguez, then in Seattle with the Texas Rangers. She was interrupted three times. After the third interruption, Rodriguez looked up at the person who cut her off and firmly said, "The lady is speaking," and turned his focus to Drayer.

But the comfort zone is still not 100 percent. A mild undercurrent exists where more conservative or religious players and field personnel still look askance at women in the locker room. But the incidents that marked the first wave are gone and never flared into the practically criminal assault experienced by then *Boston Herald* writer Lisa Olson with Zeke Mowatt and the New England Patriots in 1990. Players no longer parade around naked in their locker rooms, using towels to cover up their midsections as they emerge from the showers. They deftly change into at least some skivvies before they toss away the towels.

I first checked into the issue in 1997 for the *Times of Northwest Indiana*. At the time, more players were uncomfortable with women coming into their inner sanctum. But in spite of the whispered negatives, the women by then had a workable situation. That's in contrast to the 1980s, when Toni Ginnetti of the *Chicago Sun-Times* had to interview Cubs pitcher Scott Sanderson, who had deep religious beliefs, outside the locker room, thus playing havoc with tight deadlines. Ginnetti and other women sometimes had to avert their eyes from a small core of bad-boy exhibitionists who'd drop their towels when the women came in.

The anti-women dictums crossed all sports. *Boston Globe* columnist Jackie MacMullan found her entrée to the Celtics locker room barred by NBA legend Red Auerbach in the late 1980s. She had to enlist NBA commissioner David Stern's support to open the door while Auerbach issued bathrobes to his players. Another time, MacMullan walked up to a group interviewing the late superstar lineman Reggie White outside the locker room in Foxboro, Massachusetts. "He stopped the interview when I walked up to the group," she recalled. "White said he was married. I said, 'Congratulations, so am I.'"

Women still are under close scrutiny and have to be prepared to handle anything around a baseball team. They must be much more careful about their apparel. High heels, lower-cut blouses, and any hint of bare midriffs are verboten. Younger women almost fresh out of college are counseled that outfits that are fine for an after-hours club won't cut it around a ballpark.

Sportscaster Peggy Kusinski of NBC-owned WMAQ-TV in Chicago said she had to ditch a jacket that was "a little too hip" and another that "was too fluffy up front."

"You have to be careful about anything that is distracting from what you are saying, if you're being looked at because of that instead of for what you're saying," Kusinski said.

A few bad apples spoil it for the entire bunch with unprofessional behavior. One story circulating had a female Boston radio reporter showing up in the Red Sox clubhouse without ever turning on her tape recorder and wearing what was described as "questionable outfits." Suspected of sightseeing, the reporter one day encountered a Red Sox player who wanted to put her to the test. According to the story, he purposely dropped his towel and caught the woman peeking. She wasn't quite "exposed," but she was apparently put on notice to shape up.

Rumors pop up periodically of one or two female reporters going even further, to romantic relationships with players while still on the job.

"That happens in every office in America," Kusinski said of the rumor-mongering. "A good-looking woman talking to a player or manager, there will always be gossip. We as women will only be able to prove ourselves on an individual basis."

Kristine Charboneau, an assistant director in the home TV broadcast booth at Wrigley Field, is attractive by any measuring stick. As a result of that, she has had to live down perceptions by coworkers on her broadcast crew that she's hunting for dates if she talks to professional athletes while she is working—a necessary part of Charboneau's job.

By 2005 Charboneau was a veteran of battling for personal respect. Working the Red Sox's spring training camp in 1999 for the video production on the Fenway Park JumboTron, she caught grief from then Boston media relations chief Kevin Shea. Charboneau's producer was told that if she was not specifically doing an interview, she should be sitting in the stands. She said Shea told her he wanted "to keep distractions on the field to a minimum."

"I didn't protest because I didn't want a bull's-eye on my head," Charboneau said. "A similar situation involving a man, he wouldn't be restricted [in access]."

Women are sometimes presumed to be in a subordinate role even when their presence at the ballparks is not questioned. When Cubs media relations chief Sharon Pannozzo, in charge of her department since 1990, took aide B. R. Koehnemann into the press box at Montreal's Olympic Stadium, the attendant on duty assumed the younger Koehnemann was the boss and began dealing with him. Pannozzo just shrugged off the incident as an inevitable part of working as a woman in a man's world.

True equality for women will still be decades away, if it is ever realized, in the macho, traditional baseball world. Right now a glass ceiling exists for women working in baseball broadcasting. They have multiplied quickly as pre- and postgame hosts and on-field interviewers. Obviously, broadcast management nationwide is following a set formula in the same manner of pairing male and female news anchors at 10:00 p.m. With a heavily male audience for baseball, the more cynical of the honchos have sought and hired what they perceived as "eye candy."

"Some are very obvious," Kusinski said of women hired for their looks. "But I don't think it's all."

Women in baseball broadcast media will have truly arrived when they can not only shake off the "eye candy" stereotype, but also when they start filtering into broadcast booths as play-by-play announcers. These ranks are all-male at the moment with no female candidates in the pipeline. The situation is akin to pro football's once virtually barring the quarterback position to African Americans, converting quality black college quarterbacks into running backs or defensive backs once they hit training camp.

But why shouldn't there be controversies involving women in baseball media? It's all a part of the heavy politics of the business. No surprise here: politics, in the electoral realm, in the office, in our ballparks and in our press boxes, is America's top spectator sport.

ELEVEN

Chicago a Toddlin', But Soft, Baseball Media Town

One of those pleasant manager's office chats with Jim Riggleman was proceeding as usual as the trade deadline approached in July 1996. Getting together once every other home stand or so, we'd sit in the little office, up one flight of stairs from the main Wrigley Field home clubhouse, and chat, usually at Riggleman's invitation, after batting practice.

A man dispossessed of a raging ego, Riggleman and I would dovetail from the Cubs to baseball in general, and then on to fatherhood to politics to social mores. Sometimes we'd jaw so long I wouldn't notice that the first pitch was only twenty-five minutes away. "Gotta go, Riggs, otherwise you'd have to suit me up," I said, scurrying out the back door unnoticed into the main concourse and then up to the press box. Luckily, Cubs PR chief Sharon Pannozzo was otherwise occupied at the time. If she had discovered I was in the clubhouse area almost twenty minutes after it was closed to media with game time approaching, I would have been roasted alive. Informed of this arrangement nearly a decade later, Pannozzo laughed. Her statute of limitations had long since expired.

But on this day near the end of the first Clinton Administration— I don't think Riggleman voted for Slick Willie—the manager gave me a quiet earful. The Cubs were on the periphery of contention, bouncing around the .500 mark. General manager Ed Lynch, whose aggressive trading early in his tenure in 1995 had given way to utter caution, did not have anything hot on the fire. Nothing would be fated to heat up as the deadline passed. But in the privacy of his office, Riggleman practically pleaded for reinforcements and seemed miffed his boss was moving too slowly for the team's good.

Lynch's lack of moves prompted grumbling. First baseman Mark Grace, from whom I could obtain "A" material instead of the sound-bite friendly platitudes and quips, wondered when Lynch would swing into action. So would Grace's chum Brian McRae, enjoying his best year ever in center field. And Sammy Sosa, not yet recognized as a premium power hitter but about to lead the National League in homers for a few weeks, pondered when the complementary run producers would arrive. Of all his teammates, only Ryne Sandberg was on a twenty-homer pace. "I need some help. I can't do it all by myself," Sosa told me.

Hearing the players' moaning was commonplace, but when Riggleman joined the dissent, I couldn't wait to get to a phone to call Arlene Gill, the Cubs' longtime top executive assistant. "Arlene, something's going on in the clubhouse, I need to talk to Ed and Andy [MacPhail, the Cubs' president], as soon as possible," I said. Granted a quick meeting, I found Lynch in MacPhail's office talking over minor league call-ups. Strange, why would the team president be immersed in details about bush leaguers if he had turned all player personnel matters over to Lynch? I told the honchos of the clubhouse unrest spreading to all levels, but gave no hint that a little of it came from their own manager. My *Times of Northwest Indiana* story made no reference to specific sources, whether players or managers, mainly to protect Riggleman.

Lynch and MacPhail didn't jump out of their seats, although they professed that they were upset because their uniformed charges were upset. Lynch's inaction would come back to haunt the Cubs weeks later. Sosa broke his wrist and the Cubs lost fourteen of their final sixteen games.

Almost every year a similar story could be crafted by those covering any baseball team, especially on the East Coast, where competition for readers is dog-eat-dog and mandated by aggressive editors. But in Chicago, such "inside clubhouse" material isn't all that common. Although at least one supposedly scoop-hungry reporter was on the Cubs beat at the time, I read nothing else about the clubhouse dissent. It was not surprising, then, and became less so as the years wore on.

Whether at the end of the "dead-ball era" or early in the steroid-suspicious twenty-first century, the "toddlin' town's" sports media is regarded as "soft" by both insiders and those looking in from other cities. And the end result is not only part of the real story about their teams' being conveyed to legions of victory-starved fans of the Cubs and White Sox, but also a kind of complicity in the often-beleaguered teams' decades of losing and management bungling.

Starting with the Black Sox Scandal of the 1919 World Series and going through and beyond the "Bartman game" in 2003, many Chicago scribes, and later broadcasters, soft-pedaled stories and allowed the true purveyors of losing to get away with their gross mismanagement. Relationships between media outlets and sports owners were too close in the early and mid-twentieth century, and in a couple of cases continued into the millennium and beyond. Conflicts of interest abounded and politics was rife. The city's machine political system, in which clout, connections, and relationships were paramount over good government and merit, had long ago infested the local business community and, in turn, the Chicago media.

Pliable writers, and later broadcasters, often could not offer really informed analysis and criticism, relying instead on such stale angles as "curses" or aiming at the wrong individuals to explain away the teams' travails. More recently, they simply settled for group interviews, as multiple media outlets disseminated the same stories on the same day without much enterprise or one-on-one player or manager relationships entering the picture.

An honest consensus both in and outside the market developed that Chicago management, players, and media would not get away with their actions and reactions if they somehow could be transplanted to the hard-driving, under-the-microscope Eastern cities. Even the senior baseball official in town dealing with media recognized the cushy, cozy nature of Chicago compared to the East Coast.

"It's much more relaxed here," said Sharon Pannozzo, a twenty-three-year-veteran of her department. "It's not as competitive [as the East Coast]. There is a very Midwestern attitude here."

And what is that attitude? Bruce Miles, veteran Cubs beat writer with the suburban *Daily Herald* and a lifelong Chicago-area resident and baseball follower, may have summed it up best.

"There is less of, for lack of a better word, a sensationalistic approach to the news in Chicago than in other markets," Miles said.

"Maybe it's a sociological thing, the makeup of the people. Chicago is a pretty friendly town overall and I think the newspapers reflect it. The tone is much friendlier and much more forgiving. The fans are very forgiving and the media reflects it. If a team does poorly, that's pointed out. But if they right the ship, that's also pointed out, with balance."

Former *Chicago Tribune* sports columnist Bob Verdi agrees—to a point.

"Chicago fans are the most forgiving around," he said. "Whether that extends to the press is not clear."

Chicago had few media anarchists or bomb-throwers throughout its sports-journalism history whether analyzing the Cubs, White Sox, or any of the other star-crossed franchises in town.

"There were a lot of powder puff softballs tossed at these teams," said Richard Lindberg, the White Sox's leading historian, whose extensive microfilm studies of newspaper coverage throughout the twentieth century for his assorted books on baseball and Chicago history give him a good perspective.

But well beyond the "wait 'til next year" attitude of fans was a network of connections and relationships between teams and media that was an extension of the political system in town. Through 2004, Chicago's baseball teams had played in exactly two World Series since 1938. The media oversight of the continual bungling that kept this endless drought going was not worthy of a supposedly world-class city. At the same time, the line between writers and the sports they covered was not as well-drawn as in later decades. All-time Chicago gossipmonger Irv Kupcinet served as an NFL referee while he worked as a sportswriter for the *Chicago Times*. Longtime baseball writer James Enright of the *Chicago's American* and *Chicago Today*, the Tribune Company–owned afternoon dailies, picked up extra cash in the winter refereeing college basketball games.

The initial tone for Chicago as a soft media market was set during the Black Sox Scandal of 1919, the worst in baseball history. In the 1988 movie adaptation of Eliot Asinof's book *Eight Men Out*, Ring Lardner, the *Chicago Tribune*'s sports columnist, is depicted walking through a railroad car full of White Sox players crooning, "I'm forever blowing ballgames." Lardner and fellow Chicago scribe Hugh Fullerton are shown going about their work with apparent knowledge of the World Series fix, even circling suspicious plays on their scorecards. Yet not a word about the scandal was published until the mess began leaking out in dribs and drabs during the 1920 season.

All along, most of the writers had been coopted by White Sox owner Charles Comiskey, who regarded them as his inner circle, as part of his Woodland Bards social club.

"The attitude toward sports was much different than it is now," said Lindberg. "It was not so much news reporting as much as reporting on a leisure-time diversion. It was entertainment play-by-play.

"The media did not want to offend [the owners]. It was not taken as so-called serious news. Sure, there was a lot of veiled innuendo in Lardner's *In The Wake of The News* column. But also there was a lot of camaraderie between players and writers. They traveled on trains together. They were card-playing partners. There was a particular fondness Lardner had toward these players. It was a soul-searching situation he found himself in. What he did was laid the clues, put down enough clues, so the public began to suspect [in the 1920 season]."

Lindberg claimed that the overall newspaper philosophy of the day would not have lent itself to exposing a sports scandal.

"It was more or less a gentleman's agreement," he said. "The *Tribune* was not a sensationalistic newspaper. Their relations were cordial and friendly with Comiskey. The more sensational newspapers in Chicago had much smaller sports sections with no bylined articles of anyone doing analysis. These afternoon papers reported on game results, had small player profiles in the Sunday section, and did not have any room for investigative reporting.

"It was a different mindset. Writers were real genuine fans of the game. Baseball was the only real pro sport then. I don't think they were of a mind to upset something they looked up to, something they revered. Baseball had been a revered institution throughout its history."

Comiskey tore apart the White Sox after the 1920 season as the fixer-players were banned from baseball. The team would not recover competitively for more than three decades. The White Sox soon became a poor-soul franchise, limited by the Comiskey family's diminishing financial resources. Rather than criticize management for years of ineptitude, the local media took on a sympathetic tone, Lindberg recalled.

"For the thirty-year period following the Black Sox, there was a sense of victimization of the White Sox," Lindberg said. "There was a sense of pity these writers felt. They had a deep, abiding affection for the club and also thought the club was cursed. The writers thought it was the poor White Sox and what can we do to help them. It was a feeling that the White Sox deserve a better fate, they've suffered long enough. There was very little criticism. In general they were boosters. That's why 1951 [the dawn of the 'Go-Go Sox' era] was such a big deal."

The longest running White Sox fan was John P. Carmichael, proprietor of the *Barber Shop* sports column in the *Chicago Daily News*. Working from the "Front Page" newspaper era into the 1970s, Carmichael's column was not the source of criticism and analysis of the White Sox's foibles.

"John Carmichael was a die-hard White Sox fan," Lindberg said. "He broke bread with the Comiskey family and Bill Veeck. He just traded barbs with fellow writers and Cubs fans. That was the only kind of controversy he had."

Meanwhile, David Condon, conducting the biggest column bully pulpit in town, as Lardner's successor several times removed, with the *In the Wake of the News* in the *Tribune*, preferred to be the power brokers' drinking buddy. Condon rarely took after owner-management authority, instead preferring to be whimsical, often penning columns supposedly authored by his perennially twelve-year-old daughter, Barbara.

Carmichael's and Condon's styles were typical of the Chicago sports columnists of the pre- and post–World War II era.

"I couldn't believe what I was reading. All the columnists were in the bag [with the teams]," recalled Steve Friedman, former executive producer of *The Today Show* and cbs's *The Early Show*, who grew up on Chicago's North Side in the 1950s and 1960s and hung out in Wrigley Field's right-field bleachers.

While the writers took pity on the South Siders, the increasingly incompetent management of the wealthier Cubs did not come under fire from compliant writers. Philip K. Wrigley was unprepared to run a big-league franchise when he inherited the Cubs from his father, William Wrigley Jr., in 1932. Worse yet, the younger Wrigley was not a baseball fan. He was a reluctant inheritor of his father's fortune and, as a mechanically inclined tinkerer, would rather have been a garage mechanic. Wrigley was the best thing that ever happened to the ballpark that bore his name, putting enough money into off-season maintenance to keep it relatively well-preserved. But at the same time, the gum magnate was the worst possible owner from a baseball-management standpoint. He wanted to be different, but not better, than his competitors. He should have been driven from his ownership by a hyper-critical media that never reached that state of agitation.

In *Wrigley Field: The Unauthorized Biography*, Stuart Shea relates a 1934 anecdote about the owner calling the press together. "I don't know much about baseball, and I don't care much about it, either," Wrigley said. But he was convinced by the baseball writers themselves not to permit that comment to be published, according to the Shea book.

And over the next four-plus decades, Wrigley was treated as someone between a tinkering eccentric and a "sportsman," to use the favorite mid-twentieth-century vernacular for a sports owner who wasn't totally profit-motivated. While his managers and players took the brunt of any media criticism, Wrigley often caught a break because he simply answered his own phone, whether in his Wrigley Building office or at his Lake Geneva, Wisconsin, estate, when reporters called for comment.

"Writers, including James Enright, liked Wrigley," said Ed Stone, retired sportswriter with the long-defunct *Chicago's American* and *Chicago Today*, afternoon dailies owned by Tribune Company. "I called Wrigley and he answered his own phone."

The media never aimed both barrels at his gross mismanagement of the Cubs, led by an early neglect of the farm system, Wrigley's unwillingness to spend a portion of his fortune on building the club, a series of wacky schemes that went against all conventional baseball logic, and his inability to hire the best and brightest in the game to run the franchise on his behalf.

"The only time when there was a hardened media attitude toward the Cubs was under [Leo] Durocher," Stone said.

Perhaps grateful for such treatment, the shy Wrigley, who was not tapped into the usual lines of baseball personnel networking, hired sportswriters into the organization instead of capable baseball men. He tapped Jim Gallagher to be general manager at the beginning of the 1940s. Enright was made Wrigley Field public address announcer after his forced retirement from his newspaper in 1974. Howard Roberts, a longtime *Chicago Daily News* scribe, spent part of his retirement years handing out passes at Wrigley Field's gate.

By the time Wrigley assumed stewardship of the Cubs, the tone of media coverage in Chicago had been emblazoned in stone as soft and often deferential—and the pacesetter was the largest newspaper in town, the *Tribune*. The Midwest's bastion of rock-ribbed Republicanism under publisher Col. Robert R. McCormick, the paper wielded enormous influence in selling one million copies per day. Radiating out two hundred miles in every direction from Chicago, almost every farmer's mailbox stood side by side with a blue *Tribune* box. Ripping Franklin D. Roosevelt's New Deal at almost every turn while upholding the conservative, every-man-for-himself, trickle-down business establishment, the *Tribune* hardly was going to rock the boat of wealthy men who ran sports franchises. In some cases, the newspaper befriended them. And while other newspapers opposed McCormick's reactionary politics on the editorial and news pagers, they somehow played follow-the-leader in the toy factory of sports. The *Tribune* set the tone of sports coverage in Chicago by its sheer heft and intricate social and financial relationships with the two most important sports franchises.

In the early 1920s, owner-player-coach George Halas of the fledgling Bears of the young NFL used to drop off his own press releases to Chicago newspapers' sports departments. He became friends with Don Maxwell, a rising young editor.

"Halas and Maxwell were close friends," said Ed Stone, who would find out just how close during the course of his own career. "In the early years of the franchise, Maxwell as sports editor gave Halas publicity when no one else publicized the NFL."

The *Tribune* had other close football connections. George Strickler, a Maxwell successor as sports editor, once had been Notre Dame's publicity man, so college football became king at the paper on weekends. Meanwhile Halas, who would hold court with writers after games over libations in Wrigley Field's Pink Poodle press lounge, also befriended Luke Carroll, managing editor of Stone's paper, the Tribune-owned *American*. Carroll even picked up Halas at the airport when he returned from a road game.

By the mid-1950s, Halas's Bears were established as a money-maker while Maxwell was McCormick's hand-picked successor to run the *Tribune*'s editorial department.

"It was an unholy alliance between the *Tribune* and the Bears, and it affected the way the *Sun-Times* and *Daily News* covered them," Stone said.

A young, aggressive beat writer in the early 1960s, Stone criti-cized Halas for pulling starting quarterback Billy Wade too early in a game in 1963 in San Francisco—the Bears' only defeat that cham-pionship season.

"I wrote that Halas choked," Stone said. "The next week, I was in the office writing the home-game advance story. Leo Fischer [sports editor] gets a call and runs down the hall to Luke Carroll's office. He comes back and says, 'You're off the beat.'

"I told him everything I wrote was the truth. Fischer said, 'You can't always write the truth.' "

Stone's demotion gave a break to a twenty-three-year-old writer a year out of Northwestern—Brent Musburger. Four years later, when Musburger was promoted to columnist, Stone got his Bears beat back. But worse yet, it served as a kind of warning about critical or really objective coverage to those who still manned beats or wrote columns in Chicago.

The connections between the *Tribune*, Halas, and Wrigley al-most formed a 360-degree circle where the newspaper's ownership of WGN TV and Radio was concerned. Halas had rented Wrigley Field for fifty seasons from the Wrigley family starting in 1921. Phil Wrigley said if he ever sold the Cubs—only a remote possibility—Halas, who was interested, would not only get first right of refusal but last right of refusal. The two teams shared the WGN airwaves. Broadcaster Jack Brickhouse handled both Cubs broadcasts on TV and Bears games on radio, while helping negotiate rights fees with both.

The *Tribune* and WGN were hardly going to criticize Halas and Wrigley when both owners enabled the company to reap advertis-ing windfalls off their games. In particular, WGN was getting Cubs radio and TV rights in a near giveaway. Wrigley's business manager E. R. "Salty" Saltwell said the owner, who believed in widespread broadcast exposure for the Cubs, charged WGN a "phenomenally low" rights fee for the broadcasts. WIND-Radio paid just forty thousand dollars a year for rights in the 1950s, according to then WGN chief Ward Quaal. That increased to seventy thousand dollars annually when WGN snared the radio rights away in 1958. The late baseball TV producer and director Arne Harris recalled a fee of five thousand dollars per video game in the 1960s. The broadcasts were guaranteed annual moneymakers for Tribune Company with the usual lineup of beer, gasoline, airline, and other sponsors.

Not willing to look away from such a gift horse, Brickhouse was Wrigley's perfect public relations pitchman on his broadcasts, urging fans "in the neighborhood" to come out to beautiful Wrigley Field while busting his vocal chords with "Hey Hey" home-run calls for Ernie Banks. He legitimately built interest and enthusiasm in the Cubs even through the endless bad seasons. Despite my disagreements with some of his sunny philosophies during dark seasons, I gladly helped assemble a Brickhouse exhibit at Chicago's Museum of Broadcast Communications in 2000 and 2001. Much of my own interest in baseball when I was young was stoked by Brickhouse's broadcasts.

To be sure, Brickhouse was no total Pollyanna. Privately he was frustrated by Wrigley's incompetent management. He wondered to friends what it would take to purchase the Cubs. But keeping those feelings to himself to protect his stations' franchise programming, Brickhouse became a Wrigley acolyte for public consumption. Grateful for such service, Wrigley even considered appointing Brickhouse team president in the mid-1970s. But the broadcaster, by then a WGN lifer, wanted nothing to do with such an inherently insecure job running a baseball team.

The archetypal Brickhouse for-the-record stance toward Wrigley and the Cubs took place early in 1963. In another of his goofball schemes, Wrigley had just appointed Col. Robert Whitlow, former athletic director of the Air Force Academy in Colorado Springs, as baseball's first and only "athletic director." Whitlow had visited a friend who was Wrigley's cousin while the latter worked at the Wrigley Building in October 1962. The cousin introduced Whitlow to the owner, who was reeling from the team's record-breaking 103-defeat season just concluded and the failure of his wacky "College of Coaches" system. Another light bulb went off in Wrigley's head: We'll have an athletic director run the Cubs.

Brickhouse announced Whitlow's appointment live on his 5:45 p.m. WGN TV sportscast and introduced the new executive. Whitlow was earnest, but appeared totally uninformed about the operations of a Major League baseball team. He even suggested that the best defense in baseball was a good offense. Whitlow appeared almost befuddled.

"Phil Wrigley abhors losing," Brickhouse opined after Whitlow departed the studio. "To Wrigley, losing is a personal plague. He wants a return to the Cubs' glory days and let convention be hanged if it stands in front of his objective."

The announcer then inadvertently damned Wrigley by revealing he had more financial resources at his disposal than any other baseball owner of the time. Brickhouse said the Wrigley Gum Company had $100 million in sales the previous year and no debt.

Left out of the Brickhouse commentary was the total chaos the College of Coaches had created in the Cubs organization. Also omitted was Wrigley's early 1962 dictum that no new players were to be signed out of high school or college. The owner apparently was upset at bonus money that had gone to waste on prospects who had flamed out. Cubs scouts could still gather information on young players but could not take overnight trips. The effect was devastating on the farm system for years to come. Eventually Wrigley relented. A total of eight young players ended up signing organization contracts before 1962 came to a close.

With writers concentrating on game play-by-play, the rotting-at-the-core condition of the Cubs organization largely was overlooked. The ultimate Wrigley "yes man," general manager John Holland, should have been continually roasted during his 1956–75 tenure. But he wasn't, even though the often-secretive, media-averse executive presided over a pair of 103-defeat seasons in 1962 and 1966, was too quick to call up players, and in turn too hasty in trading them, and was far in over his head.

Former Cubs public relations chief Chuck Shriver said in 1999 that the Cubs simply could not win with a combination of Wrigley and Holland running the team. Another Cubs front-office veteran of the time said Holland simply should not have been general manager; farm director might have been the highest-level job he could have competently handled. With help from the often-meddling and surprisingly unstable Tribune Company successor ownership, the Cubs finished under .500 a total of forty-one times between 1947 and 2003. That's in contrast to the supposedly cursed Boston Red Sox's failure to reach the break-even mark in just seventeen seasons during the same period.

Oddly enough, during the Cubs' darkest years from about 1950 to 1966, no writer or columnist wrote about their own curse, that of the "billy goat," from the 1945 World Series and connected it with the Cubs' losing when it should have been fresher on their minds. That tall tale was revived in the late 1960s by columnists Mike Royko and David Condon, both regulars in the Billy Goat Tavern, underneath their newspaper offices on N. Michigan Avenue. The curse took on a life of its own through ensuing decades to become a central part of the Cubs' existence by their 2003 National League Championship Series collapse.

Cursed or not, Cubs fans never accepted losing, despite theories to the contrary by uninformed media. They did not totally abandon their favorites, but they weren't going to endorse ownership's blunders either. The cusp of the 1960s might have been a perfect time for a concerted media effort to put pressure on Wrigley and Holland. Fans were increasingly restless after a decade and a half of mostly bad baseball. Wrigley Field attendance eventually fell to the six hundred thousand level, a disgraceful number in a city of Chicago's size. In the *Voice from the Grandstand* column, authored by William Barry Furlong, in the *Chicago Daily News* in July 1959, fans criticized Wrigley for the operation of the Cubs and the lack of night games at Wrigley Field. The owner responded with his own letter, advising one particular fan to not get so lathered up. "What puzzles me is, feeling the way he does, why he doesn't direct his time and attention to something else that would not get him so stirred up."

Furlong, later a *Sports Illustrated* writer, journeyed to Wrigley's Lake Geneva estate to find the owner working under a car, his true passion. Pitcher-turned-author Jim Brosnan just missed out doing a book on Wrigley and the Cubs at around the same time. Forty-five years later, Brosnan said he would have relished the chance to query Wrigley and determine, as an ex–big leaguer, whether the magnate really understood baseball.

Daily News beat man John Kuenster, not wedded to the quoteless, play-by-play deadline game story, and working for an afternoon daily, probably went the furthest in exposing the problems of the Wrigley-Holland stewardship. Before the August 25, 1959, game at Crosley Field in Cincinnati, outfielder Walt "Moose" Moryn lashed out at Holland to Kuenster, claiming the GM dictated the lineups that manager Bob Scheffing put on the field.

"I don't think Wrigley knows what's going on," Moryn told Kuenster. "Maybe this is one way he'll find out."

Moryn also criticized Holland for playing poker with the players on the back of the team chartered flights and alleged trips to Chicago-area race tracks on off days.

After Moryn was finally traded to the Cardinals on June 15, 1960, he let loose again to Kuenster, claiming the only way the front office would change would be under new ownership.

For his labors, Kuenster was ripped by a Cubs coach as he got on the team bus and was denounced for his negative reporting by Brickhouse on TV.

All the while, the negative racial undercurrent of the Cubs organization was largely swept under the rug. Wrigley drew some media criticism when he was slow to integrate his roster after Jackie Robinson and other pioneering African Americans came to the majors. He finally broke his own color line with the debuts of Ernie Banks and Gene Baker near the end of the 1953 season. But there was a price for being an African American with the Cubs. And breaking out of the narrowly defined code of behavior—silence was preferred—meant benching or banishment.

Around 1961, hard-hitting outfielder George Altman, a true gentleman, believed he had his teammates' support to become player representative. When management caught wind of this move, they announced that white outfielder Bob Will would assume the role. Then, in 1962, the great Buck O'Neil was appointed the first African American coach in the majors with the Cubs. There was a caveat—O'Neil would not be able to run the team even temporarily in the rotating coaches' scheme, even though with his total baseball experience he was the most qualified individual in the organization available to manage the Cubs.

Personal relationships were an even bigger tripwire. An African American player dared not consort with a white woman. Young outfielder Oscar Gamble was traded after the 1969 season because he crossed the color line for dates when he was called up that season. Altman felt a coolness from his bosses when his light-skinned wife was seen in the stands in 1966. Rookie outfielder Wayne Tyrone found himself on the bench in 1976 when his girlfriend, who was white, showed up at Wrigley Field to watch games.

Such an ossified, backward attitude was carried to an extreme when soft-spoken, right-hander Ray Burris, never a "troublemaker" in the vernacular of the times, was seen by a front-office type engaged in innocent conversation with the white female who headed his fan club in the Wrigley Field parking lot after one game. Burris was then told by the honchos upstairs not to be seen with the woman again in public. He also recalled a front-office representative traveling on the road to monitor players' off-the-field activities—especially the African Americans.

The Burris situation was yet another example of how the media never picked up on the restrictive dictums under which Cubs of color operated.

"No one asked," Burris replied. Bob Verdi, then on the Cubs beat for the *Tribune*, said no writer could have expected to read Burris's mind. Perhaps he should have taken one of the writers aside in confidence. *Chicago Sun-Times* beat writer Joe Goddard once said his "juices would have been flowing" to latch onto such a story. Civilrights major domo Jesse Jackson already had threatened to picket the Cubs for not naming Ernie Banks manager, so the potential for a tinderbox was present had the media done its job.

But this was the tail end of the era when the writers penned little more than the game. Goddard began tacking on regular notes or tidbits to the end of his stories during the 1970s. That upset Jerome Holtzman, later regarded as the dean of baseball writers, who did not particularly care for adding notes to his own game stories in the *Sun-Times*.

One writer who actually dug into stories strayed from the *Tri-*

bune's house-man style. Richard Dozer actually seemed to out-report Holtzman, long noted for his insider's reputation.

Near the end of the 1961 season, Dozer reported that outfielder Lou Brock and second baseman Kenny Hubbs, making their big-league debuts at the time, were ticketed by the organization to have one more year in the minors. Both were extremely raw at the time. But both Brock and Hubbs became regulars to fill gaping holes in the 1962 lineup. Hubbs won National League Rookie of the Year honors, but Brock struggled mightily until he was traded two and a half years later.

Dozer also broke the story of the eventually disastrous trade of Brock to the St. Louis Cardinals. On May 26, 1964, three weeks before the deal was consummated, he reported that Holland was offering Brock to the Cardinals for an unnamed pitcher. He also quoted Holland as saying that he had helped St. Louis previously, and he might help them again. Luckily Holland was a slavish Wrigley loyalist; such a quote could get a present-day Cubs or Cardinals GM fired.

In 1969 Dozer asked Leo Durocher in a postgame interview whether the first-place Cubs were starting to get tired as August drew to a close. Angered, Durocher dragged Dozer and the other writers into the clubhouse. The manager challenged Dozer to ask the players directly whether they were tired. Fearing Durocher's wrath, no one answered Dozer's question. Two weeks later, the Cubs, exhausted by Durocher's lineup management that included sparse use of his bench and bullpen, staged one of the most painful collapses in their history.

Durocher's imperious rein as manager, as Ed Stone recalled, prompted the writers to get tough for once in their lives. The most amoral man in baseball, Durocher disliked the writers and sometimes fed them false information. Relations were constantly in a state of tension.

Durocher and Holtzman, a former World War II marine, nearly came to blows once in the manager's office. Clowning around one day during his pregame WGN-Radio show taping with Lou Boudreau, Durocher recorded rips of all the writers: Dozer was a wandering Romeo; James Enright was a penny-ante politician; and Edgar Munzel of the *Sun-Times* was a barfly. Only Ray Sons of the

Daily News was spared. Durocher called Sons a "nice boy," but urged his editor, Roy Fisher, to "fuck himself." Sons was not totally spared; Durocher ripped a piece of copy paper out of Sons's typewriter on the Cubs' chartered plane, urging the scribe to write a new story. The manager also grabbed radio announcer Vince Lloyd's pipe and tossed it into the plane's bathroom sink. By the time Durocher began his last season as manager in 1972, the Cubs had to appoint Hank Aguirre as a media-relations coach to act as a go-between for Durocher and the writers.

The writers sometimes would get a break from Durocher at season's end. Setting a pattern that still exists today, the Chicago papers did not use sports, and baseball coverage, as a primary focal point of competition for the reader. When either the Cubs or White Sox dropped out of contention near the end of the season, the papers would pull their writers off the road. That's why I witnessed the *Tribune*'s Bob Logan covering a Cubs-Padres doubleheader in San Diego via the office TV set before August was finished in 1974. In several other instances, Cubs home game stories did not have a byline in the *Sun-Times* in 1965.

The size of the traveling writers' group got cozy for season-long stretches starting in 1978. The *Daily News* folded as spring training began that season, three and a half years after the Tribune Company pulled the plug on *Chicago Today*. With suburban dailies not yet large enough in circulation and revenue to travel full time with the Cubs and White Sox—the Chicago suburbs developed decades later than those in other northern urban centers—only the *Tribune* and *Sun-Times* could afford season-long road coverage over the next decade. A metropolitan area as large as Chicago's, featuring only one-third the number of traveling writers of Boston or San Francisco, seemed a pitiful situation. In reality the shaky competitive level was reduced even further.

The *Sun-Times*'s Goddard and the *Tribune*'s Fred Mitchell manned the Cubs beat through a chunk of the 1980s. They did not go after each other dog-eat-dog for stories. Goddard did get some inside stories with some of the best one-on-one relationships with players and executives of any baseball writer in the team's history. But he also described himself as a "gentleman" writer.

"They were pretty friendly to each other," the Cubs' Sharon Pannozzo said of Goddard and Mitchell. "They were never adversarial, which you get in New York."

White Sox fans were distracted by this cut in competitive coverage as their ownership shifted from Bill Veeck to the group headed by Jerry Reinsdorf and Eddie Einhorn in 1981. And they were still in a state of agitation over Veeck's charges that the city's baseball coverage in the late 1970s was tilted toward the Cubs. Veeck even measured column inches devoted to each team to back his claims. Reinsdorf and Einhorn did not disagree with Veeck's analysis.

"The White Sox were placed at a competitive disadvantage he believed impossible to overcome," Sox historian Rich Lindberg said. Lindberg, no great fan of Veeck, actually believed the trend of imbalanced coverage continued in 2004, holding up marked-off sections of newspapers while on dual speaking engagements with me throughout the Chicago area. But he still had to face the inescapable truth that the Cubs were far more popular than the White Sox, even after the latter team's amazing World Series run in 2005.

I posed the question to *Tribune* sports editor Bill Adee in the U.S. Cellular Field press box in 2002. "The Cubs have more fans than the Sox," Adee said in a simple explanation about the additional ink devoted to the North Siders. Three years later, the *Tribune* would go out of its way to give the Sox their just due in publicity with the Fall Classic triumph.

But even before he and his team dominated both headlines and broadcast coverage, Reinsdorf refused to be backed into a corner in the same manner as Veeck. The Cubs' publicity advantage was ingrained, but the Sox chairman had some media power of his own through influence at the team's cable television and radio outlets. He was no George Halas, but he still had some reach into the personnel and editorial decisions of outlets that had a financial relationship with him. Chairmanship of a second team, the NBA's Bulls, and a long-standing alliance with owner Bill Wirtz of the NHL's Blackhawks gave him additional clout.

Brooklyn-born and self-made, Reinsdorf perhaps is sports' best man for working financial numbers. He offers up a powerful one-two business punch as an attorney and certified public accountant. But he's also a media junkie. Reinsdorf reads almost every baseball article within his grasp. He's been known to scrawl comments on clips returned to his front office. One time, he suggested to Goddard that he had questionable grammar in one of his articles.

Through the 1980s, Reinsdorf's common-man background served him well in media relations. He was one of sports' most accessible and quotable owners. Sportscaster Chet Coppock asked him to do a video gig, and Reinsdorf responded, "When do you need me there?" On several occasions during their first years as owners, I simply strolled from the old Comiskey Park press box, past the broadcast booths and into the private box of Reinsdorf and Einhorn to talk to them during games.

But the controversy over the White Sox's threatened move to St. Petersburg, Florida, and the bid for state funding to build what is now U.S. Cellular Field in 1988, caused Reinsdorf to dramatically reduce his media profile. He grew distant, limiting his on-the-record media exposure to a few favored writers and sports-talk-show hosts. Lindberg called him "shell-shocked. . . . The privacy of the owner's suite suited him just fine, and he never would be seen hobnobbing inside the press box unless there was a major storm brewing, like the impending 1994 players' walkout forcing him to articulate his position among baseball powerbrokers at an impromptu interview session."

White Sox vice president Scott Reifert, who now acts as a spokesman on behalf of Reinsdorf on most occasions, disagrees with the perception that Reinsdorf is distant.

"Being the owner who's involved, he makes decisions that are unpopular at times," Reifert said. "He's willing to make the right decision on behalf of the organization even if it's unpopular. The safest route is just not to talk. He believes very strongly that the fan coming here doesn't want to hear from the owner. He wants to hear from the players, manager, and general manager.

"He told of the time he came out and was very complimentary of the coach [the Bulls' Doug Collins], and two months later he had to fire him. He feels you should let the daily comments about the team stay functioning with the people running the team."

Reinsdorf respectfully declined an interview request for this book but came out of his shell to hobnob with media around the batting cage throughout the 2005 postseason. Even in his glory, he had strong opinions about those who cover his teams. I saw firsthand how approaching Reinsdorf at the wrong time and in the wrong place could have consequences.

On Labor Day night in 1993, I spotted Reinsdorf standing near the batting cage at U.S. Cellular Field. At that moment, I had to prepare a feature on the upcoming Bulls season for a local magazine, which required two months' lead time from handing in the article to publication. So for convenience's sake, I asked Reinsdorf, as Bulls chairman, for several comments. He responded to call him at the office after the holiday.

Somehow I agitated Reinsdorf with my interview attempt. Working on a day-to-day credential because of a recent job change, I discovered the White Sox had denied my request for a credential for a game at the end of the same home stand. Media relations chief Doug Abel, standing nearby when I approached Reinsdorf, explained I was at the ballpark to cover baseball, not conduct basketball interviews. I had to go through the Texas Rangers media relations department to obtain a credential to do an interview of one of their players when they came to Chicago. When the Sox made the 1993 American League Championship Series, I was granted a credential by the AL; passes were out of the White Sox's control.

Just as mysteriously, the following January I was granted a season's credential for the upcoming 1994 campaign. I had possessed a season's pass from 1980 to 1992. I wondered if the restoration of access rights had something to do with publicity over the debut of my weekly radio baseball program that eventually was called *Diamond Gems*—or whether it was deemed that I had served my penance for inopportune pestering of the chairman.

My credential hassle gave some credence to a popular theory that Reinsdorf has tentacles into some media outlets. Unlike George Halas, he cannot place a call to an editor chum to get a too-aggressive writer removed from the beat. But he did possess leverage simply because of his chairmanship of two teams.

Sox historian Lindberg believes too much credit is given to Reinsdorf's influence.

"The chunk of sports Jerry has influence over is the weaker half of Chicago sports—the Sox, Bulls, and Blackhawks," he said. "They're the weaker sisters compared to the *Tribune*, Cubs, and Bears. They have the stranglehold of power in Chicago. There's fear of Jerry, but also Jerry's fear of the media."

Reinsdorf and Einhorn prematurely started a pay cable channel, SportsVision, in 1981, with Bill Wirtz and soccer owner Lee Stern. The station eventually morphed into SportsChannel, a basic cable operation whose ownership passed to out-of-town interests. However, the White Sox and the Michael Jordan–led Bulls remained SportsChannel's core programming. SportsChannel eventually became Fox Sports Net Chicago. TV executive Jim Corno ran the operation through all its incarnations.

Those who worked for Fox Sports Net Chicago were told they were not to report negatively on the teams for which they served as cable rights holders.

In 2004, Fox Sports Chicago was gutted as the White Sox and Bulls rights, along with many on-air and behind-the-scenes personnel, shifted over to Comcast Cable's new operation. Corno also moved over to run the operation, maintaining his own close relationship with Reinsdorf. But the honchos were now virtually joined at the hip—Reinsdorf's teams, the Tribune Company, and the NHL's Blackhawks had ownership stakes in the cable channel along with Comcast itself.

Executive producer Lissa Druss Christman insisted her talent could be objective in talking about the teams they covered. Her claim was confirmed by a colleague, who said Comcast had the backing of the cable company's Philadelphia headquarters to maintain a sense of objectivity in coverage. But that analysis was going to be severely tested due to the close ties with the teams.

The Reinsdorf connection with WMVP-AM (1000), the longtime flagship radio station of the Sox and Bulls, also was interesting. For a while, the ABC-owned radio outlet seemed eager to get out from under high annual-rights fees of $7 million that guaranteed financial distress when Reinsdorf's teams had losing seasons. And when U.S. Cellular affixed its corporate naming rights on Reinsdorf's ballpark in 2003, the communications firm suddenly had no advertising dollars left over for the radio station, which was not allowed at first to make a deal with a competing cell phone company. A weekly Sunday-morning show on the Cubs made its debut on WMVP, no doubt to Reinsdorf's chagrin since WGN, the Cubs' radio flagship, had no similar Sox program. Criticism of Reinsdorf and the Sox was heard, particularly from the hyper-opinionated, mid-morning host Jay Mariotti, a longtime jabber of the chairman in his *Sun-Times* columns. Mariotti also publicly feuded with Ken "Hawk" Harrelson, the Sox TV announcer and Reinsdorf associate.

But by the end of 2004, the sands had shifted at WMVP. The Sox and Bulls rights were coming up for renewal. Suddenly management desired continuation of the play-by-play deals, considered a centerpiece for sports stations even as a "loss leader." The Cubs show was transformed into a generic Chicago baseball program. Mariotti's continual vitriolic presence, despite climbing ratings, could have been seen as an impediment to retaining the rights. If so, WMVP management had a right to be nervous when sports-talk competitor WSCR, possessed of a superior thirty-eight-state nighttime signal at 670 AM, was linked to interest in the teams. Later WSCR hired Mitch Rosen as program director, a decision that could not have hurt their bid to Reinsdorf. Rosen held that same position at WMVP at the dawn of the millennium when the station's relations with the Sox and Bulls seemed friendlier. Rosen called himself a Reinsdorf friend in an interview with Ted Cox of the suburban *Daily Herald*. In between radio management jobs Rosen worked as an agent, with Sox manager Ozzie Guillen one of his "name" clients.

Something apparently had to give—and it was Mariotti. After the 2004 season, he claimed he had received management edicts to soften his on-air criticism of the Sox and Bulls. At the end of 2004, just before a contractual clause would have vested Mariotti for six months' more pay at WMVP, he had a forced parting of the ways with the station. WMVP management declined comment at the time, while the Sox's Scott Reifert said Reinsdorf had no prior knowledge of Mariotti's departure.

On April 4, 2005, Opening Day at U.S. Cellular Field, Reinsdorf proved on the air that informed, borderline-tough questioning was not welcomed on his team's outlets, especially when he was involved. Expecting just a softballs-filled chat in an interview with Mariotti successors Marc Silverman and Carmen DeFalco, the chairman took umbrage at the line of questioning, which included steroids and whether he would negotiate with agents for his team's coaches and managers. Silverman asked Reinsdorf if the Bulls' improved season was his biggest surprise of the year.

"The biggest surprise I've had is the nature of this interview," he told Silverman. "I thought it would be a nice chat about Opening Day, and you guys turn it into '60 Minutes.' These are not questions we were supposed to discuss." Reinsdorf added he would not appear with Silverman and DeFalco again.

Toeing the Sox line did not help WMVP in the end. Reinsdorf awarded the radio rights to WSCR—at a reduced fee compared to WMVP's payout—in the early summer of 2005.

Meanwhile, another long-term accusation of conflict of interest in Chicago sports did not live up to its long-advertised reputation, with a couple of possible exceptions. The Tribune Company had purchased the Cubs from an inheritance-tax-beleaguered Bill Wrigley in 1981 to protect its WGN TV and radio deals. Almost from the start of its parent company's baseball ownership tenure, the *Chicago Tribune* was accused of not covering the Cubs objectively. But that proved not to be true, as *Tribune* columnists, especially Rick Morrissey after 2001, offered up critical Cubs coverage. And while the daily beat-writer work was just average through other writers' tenures, the likes of Alan Solomon in 1988 and Paul Sullivan in 1997 produced some of the more insightful, aggressive reporting in town. When queried, *Tribune* writers over the years have said they've never had directives to go easy on the Cubs. The only exception was a 2003 story, jumped upon by Greg Couch of the *Sun-Times*, detailing how the Cubs scalped their own tickets through a dummy corporation set up a half-block north of Wrigley Field. Little was written in the *Tribune*. When asked if he could cover that same story, one *Tribune* writer responded cynically, "Not if I want to keep my job."

Sullivan was nipped by the other fly in the ointment. A favorite guest on TV and radio shows, he was summoned to help broadcasters Chip Caray and Steve Stone fill time during a rain delay of a Cubs-Giants game on August 23, 1999, at Wrigley Field. With the Cubs in the middle of a horrific 6-24 month, Sullivan was asked if manager Jim Riggleman was getting the ax. He responded that it wasn't all Riggleman's fault, that top management in the form of team president Andy MacPhail and general manager Ed Lynch should take their fair share of the blame. Apparently, freedom of opinion did not apply to beat writers. After the season, Sullivan was threatened with transfer out of the sports department, possibly to the journalistic Siberia of suburban news coverage. Eventually he accepted a switch to the White Sox. John Cherwa, the sports editor in 2000, soon was moved out of Chicago to another Tribune Company job in Orlando. Sullivan enjoyed his Sox seasons, then returned to cover the Cubs starting with the eventful 2003 season.

The *Tribune* did not know what it was missing on the Cubs beat with Sullivan's absence. When they had hired Mark Gonzales of the *Arizona Republic* to cover the Sox in the spring of 2005, they fielded two of the strongest baseball writers in the country. Although he angered some Cubs like LaTroy Hawkins with his prying and sometimes sharp language in print, Sullivan distinguished himself from many of his colleagues by developing one-on-one relationships with players and coaches. He broke off from the crowd of regular writers, who have fallen into a new trend in baseball media coverage: moving around in a group, even a kind of journalistic cartel, seemingly avoiding one-on-one interviews and relationships with baseball newsmakers. Although much information in the daily ebb and flow of working a clubhouse can only be obtained in a group setting, the differentiation of stories and reportage steeply declined as the millennium began.

An example of overdoing the group concept happened in spring training 2001. A middle-level Cubs pitching prospect named Courtney Duncan was trying to make the parent club. On a Sunday all the writers present in Mesa, Arizona, interviewed Duncan. The next day, all the features out of camp were variations of the Duncan talk. Innumerable other examples have been featured in ensuing years on themes that were not especially breaking news and available only in a group-interview setting. The *Worcester Telegram and Gazette*'s Bill Ballou, senior Red Sox beat writer, calls the mass production of the same stories "socialized journalism."

None other than Cubs pitcher Kerry Wood believed the baseball consuming public lost out by identical stories fanning out over all media outlets.

"It's an injustice to the fans," Wood said. "They pick up three different papers and they all have the same quotes. Why do they have to buy three papers? They can read the same quotes in one paper. The herd walked over there and got all the same quotes and wrote the same stuff."

Also noticed by players, team officials, and other media was the preponderance of clumps of media standing around the clubhouse or the dugout during batting practice, not making a move to work unless a group-interview subject presented himself or a baseball executive ambled by for a briefing. Chicago seemed the most outstanding example of such media behavior, but the same scene was also noted in other cities. The media would spend more time chatting among themselves and watching the passing parade of players instead of fanning out to work the team on an individual basis.

"They stand around, because nobody's talking to anybody," Wood said. "One comes to talk and then there's a group of twenty people around them."

Cubs media-relations chief Sharon Pannozzo, who had to try to thin the media herd in 2004 after the Cubs near-miss World Series season, wonders about the intentions of some of those gathered at one end of the clubhouse, not making a move to talk to players.

"A lot of people are in the clubhouse and not doing anything," Pannozzo said. "If people are just standing around not working, they [the players] wonder why they're standing around. It's the players' office. You don't come into our office and stand around."

The *Daily Herald*'s Bruce Miles would prefer to conduct his interviews one-on-one. "But in this climate and day and age, it's becoming harder and harder, unless you wait till after batting practice and everyone goes upstairs, or when they first open [the clubhouse] for the day," he said.

Wood and Pannozzo weren't the only ones noticing the pack of media types hanging around the clubhouse and dugout.

The traveling writers were seen waiting around for manager Dusty Baker at the Great American Ballpark in Cincinnati while other interview possibilities swirled about them. Indeed much of the daily notes material has consisted of transcripts of Baker's pregame media briefings, as they did of predecessors Bruce Kimm and Don Baylor. Readers would much prefer to hear from the players instead of endless manager homilies. Without a deep psychological probe, the group behavior appeared to be part safety-in-numbers, high-school lunchroom clique, and part fear of breaking away to establish any kind of one-on-one relationships with players.

Miles insists that the regular crew of writers works individually, without collusion or agreements that an agenda should be set each day of what information to convey. One popular feeling within the sports-journalism community is that informal "no-scoop" agreements exist among some teams' group of covering writers, in various sports, to ease the grind of the long season and the daily demands for copy.

"There's never been any concerted effort to say, 'Hey, let's spin the story this way, everybody make their lead note this, or write a feature this particular way,'" Miles said. "Get it as you can. I've never seen a concerted effort to say, 'Hey, let's all protect each other.'"

Although the group/cartel concept seemed to strengthen after the Cubs endured second-half death marches in 1999 and 2000, Miles said the traveling crew did not decide to ease their collective pain through cooperation.

"No, because there's a lot of interest in stories that come out of losing," he said. "Somebody might be playing out the string, trying to win a job for next year. The Cubs beat has a lot of collegiality, but it's competitive. It generates more copy than any other beat in the city. There are days when we write three, sometimes four stories. The work ethic is very high on the beat."

Some of the best "inside baseball" stories are gleaned through relationships with baseball figures. Even a big name like Wood, never an interview-hungry type, will be helpful. Yet a reporter needs to spend time establishing credibility with such players and managers in noninterview, nonpressure situations. That means breaking away from the media clique and chatting informally with them, establishing your reputation, and proving you understand baseball while wanting to learn more. The conversations can take place in the locker room, in the dugout, or even by the batting cage, although approaching baseball types in the latter traditional conversational setting is increasingly being discouraged by teams.

"Some players don't want to be bothered while they're hitting," Miles said. "If you go to the cage and talk, you'll draw a crowd.

There are multiple dynamics at work. It's grown like an amoeba over the last several years."

One relationship a Chicago writer did cultivate was the *Chicago Sun-Times*'s Mike Kiley's personal pipeline to Sammy Sosa. The slugger was seen numerous times from 1998 to 2004 in whispered conversation with Kiley, much to the pleasure of his bosses and the frustration of his colleagues.

"I think it took Mike some time to develop that relationship," Miles said. "You live with it on the beat. You win some, you lose some. You don't like it, but what are you going to do about it? It's human nature where certain people like others more than other people."

Sosa was a prize catch for a newspaper able to convey the one-on-one thoughts of the number one athlete in competitor Tribune Company's employ. But that relationship was severed when Sosa trashed a decade's worth of goodwill with Chicago fans at the end of the 2004 season.

Carrie Muskat, a twenty-year baseball writer working most recently as Cubs reporter for MLB.com, also enjoyed some good one-on-one relationships with players, who praised her work ethic and clubhouse persona. But, overall, some of the journalistic basics were not being followed. Even in press conferences, tougher, more incisive questions often were not being asked. Sometimes pregnant pauses, as the one I encountered back in 1989 with Don Zimmer, interrupted the flow of information. The stark conclusion is that some Chicago sports media types were simply afraid to ask questions that might offend their interview subjects, in a group setting or in the much rarer one-on-one setting. Others might ask innocuous or almost apologetic questions.

Michael Miner, media critic for the huge alternative weekly *Chicago Reader*, took the traveling crew to task in his March 25, 2005, column. Bruce Jenkins, sports columnist for the *San Francisco Chronicle*, quoted a friend of Dusty Baker as speculating that some of the manager's Chicago critics did not want to see an African American in such a position of power. Miner detailed how the writers quizzed Baker on the Jenkins column, but failed to bring up the race question to the manager directly.

The flow of events made it obvious that many Chicago coverage people were not being pushed by their superiors to get to the bottom of things and beat the competition—all part of the daily routine on the East Coast. The simple guideline could have been to put together the concept of tapping into relationships, picking up the phone, and breaking away from the pack. You can come up with stories before the competition.

One example of such simple logic took place before and after the horrors of 9/11. I had followed the work of Mack Newton, Cubs manager Don Baylor's hand-picked fitness guru and motivator, who began work in spring training 2001. Preaching winning amid his rigorous workouts, Newton showed up several times to work with the Cubs in the first half of the 2001 season as the team zoomed into first place. But after the All-Star break, he disappeared. I wondered, and wondered, and wondered. After a while, when I didn't read anything about Newton in the daily coverage from the traveling writers, I called him at his Phoenix office for a story in the *Times of Northwest Indiana*. Newton said the players didn't want him around anymore. He was virtually run off. I confirmed that fact from Cubs players Eric Young, Matt Stairs, and Kevin Tapani.

After also discovering that Baylor was granted a fund of nearly two hundred thousand dollars by the Cubs to partially pay for Newton's services and other scouting help, I filed the story for October 3, 2001, publication. Unknown to me, Baylor had just dumped emotional pitching coach Oscar Acosta, who leaked the firing to Miles and Kiley in a kind of package deal. I had witnessed Acosta helping out both Miles and Kiley previously. The two unrelated stories merged into a kind of clubhouse conflagration. Acosta's pitchers were extremely angry that Acosta was canned. Wood threatened not to make his final 2001 start until Jim Hendry, then second in command in the front office, talked him back onto the mound.

I had a certifiable scoop, but the same story was available to any regular writer who could have deduced something was up by Newton's absence a month earlier, had called him, and worked the clubhouse one-on-one. '

Merely breaking away from the media pack standing at one end of the clubhouse or by the dugout also can net some easily attainable inside stories.

Twice during July 2004 I approached Cubs second baseman Mark

Grudzielanek—a straight shooter—one-on-one by his locker. The first time, he suggested that a players-only meeting to hash out the team's troubles might be called during an upcoming road trip, away from the media fishbowl in Chicago. On the second occasion, Grudzielanek said he would have been willing to shift to third base to keep him and Todd Walker both in the lineup at the same time. When the Cubs lost slugging third baseman Aramis Ramirez to a groin injury at the beginning of the month, manager Dusty Baker used non-sticks Ramon Martinez at third and Rey Ordonez at shortstop. At the same time, Baker benched either Grudzielanek or Walker, refusing to weaken the infield defense, or so he thought. Grudzielanek reminded me that he had played third base as a rookie and could make the switch with a few days' infield workouts. Both stories were available to anyone else who asked. Only WSCR-AM's George Ofman, tagging along on the second visit to Grudzielanek, ran the information.

"Maybe some players give off an air of intimidation," Miles said. "I heard one player say, 'I think a lot of people are afraid to come up and talk to me.'"

Call it afraid, underdirected, undermotivated, or just not people-savvy enough, the gap between players and media is not being bridged in Chicago. The fault, in the end, is not with the writers and broadcasters huddling in a group, but with their editors and program directors in not demanding creativity, original coverage, and common-sense competition to go beyond the usual necessary stories available to everyone.

Such a style can help shed light on the why's and how's of Chicago's baseball teams. If practiced—and that's a big if—that should enable fans to become much more knowledgeable and informed about a game to which they've given their hearts and souls.

TWELVE

No-Shows in the Press Box and Clubhouse

S tarting about 1990, the same complaint repeatedly was uttered, whether by players I regularly covered or those visiting Chicago. You'd be deaf, dumb, and blind if you didn't spot the trend.

Covered every day by newspaper beat writers, Major Leaguers were upset that these same publications' sports columnists would rarely come down to the clubhouse, if they even showed up at the ballpark in the first place. Yet at the same time, the columnists were offering critiques of individuals and teams without doing any necessary background information, without talking to any of the parties firsthand.

The complaints then shifted to a new genre of commentator as the 1990s wore on: radio sports-talk-show hosts. While more columnists were spotted here and there, only a small fraction of airwaves gabbers bothered to show their faces in press boxes and clubhouses, even though they usually did not put in a full eight hours at the office, factoring in their three- or four-hour broadcast shifts and "show prep time."

"There's no question that players get upset when criticized by people who aren't around," said Drew Olson, former baseball writer with the *Milwaukee Journal Sentinel*. "The 'hit and run' method employed by many columnists and most talk-radio hosts probably has played a role in eroding some players' relationships with the media."

And as a new century really got rolling, the two genres merged, almost akin to a cross-pollination of media. Image-hungry sports-talk stations and ESPN began hiring the top columnists in major cities to handle either daily three- or four-hour radio shows or video shoutfests. A few, like the *Chicago Sun-Times*'s Jay Mariotti, did all three—a column, daily radio, and daily national TV. That logically left even less time for in-your-face visits to ballparks and provided more opportunities for basing commentary on secondhand information, now repeated on more outlets.

The trend was by no means confined to one city or region. Almost nationwide, the scuttlebutt told of columnists and radio talkers using second- and thirdhand information to comment on and analyze their sports subjects—tapping into material already accessible to their readers and listeners. Branded as "experts" by their hype-conscious management, the opinionmeisters ran the risk of putting forth inaccuracies at the worst or lazily recycling information at the least.

The matter-antimatter mix of overly affluent, arrogant players on one hand and undermotivated, sometimes inexperienced reporters on the other did a lot to pry apart two parties who in fact need each other. But the print and radio no-shows in the clubhouse and press box made matters worse, causing the players to further withdraw from media contact and thus making the job harder for the diligent portion of baseball reporters.

Just as noticeable to the players as the clumps of reporters who gathered, high-school lunchroom clique-style, by dugouts or at one end of clubhouses were the absences of commentators who were too lazy, too scared, or too proud to get the players' side of the story beforehand or face their subjects afterward.

In many ways, the two sides are dug in and won't budge from their positions. Cubs media relations director Sharon Pannozzo felt more strongly about the issue than many of her players.

"I think they're cowards," Pannozzo said. "If you don't come to the park ever, not to the field, don't go to the field or the press box, you're getting [information] secondhand, what happened, what somebody's really like. You don't know that person. Credibility is the key. Somebody on a talk show wants to sit there and rip [a player] and doesn't come out here, you really don't have a right in my opinion. [Players] feel you're not a man, you don't have the guts to come and talk to my face.

"It's no different than being in a courtroom and having the right to face your accuser. If you feel you have the right to go on the air, say whatever negative things you want about an individual or player, that's fine. That person has the right to be in the same room at some point and you actually face that person. There are people who want to write negative things and the furthest they ever go is the press box. That's as far as they go."

Typical of the opinion of the opposite side were the afternoon drive-time sports-talk duo of Terry Boers and Dan Bernstein on wscr-Radio in Chicago.

"If you're a comic and you're making fun of the president or a senator, do you go spend time with the president or the senator?" asked Boers.

"Does David Letterman have to go to a press conference?" inquired Bernstein. "Does Jon Stewart have to go to a House committee meeting?"

Other analogies used by columnists and sports-talk-show hosts included George Will not having to attend every session of Congress to pen a column, Roger Ebert not being required to face studio heads and directors after he pans a movie, and a restaurant critic not visiting the eatery the day after he savages it.

"I was a reporter [in the 1990s]," Bernstein said. "We're doing commentary. I turn on my tv, go to a game with my family, and see Moises Alou doubled off second base and I hear Dusty Baker spewing a line of bullshit about being aggressive. Why do I have to go to the locker room afterward? I go on the air and tell people what I think.

"That's [the locker room] their territory. Of course they want people in their clubhouse, with their public relations people there. There are two sets of tilted ground here. If it means they pick up a phone and call our show, which means that's our territory and we control the discourse, yes, we have a position of power. But, similarly, they're in a position of power if they want us to stand in front of their locker when they've got pr people, media relations people, policing the questions. I don't want to hear that's a sacrosanct even playing field in the locker room."

So if their absences are notable now, how frequently should the no-shows ideally work the press boxes and clubhouses if they're not required to cover teams on a daily beat basis?

"Once a home stand would be nice," Pannozzo said. "All these people have a telephone. They're not afraid to call me for other things, like when they purchase tickets. They're happy to take the benefits of the services we can provide. You'd be surprised what people are not afraid to ask for. They're not afraid to ask for playoff tickets. It's a service I offer, so I would be fair."

Another Chicago sports-talk-show veteran is in full agreement with Pannozzo.

"Anybody who criticizes talk-show hosts and columnists for not coming to the ballpark are absolutely justified and correct," said Tom Shaer. "You should be there at least once or twice per home stand. They know who you are. You can go up to a guy without a tape recorder or notepad, you build a little trust."

There are shades of gray in between the stances of Pannozzo and Boers-Bernstein. What shakes out in the end is that player-media (and fan) relations would be better off if more of those who put on a jock got to know those who aren't so well-protected, but make it a point to comment from a distance.

"It's a lack of understanding on all sides," said Mike Fannin, sports editor of the *Kansas City Star*. "Players don't seem to understand you can have an understanding with a writer and he can still write something critical. And columnists don't like to be yelled at. The relationship has changed so dramatically. Some columnists say, 'I can swoop in and swoop out and go on to the next topic.' I don't think players relate to journalists as well as in the past. And I don't think columnists relate as well to players."

But to Chicago's Jay Mariotti, the athlete scarcely comprehends the role of the columnist.

"I think most baseball players are into political ways of things and cliques, the bullshit ways of things," Mariotti said. "The problem is that too many of them lump us in together [columnists and beat writers]. My job is to write about them one day, then go to the British Open, then go to the Bears and a tennis tourney. They don't understand. The smart guys understand what the role of a columnist is."

Whether they were off to Scotland or Wimbledon or Platteville, I picked up on the no-show factor when I began covering the Cubs on a daily basis at home in 1994. Often a home stand would pass with the appearance of a columnist just once or twice. To be sure, summer is the least busy season of most columnists, as I noted in a

1995 feature in the *Times of Northwest Indiana*. They're taking vacation time after a busy previous fall and winter of NFL, NBA, and college basketball coverage; few columnists will ever miss an NFL regular-season or playoff game. Golf tournaments that almost double as quasi-vacation junkets beckon in all parts of the world. Then the sacred rite of the hottest part of July always bursts on the scene: NFL training camp.

Baseball often can wait until something compelling takes place, like a pennant race or great individual accomplishment. Never mind that no matter how much a columnist believes he's his own conscience or that of his readers, he still remains a reporter when it comes to the basics, the standards of the business still applying. And the concept of developing sources and getting to know the people being written about—and criticized—still apply.

"Red Smith, the greatest sports columnist who ever lived, said the most important thing is being a reporter," said Ira Berkow, longtime *New York Times* sportswriter.

"You have to have the facts to come to a logical or knowledgeable opinion. You have to be talking to people and getting it for yourself. All good columnists have sources. You need people who trust you and give you stuff. All good journalists must follow that if you want to have a decent career."

Discerning readers agree. Sylvia Ewing of Chicago was referring to news-side columnists, but her opinions apply to sports analysts, too, in a letter to the February 18, 2005, *Chicago Reader*.

"Hopefully, a great columnist never forgets that he or she is a reporter," Ewing wrote. "The opinions that they share should start with facts. At best, they are not narrowly preaching to the choir, or simply railing against those who disagree with them, but rather stating their views so that the vast majority of folks who are undecided, who have no opinion, will have a reason to care. The first step to being a great columnist is to give a damn, and that includes getting out of the office to see what is going on in the world."

Cubs spokesperson Pannozzo abhors the packaging of columnists as on-site, inside-baseball experts when the reality just isn't so.

"I just don't think we were as much fodder for them," she said. "They write from the perspective that they are here. They give their readership the idea that they are at the park, they know these people, they know what's going on. Most of these columnists get [material] secondhand. If they write about an incident that happened and they weren't there, they got it from somebody else. You can trust your source all you want, but one perspective on something may not be exactly how it happened. You could be writing a falsehood. That's the risk you have to take. But your readers are [following] it as if you were there."

One prevailing view is that many of their brethren can either take baseball or leave it—more of the latter.

"Some columnists don't like baseball," said the *Boston Globe*'s Dan Shaughnessy, as much a part of the Fenway Park scene as the Green Monster. "Mitch Albom doesn't like baseball and writes very little on the Tigers. But in Boston, it's very heavy baseball."

Perhaps the no-shows and ennui about baseball is a Midwest or West Coast type of phenomenon. With few exceptions, the columnists in the "blue states" of baseball journalism had better show up or face derision or even demotion if their rivals craft a better piece firsthand.

"It doesn't hold true in New York," the *New York Times*'s Ira Berkow said. "The columnists are there. The papers demand that they are on the scene. It may be true in other venues, but not in New York."

While I slaved away the hot press-box afternoons and occasional nights at Wrigley Field in the mid- and late 1990s, I rarely spotted *Chicago Sun-Times* columnist Rick Telander. Cubs manager Jim Riggleman said I wasn't imagining things. "I rarely saw Rick," he recalled.

Although Telander had authored several interesting baseball features for *Sports Illustrated*, he seemed to be militantly a football and basketball guy. His books reflected those interests. Once a college defensive back at Northwestern, Telander tried to latch onto Hank Stram's Kansas City Chiefs as a rookie in 1971. Telander did not make the cut, but the experience provided fodder for another book. Setting the book's premise, Telander said baseball was America's pastime, but football was its passion.

But as the Cubs improved in 2003, more frequent Telander appearances almost became mandated at Wrigley Field. He found himself on duty the night Sammy Sosa was caught red-handed with a corked bat. In the tense questioning afterward, Cubs manager Dusty Baker was irked by Telander and called him "dude." Telander also jumped aboard for the White Sox's 2005 World Series express.

Despite his increased baseball attendance, Telander still is clear about his priorities and baseball's ranking among them.

"Baseball's a whole different animal," Telander said. "By the time they were done, the Red Sox played 180 games [in 2004]. Baseball goes on every day. It's not even remotely like football. Sixteen games in baseball is equal to one in football."

While Telander worked elsewhere during summer afternoons in the 1990s, I was also astonished at the will-o'-the-wisp sight of the *Chicago Tribune*'s Bernie Lincicome when he did show up. I'd call over to Lincicome in the press box to ask if he needed directions downstairs, and whether the players would be nervous knowing he was in the house. Charged with being his sports section's voice of sarcasm and satire, Lincicome did not feel the need to do a lot of clubhouse face time to provide accurate grist for his zingers.

As a result of his spotty attendance, one day in 1986, Keith More-land guided Lincicome around the Cubs clubhouse, introducing him to his teammates two years into the columnist's Chicago tenure.

"I probably averaged ten to twelve games per year," said Linci-come, who moved on to the *Rocky Mountain News* in 2000. "When they're doing well, when they're the story, you go to more. The years that the Cubs were good, I'd be out there twenty-five times a year. When they're not, I find other things that are interesting. The columnist's duty is to be interesting that day. If the team is not interesting, you pick something else to write about."

Moreland's locker-room tour was part of a tense situation.

"The Cubs opened the season badly," Lincicome said. "I had written a column in my fashion, tongue-in-cheek. Postgame, here comes Don Zimmer [then a Cubs coach] fresh from the shower, pink and rosy. He's charging at me like an umpire, and he's naked. 'You can't get me, you can't hurt me.' I didn't know what the hell was going on.

"Then there was Moreland saying, 'I'll show you the guys you're insulting.' I must have said to Moreland that I know you, I've been here two years, I know all these people. Problem is, you don't know me."

The hard feelings of the afternoon did not last. Several years later, promoted to Cubs manager, Zimmer called Lincicome into his office and fixed him a ham-and-cheese sandwich.

"We made up over cold cuts," Lincicome said. "He told me to tell everyone in Boston he said hello. He thought I was from Boston."

Lincicome said he is comfortable in his nonreporting role.

"I'm not in the scoop business, not in the inside-story business," he said. "I'm in the perspective business, with humor and a goal to entertain. All of that doesn't require me to be down there [in the clubhouse]. You try to fit that day's game into your view of it. Otherwise if you get into numbers, plays, that's the job of someone else. My objective is not to be a friend of the players, not to be a stenographer."

Obviously with the support of management, Lincicome forged a niche on the *Tribune*. Fellow columnist Bob Verdi played opposite him as the print lyricist and chronicler of athletes and coaches. Thus his mindset in ballpark attendance stood out in contrast.

"I followed guys I grew up reading and admiring," Verdi said. "Red Smith said there's no substitute for being there. Some feel a columnist is allowed to sit home and pontificate. If a columnist repeatedly writes opinions and never goes to the ballpark, it's a little curious. Is he or she serving the reader, just writing off the top of the head? It has to be an informed opinion. There's a certain respect if you come and face the music. You're not asking them [athletes] to go to dinner.

"When they put my picture in the paper, I didn't stop being a reporter."

Hazards are encountered in not obtaining information directly from sources, even in crafting critical opinions, according to *Boston Globe* columnist Jackie MacMullan.

"As a beat writer covering the Celtics, I covered John Bagley, who was overweight," MacMullan said. "People loved to make fun of him. He wasn't quick enough. I'm talking to him one day and he went on to say how hard it was. I asked him if he was trying to do something [to solve the problem]. He said isn't it nice that someone asked me if I was doing something. It was a medical situation [thyroid]. If ever a time it was driven home that you have to be there and talk to them, that was it. I think I got more response than anything I've written.

"That's what they pay us money to do. That's our job, to get to know athletes."

Despite the cynicism and even fear that athletes would lure them into the locker room to verbally ambush them, or worse, for critical comments, the general consensus is that familiarity would not breed all that much contempt. And, in fact, the athlete must learn to live with criticism as part of the price of being a Major Leaguer.

"You have to be more careful when you decide to rip on somebody without knowing the person as a person, not a piece of meat ballplayer," said former relief pitcher Rod Beck. "If you're there day in and day out, you'll see if a guy is lazy or if he busts his ass.

"If you can't handle criticism, you shouldn't be playing the game. The game is out there for public comment. If the game is out there for public comment and scrutiny, it's very much the media's job to report what's going on. As long as it's the truth, how can I sit there and say anything about truthful criticism?"

Cubs pitcher Kerry Wood is guarded about his craft and maniacally protective of his private life. But those who put in the time—and it might take at least several years—getting to know Wood will get past his first line of defense.

"I think you've got to do more than talk a couple of times to earn the trust," Wood said. "What bothers me the most is writers personally don't take the time to get to know me, but write opinions about my character, or any players for that matter. That bothers guys."

Suggesting Wood go for outs instead of strikeouts to save his arm is a fair comment to him.

"But calling [Carlos] Zambrano 'Straitjacket-worthy Zambrano' is not fair comment," he said. "You're insulting the guy, calling him names, insulting his intelligence, everything about him. It's weak. If you have something to say, come in and talk to the person.

"If you're going to do your job to the best of your ability, which would mean coming in actually interviewing players and taking time out of your schedule instead of just brainstorming about what you're going to write, it would be more acceptable [to players]. It's a respect issue. It's an honor to be in a big league clubhouse."

Anything beyond firsthand information starts the yellow light flashing to players.

"That's what bugs me," bullpen veteran Ray King said. "As a reliever, we sit in the clubhouse for three, four innings and listen to the radio or TV broadcast, and all of a sudden someone says, 'I was sitting and talking with Ray King today and he said this.' But he was sitting at the end of the bench. He just heard me and you talking. That would really agitate you, because we didn't say hello to each other.

"It really bugs you. You tell one person something, by the time it gets to the tenth person, it's blown way out of proportion."

Many media types have no problem discussing problems with players even amid the inherent tense atmosphere.

"Dan Shaughnessy taught me right away," Boston's Jackie Mac-Mullan said. "If you ever write anything negative about somebody, show up the next day and take whatever it is they give you. Some can, some can't."

"I learned long ago that whatever you write, you are as accountable to them as they are accountable to you," *Chicago Sun-Times* sportswriter Brian Hanley said. "If you write something that's strong, you're there the next day in case someone has a problem."

But that accountability remains sporadic. And it makes the jobs of the daily beat writers, on whom the columnists often lean for filler quotes and other tidbits, more difficult.

"They're 'hit and run,'" Hal McCoy of the *Dayton Daily News*, the dean of all major-sports beat writers, said of columnists. "They create a lot of ill will. Beat writers are covering their tracks every day when columnists don't come out and see the club [regularly], don't talk to the players, and write things that are way off the wall. It's everywhere. I notice that columnists almost never come to night games. They don't like writing on deadline. If you have a day game in Cincinnati, every columnist from miles around is there."

"Players get used to seeing beat writers every day [from spring training]," said Bruce Miles, the Cubs writer for the suburban Chicago *Daily Herald*. "They know if the beat writer writes something, he or she is there every day to take the heat or discuss something. It's a culture where they like accountability. If they see somebody take a shot at them, they'd like a chance to rebut that in person."

Seeing how the rift was only getting worse, I posed the question to controversial Chicago "opinionist" Jay Mariotti several years back.

Why not establish one or two "go-to" guys on each team on whom he could rely to provide the background for his commentary?

Mariotti did not believe that idea was practical, and reiterated his stance more recently.

"It's difficult for a columnist to maintain relationships," Mariotti said, citing a rapport with former Bears coach Dave Wannstedt. "Deep into his tenure, when he started to fail, you became critical, he believes you're backstabbing him. You lose that guy for life. It was the same with Sammy Sosa. You hang around with him. You give him good coverage, interview him in a limousine, then things become sour. The player expects that relationship all the time.

"On many occasions, it becomes so ugly that you learned the lesson not to get too close. The only athlete I dealt with who seemed to understand that was Michael Jordan. He'd be mad [at what was written], but he'd talk to you. You do that in a parking lot in front of a gym, not in front of him in the locker room."

Attributing the tension of the locker room to the interminably long season in which nerves get more frayed by the day amid close quarters, Mariotti rarely descends into Chicago baseball home locker rooms even though he probably recorded more frequent ballpark attendance than any other columnist in the city. He cited a series of ugly incidents involving players seeking confrontations with him for his avoidance of personal contact with players. Mariotti even tussled with White Sox announcer Hawk Harrelson in the press box in the Metrodome in 2004.

I sensed a familiar personality behind me while I was waiting to interview Houston's Roger Clemens in Wrigley Field's visiting locker room that same season. Sure enough, Mariotti stood there with a grin. But he would not go across the field to the Cubs clubhouse, preferring to take quotes off the closed-circuit video feed in the press box.

Columnists, of course, have built-in alibis about why they can't be more frequently seen around the press boxes and clubhouses. They must cover all sports and the flow of assignments takes them away from ballparks, preventing more frequent attendance.

Sports-talk-show hosts don't have that excuse. Unless they travel for remotes like the Super Bowl, other championship events, or NFL training camps, they usually are studio-bound. But even with the show-preparation time, they could get out to one or two games a homestand.

A minority of hosts do just that, introducing themselves to players and executives, even doing their own guest-booking. Yet the far greater number—in all markets across the country—take almost a professional pride in staying away, relying instead on broadcast observations of games, newspaper clippings, Internet printouts, and off-kilter observations of callers. Their listeners have access to the same information. So rather than enlightening the audience, many of the hosts' rants lead them astray instead. Recycling others' works ends up with inaccuracies as the misinformed lead the misinformed.

If such a stance is taken, it would promote a venture into dangerous territory, said Chicago sports voice Tom Shaer. He cited one example of a "complete lack of knowledge" about real-life events.

"The White Sox got rid of [shortstop] Mike Caruso because he was not committed to being in baseball shape," Shaer said. "I heard a guy on a sports-talk show rip the Sox for giving up too early on Mike Caruso. I had information from other players that confirmed Caruso wasn't interested in taking care of his body. What's Mike Caruso done since the Sox got rid of him? Not a fuckin' thing. At the time, if [the on-air person] had been around the ballpark, he would have found out talking with people who had personal interaction and by what Caruso did."

To Shaer, ballpark attendance isn't absolutely necessary. But any sports-talker dedicated to excellence will make the appearances.

"They don't go because they're lazy and don't have the same standards," Shaer said. "They don't have to go to the ballpark to do every element of their show, but they do have to go if they want to discuss inside stuff. You should strive to be the best. A four-hour talk show, guys prepare one and a half hours at home and one and a half hours at the office. You've got to go the extra yards, make the extra effort.

"You don't have to be at the ballpark to do a pretty good job. To do the best job, yes. Talk-show hosts say they don't want to get to know guys, just observe and be like a fan. Fine. But when you get into the areas of inside information, you should be at the ballpark."

Chet Coppock had the only nightly sports-talk show in Chicago at the dawn of the 1990s on what is now WMVP-AM. More recently he's been a weekend host at the Sporting News Network. He goes further than Shaer in criticizing many of his fellow hosts' no-show policies.

"Number one, they're gutless," Coppock said. "Number two, they have no knowledge. Number three, they're surrounded by the worst kind of court a king can be surrounded by. They're the great unwashed who are calling them on a regular basis, praising them regardless of what they say, no matter how stupid, how illogical it is.

"Most of these guys just really don't have the stones—put that in bold type—the rocks, the onions, to walk into a clubhouse and confront a ballplayer or manager for two reasons. One, it scares the hell out of them. Two, they know if they're asked a legitimate baseball, basketball, or football question, they're going to be completely exposed. So as a result, it's a lot safer to stay in your studio, holler over a microphone, have no idea what you're talking about, and point to a rating book that says our twenty-five to fifty-four demographic shows we are the Vito Corleone family instead of going out to the ballpark."

Top hosts Chris Russo and Mike Francesa of New York's WFAN, the country's top sports-talk station, were not often seen at baseball games in the Big Apple. Neither were most of their gabber colleagues.

"In fairness to them, I feel they should go more often, maybe a game a home stand," said WFAN Mets reporter Ed Coleman. "They do a five-hour talk show and also spend a lot of time doing remotes. They both have family obligations. But you don't have to stay for an entire game.

"Maybe guys feel they're better served sitting in front of TV. They feel they're boxed in if they go to one event."

Ninety miles down I-95, the majority of pontificators at Philadelphia's all-sports WIP-Radio view baseball from afar.

"There are hosts on our stations who don't go to lots of games," said WIP general manager Marc Rayfield. "Others go to many. Absolutely, I can see why the players feel that way—but players often times don't tell you anything. The responsibility of the sports radio station is to voice the opinion of the fans. Our responsibility is to the fan, not the player. If the fan criticizes him, the player will avoid [media contact]. The player will give a no comment or soft comment. Those who do comment are the exceptions, not the norm."

Two of Rayfield's management contemporaries in other markets believe hosts boost their credibility by showing up.

"They're being lazy," said Greg Rakestraw, program director and host at wxlw-am in Indianapolis. "There is also this sense of accomplishment with some people where that's beneath them. My opinion doesn't require me to go out there. It's a sign where they think they've paid some dues."

"I honestly think for the talent's overall well-being, he or she should make appearances at the game [whatever sport]," said Tim Spence of Denver's kkfn-am. 'They never show up at a game, so they can't know what's going on,' is ludicrous. It sounds like the players can't take the heat."

Few take the lead of wip host Howard Eskin, who sticks out among his stations talkers as a regular at Phillies games.

"That's the way I came up through the business," Eskin said. "That's the way you're always supposed to do it. As a [tv] sports anchor, I always thought it was important to interview players myself. Even on my days off, I go down there. More importantly, I enjoy it.

"When it comes right down to it, it's too easy in the business [to be a no-show]. With the Internet, it's created a laziness in the broadcast industry and even in print. There's a lack of accountability. If I don't have to do it, why do it? If you are critical of a player on the air, no question they really resent it when they can't discuss it with you."

The archetype for the no-show host seems to be the rabble-rousing Mark Madden of weae-Radio in Pittsburgh. Madden is notorious around town as a regular in his favorite Pittsburgh Penguins locker room, but an invisible man around the Pirates and Steelers dressing quarters.

As acerbic away from the mike as on the air, Madden, who doubled as a national weekend host on espn-Radio, said he won't answer the call of players to be personally accountable for his commentary.

"Players feel this way because they're pampered little idiots," he said. "Beano Cook said he'd rather associate with Nazi war criminals than Major League players. He's right. In today's era, any information you want is possible in the newspapers and on tv. You don't need to be anyplace to get information. They want people like me to show up in the clubhouse to yell and scream, to retaliate for slights, real or perceived.

"The players don't want you to get advance information. They want to intimidate you in advance or dress you down afterward. The idea of a sports-talk-show host being at every clubhouse is ludicrous. Is it preferable? Probably. But I don't think it's necessary. Athletes are getting tougher and tougher to deal with."

But Madden claims not all of those who show up in the locker room take advantage of that access.

"I've been in the Penguins' locker room for years," he said. "I've seen reporters there the entire year not ask one question. Maybe it's because they're lazy or maybe they're intimidated by being in the locker room. Smaller media are getting glorified fans [as sportswriters] who get into games for free. They are lesser lights who congregate."

Meanwhile, Chicago sports talker Dan Bernstein said the best information he gets is over the phone, tipping a few with sports types in bars, or even getting briefings from the bartenders themselves. That's how Bernstein was able to follow eccentric reliever Kyle Farnsworth's nocturnal wanderings while a Cub from 1999 to 2004.

"The most valuable stuff isn't necessarily [gathered] . . . by standing around a clubhouse waiting for a media-relations person to bite my dick off," Bernstein said. "Unless you have that natural curiosity, you're going to be a terrible talk-show host."

If all involved weren't aggravated enough, they could get upset even more by the early twenty-first-century trend of creating a hybrid—a newspaper columnist who gets even greater exposure via daily radio and TV talk gigs. But at the same time, that leaves even less time to get out to live events and to seek out face time with the people they cover.

Chicago's Jay Mariotti endorses such a trend.

"Newspapers have no choice in the Internet age but to let their high-profile people do outside work," he said. "They're all interconnected jobs and they all help each other. I became a better writer because I did a radio show."

Fellow Windy City pundit Rick Telander at least is honest when he explained late in 2004 the motivation for multiple dipping from the same fount of opinion.

"We're all trying to maximize everything," he said. "We're all trying to make money, to tap into new channels of cash flow. It's a money grab, no question. You're not going to do what people did in Red Smith's days—that's long, long gone. I spent thirty-three years writing about sports. I consider myself an expert. Experts should have the right to pontificate."

But Telander's ability to pontificate based on inside information that he gathered for his books and *Sports Illustrated* features was severely compromised by his daily on-air shift on wscr-Radio in Chicago. Teamed with two other co-hosts, Telander was on the air from 2:00 to 6:00 p.m. Such hours precluded him from getting out to pregame media access for both day and night sports events. Telander claimed he could take off parts of his program as events warranted. Yet that meant a diminishing quality of the radio show if the lead host often had to bail out early. If he stayed the entire four hours, he'd be rushing to make first pitch or tipoff for a night event.

After a half-year on the air, the schedule proved too much. At the end of one program, Telander unexpectedly announced he was quitting to increase his family time.

During 2004, Mariotti worked the 9:00 a.m. to noon shift on wmvp-am (1000), sometimes taping the last half-hour ahead of time so he could get away to the *Sun-Times* to tape *Around the Horn* at midday. He could thus still make it out to both day and night sports events. Occasionally Mariotti would stay in a downtown Chicago hotel to cut down on the early morning commute from his north suburban home to wmvp. Several times during the 2004 baseball postseason, Mariotti flew to New York, covered the game, then hopped the first flight back to Chicago the next morning to do his show in the studio. How he avoided total exhaustion is beyond human comprehension.

"All you're doing is talking about sports," Mariotti said. "It's exhilarating. If you're not on the radio, you'd be on the phone talking to friends. The hardest thing to do is a column. Talking is immediate. I don't believe a radio show can be mailed in. A column absolutely can be mailed in, if you're not careful.

"I think the only conflict is if you break your stories on the radio [and not in the column]."

But something had to give with the multimedia stars. Face time with athletes and sports executives was one of those things. Total effort and excellence was another.

"I used to work two jobs—WMAQ-TV and The Score (WSCR)," Chicago's Tom Shaer said. "When you work two jobs, it's a physical and mental impossibility to give 100 percent to each. Anyone who tells you they're doing the best possible job on each job is lying to themselves. They sincerely believe it, but it's not true. Can you give 95 percent to each? Yes."

Something serious did give in Detroit with an overcommitted columnist. During the 2005 Final Four, *Free Press* columnist Mitch Albom, by then more famous for his book *Tuesdays with Morrie* and TV screenplays, faced a nightmarish Friday April Fool's Day in which he had to write two columns and work his four-hour WJR-AM talk show. This time, the dizzying pace caught up with Albom, creating a national media uproar.

Pressed for time with a deadline looming for a section printed before the Saturday, April 2, game, Albom wrote that NBA players Mateen Cleaves and Jason Richardson attended—past tense—the NCAA semifinal between their old school, Michigan State, and North Carolina. Problem was, by the time the column came out Sunday, Cleaves and Richardson had not been at the game due to scheduling conflicts. The overextended Albom did not take care to write around the fact that Cleaves and Richardson indeed might not be in the stands.

Perhaps if he wasn't pulled in so many directions, Albom would have paused to consider how to word the column more carefully. He was suspended briefly while his paper apologized for yet another in a series of latter-day journalistic hoaxes and serious errors. Albom issued a printed mea culpa.

In the end, the answer must be to make columnists choose which is to be their number one medium—print or broadcast. They may have to cede their own star system if the suggestion of at least one broadcast executive is followed.

"To me the best scenario is a [radio] host that's full time, with a columnist as secondary host so he can take off [on assignments]," said Greg Rakestraw of Indianapolis's WXLW.

The double-dipping and no-show trends also attracted the attention of Stephen Rodrick in the January 25, 2005, edition of *Slate*.

Rodrick described how *Philadelphia Inquirer* columnist Stephen A. Smith appeared regularly on NBA *Fastbreak*, *ESPNEWS*, and *SportsCen-*

ter, while also serving as a judge on ESPN's *American Idol* mimicry, *Dream Job*. Rodrick said Smith wrote his NBA draft column on a BlackBerry in between TV appearances. ESPN, Rodrick reported, even wanted Smith for an hour-long daily show. He also listed *Miami Herald* columnist Dan LeBatard's "Mel Moonlight" gigs: a daily drive-time show on a Miami sports-radio station, a Sunday morning show on ESPN Radio, guest-hosting chores on PTI, and a twice-monthly column for ESPN *the Magazine*.

"How can you be on the radio with Stugotz [his co-host] and stake out Shaq's stool at the same time?" Rodrick asked. "For the Stephen A. Smiths of the world, sports television turns their columns into shrill, nonreported versions of their televised rants . . . the time suck of countless side projects cheats their readers."

A column is now only an appetizer to a couple of other journalistic courses.

"Being a columnist at a major daily paper was every sportswriter's dream job," Rodrick wrote of the good old days. "Legends like Jim Murray at the *Los Angeles Times* and Shirley Povich at the *Washington Post* were the most beloved guys at their papers. They'd write a cherished column for thirty years, and that was it. There was nothing else to do, no higher job to attain. No, a sports column is nothing more than a springboard, a gig that starts you on your way to becoming a multimedia star."

ESPN employed a rotating group of four columnists for its daily *Around the Horn* program, installing cameras in the scribes' respective newspaper offices. The papers obviously did not object with their mastheads prominently displayed and their stars pontificating and gesturing. Some gave up columning altogether. Skip Bayless, who had wandered the country from Chicago to Los Angeles to Dallas, back to Chicago, and then to San Jose, moved to New York to be a regular on ESPN2's *Cold Pizza*. He was joined on the daily morning show by an overly dramatic Woody Paige, who was allowed by the *Denver Post* to continue writing a weekly column from New York while tending to his TV duties. Eventually Paige gave up the column.

Rodrick praised Kansas City columnist Jason Whitlock and Los Angeles columnist T. J. Simers for putting their print duties first by gathering information firsthand at the ballpark, in Whitlock's case in spite of his broadcast commitments.

But what Rodrick really meant was the crux of the issue in baseball-media relations: Is the baseball consumer better off soaking up material from well-paid opinionists spreading themselves thin or hunkering down in their studios? Judging from the trends, it appears the latter group is taking care of number one first, second, and third.

THIRTEEN

Sports-Talk Radio

I didn't feel as sleepy as I thought I would, rising at 4:25 a.m. on Saturday, July 4, 1992. Eyes mostly wide awake, I rushed to get ready and jumped into the car for the fifteen-minute drive on an uncharacteristically empty Edens Expressway to the cinder-block Chicago Northwest Side studios of all-sports WSCR-Radio (The Score), on this day a daytime-only station operating at 820 on the AM band.

Months of badgering Score sports director Ron Gleason to let me do a fill-in weekend shift finally paid off. A cozy group of guys from smaller media outlets and others I frankly had never heard of had gotten the call in the six months since The Score had been on the air as Chicago's first regular sports-talk radio outlet. Maybe my number was called to get me off Gleason's back. I had contributed, for free, baseball analysis to The Score's Mike Murphy's early-evening and weekend program. So why not use such access for a long-form deal like a four-hour program?

That's exactly what I was assigned on Independence Day in the last year of the Bush I presidency. I would team with *Daily Southtown* sportswriter Paul Ladewski, who already had done some fill-in work, to handle the 6:00 to 10:00 a.m. shift signing on the station.

In the ten days before airdate I worked as my own producer. I lined up a nice guest list for the program: a wakeup call to all-time Chicago sportscaster Jack Brickhouse, Cubs outfielder Dwight Smith from his Atlanta home, and several veterans of the All-America Women's Baseball League in the 1940s. The latter's presence was timely since *A League of Their Own* was out in theaters.

I would not depend on the callers as a crutch to carry the program or a bevy of seven-dollar-an-hour, fuzzy-cheeked producers to book guests.

There was one other guest who had confirmed: network sports-caster Brent Musburger, who was willing to phone in from his vacation home in his native Montana. But in discussing the show in advance, Ladewski said something that I construed as a desire to ambush Musburger over his style of calling a game. I quickly called his agent-brother, Todd Musburger, to suggest there was a difficulty about Brent being on and that I had to abort the guest shot. Somehow Todd Musburger got the idea, and we parted without acrimony.

The program started slowly. I didn't book the guests for the first ninety minutes; you just don't do that to good people that early on a holiday morning. Ladewski and I had only a few calls in the first forty-five minutes. I verbally fumbled the sports updates several times; hey, it's not easy to read even a list of last night's baseball scores. But when we chanced upon the topic of whether pro athletes should be allowed to compete in the Olympics with the Michael Jordan–led Dream Team about to depart, the phones lit up. That carried us all the way to the guest times for Smith, Brickhouse, and the women's league veterans.

I felt exhilarated when I stepped out into the sunshine after 10:00 a.m. But a follow-up call to Gleason a few days later elicited a left-handed rejection of further co-hosting gigs. "It wasn't our best show; it wasn't our worst show," he said in his best management fence-straddling manner.

In further conversations with Gleason over the next few years, I realized why I didn't tickle his fancy. I had used too much of a straight-on, magazine-style, journalistically based format that holiday morning. Gleason also rejected the concept of picking up *Diamond Gems*, my syndicated, weekly baseball radio show that I founded in 1994 when I believed The Score and other Chicago stations were giving short shrift to baseball.

Gleason's explanation was a one-word answer that not only kept me at a distance, but also aggravated an entire sports spectrum full of athletes, coaches, managers, and executives. It represents the core philosophy that has driven sports-talk radio since it became popular around 1990.

"We want entertainment," Gleason said. He did not add "journalism" or "inside information."

The word "entertainment" would be repeated umpteen times as I would talk to different sports-talk types. And all it did was further anger ballplayers who became fodder for on-air criticism and satire that was part *Animal House*, part raging testosterone contest, and part gambling and drinking exploits braggadocio. Sometimes the inference of in-studio flatulence is thrown in for R-rated effect. The laughing and scratching was not all that dissimilar to the private behavior in clubhouses themselves, but this time for public consumption with few holds barred in skewering public figures. And, all the time, a free rein to callers who often added little to the show except ignorant opinions that frequently went uncorrected by cynical hosts.

Like the better-rated Rush Limbaughs and fellow hot-air mongers, the sports gabbers were selling mostly sizzle and little steak. They were generating heat, but not shedding much light. If accuracy about a public figure's personality and actions and the concept of good information got in the way of a fun time on the air, well, that's show biz.

"Sports-talk radio as you and I know it in its purest form is long gone," said Chicago's Chet Coppock, who has hosted sports-talk shows going back to the mid-1980s. "Sports-talk radio today is basically (bragging about) getting dead drunk, which strip-joint did you go to. It's no longer about sports. It's about the interjection of your own personality carrying a three- or four-hour window."

As the genre evolved through the 1990s, the format shifted. Snaring the biggest-name guests possible once was a priority. Then management went overboard in cramming as many callers on the air as possible. Most recently programming revolves around a star host who's part amateur comedian and part "mad as hell and I'm not going to take it anymore" ranter. Games and those who play them only become backdrops for the host's stage. And it goes beyond a mid-1990s trend of pushing baseball backward in the conversation pantheon while pro football is emphasized—even if the callers want to talk baseball twelve months a year.

The genre is well-defined by Tim Spence, one of the more reasonable managers in the business. To be sure, Spence went against his own inclination toward hosts interacting with callers by picking up the taped and caller-free *Diamond Gems* for Sunday-morning airings on his all-sports KKFN-AM in Denver. He has to give his on-air talent at least one day off a week. Otherwise, he runs a personality-driven operation.

Spence defines the kind of "entertainment" he's looking for in a sports-talk host as "somebody who understands how to have fun, talk sports, and relate to the audience . . . I believe that listeners ultimately want to be *entertained*. If this means it's involving a guest, multiple guests, guests with callers, or just callers, then that's ultimately up to the talent and the producer of the show. I believe in a solid mix that enables the talent to be at his or her best. It's all about the talent and all about what they can deliver. What this comes down to is simple. Guest and callers are simply tools for the talent to be at their best."

Another term used to describe the ideal sports-talk host is "compelling," according to Marc Rayfield, general manager of WIP-Radio in Philadelphia.

"We look for somebody who is compelling," he said. "We'd take compelling over knowledgeable. That's the only reason we identify with somebody. Movie stars, TV stars, athletes, something about their story is compelling. It's not just X's and O's [as a conversation topic]. We're looking for somebody who the people feel provides must-tune-in radio. People tune in to [hosts] not because they're the most knowledgeable, but because they are most interested in their opinion and relate to them."

In Chicago, the Score owner Danny Lee and general manager Seth Mason called around the Chicago market for names they'd heard, read, or who were referred to them when they put their first on-air lineup together late in 1991.

"Nobody got on just from a tape," Seth Mason said. "There were slightly different criteria for different shifts. The basic qualification was a gift of gab. They had to be quick-witted and know their sports. I did go for a variety approach and wanted a certain amount of writer types, a certain amount of radio types. It would be a two-man show, with the triangle of the listener or guest and the update guy. I started asking around about writers, and the first question I asked was who makes the press box laugh the most. The first guy they said came to mind was Terry Boers."

Such a talent hunt was the turning point in Boers's career. He junked his newspaper work and has been a mainstay of WSCR since the station signed on in January 1992.

Given the need to capture and hold a fickle listening audience with interesting on-air personalities, there still would seem to be room for good information. After all, radio is more immediate than old-technology newspapers. Yet the management belief doesn't seem to be very strong that good information and the kind of entertainment that includes personality-driven hosts can be expertly blended.

"They can coexist, but it sometimes is very difficult to make both excel to the level you'd like," Tim Spence said. "This format is all about entertainment. The 'sports information' is important for credibility, but can never be the ultimate focus of the radio station. It's all about the talent and always will be."

Once a Chicago Bulls beat writer, then a columnist at the *Chicago Sun-Times*, Boers is a self-described "entertainer." He said any shred of journalistic purity is long gone.

"There might be elements [of entertainment as a columnist]," Boers said. "But this is an entirely different approach. While I did entertain in the newspaper, the job here, nine times out of ten, is exactly that.

"New York is more hard-core sports talk. That's fine. I'm not particularly interested in doing that show. Do that four hours a day, I'd go insane. You be yourself. You don't want to be disingenuous about everything. What you'll get on the air is hopefully what you get off-air."

"We take great pains to inform ourselves as best we can," Boers's on-air partner Dan Bernstein said. "Over the years we've been together, our audience knows we don't make stuff up. But we're also a satirical radio program. Our job is to take what's in the news and have fun with it. We show up, do the show, and we have strong opinions about Chicago sports teams.

"A lot of people in this town just want to cash a check, live very happy lives, telling people what they want to hear and put the team's hat on that day. More power to that. I can't do that."

Hyper-opinionated Mark Madden of WEAE-Radio in Pittsburgh takes the entertainment concept to its logical conclusion.

"I'm not in the sports-reporting business," Madden said. "I'm in the entertainment business. I couldn't care less about the people I talk about. I owe them [listeners] honesty. To some degree I can reconcile [journalism]. But entertainment comes first.

"The first obligation of the sports-talk-show host is to win. What you say is fine as long as you can stay out of court. The more they hate, the more they listen."

But entertainment and satire by nature means poking fun and criticizing public figures. "The entertainment value is to keep bashing, bashing," said Greg Rakestraw, program director and afternoon host at all-sports WXLW-AM in Indianapolis.

When the gabbers turn serious, it's from the safety of the studio. Such a style is the biggest wedge being driven between Major Leaguers and the media and, in turn, the fans. Opinion, analysis, and commentary, much of it based on other sources of information, is hurled in the sports personalities' direction.

But amid the broadcast brickbats, the top stars of the game are expected to turn around and do live guest shots on the programs. If they lighten up and actually get on the line, the hosts more often than not turn to putty. They are obsequious, a Jekyll-and-Hyde turnabout from their typical on-air personas. Rare is the Jim Rome–style ambush of Jim Everett, whom Rome called "Evert"—in dishonor of female tennis superstar Chris Evert—in an attack on his football masculinity before Everett tried to rough up the insolent gabber.

A minority of ballplayers accept sports-talk radio for what it is—fun and games using their exploits as fodder.

"It's hilarious," said Cleveland Indians left-hander C. C. Sabathia. And the media-friendly pitcher would have more grievances than most players about satirical talk because of his weight, which he takes in stride because "I'm actually a runt in my family."

"I listen to WTAM-AM every day. Some things I take serious, some others I laugh about. It's funny. I'm in my garage listening to sports-talk about the game all the time. That's all it is, people's opinions. Most of the hosts don't show up regularly [at the ballpark], but guys [teammates] take it too seriously."

Veteran knuckleballer Tim Wakefield listens to sports-talk "once in a while, but I don't pay any heed to it." Still, he understands the modus operandi: "There are some intelligent people on some of the shows who can analyze correctly. But I understand it's entertainment and I also understand why it's there, why it exists. There needs to be some controversy. It's kind of entertaining to listen to what some of the people calling in say."

The old adage that any publicity is better than no publicity is offered up by Boston Red Sox manager Terry Francona.

"You have to keep that in perspective," Francona said. "Talk radio generates interest. Any interest in our game is good."

But for every Sabathia, Wakefield, and Francona understanding the ratings-driven motivations of radio management and talent, probably five Major Leaguers are repulsed by the format of sports-talk radio.

"I don't listen, but I heard around town that they sit there and rip people without knowing the information," said Cubs pitcher Mark Prior. "If they call it entertainment, unfortunately it's passed off as facts and a lot of people believe they are facts. If it's considered entertainment and not reporting news, then I'm definitely not going to be listening to it."

Sometimes the shock value of general talk-radio slops over to inflame the players even more. And that affects how the everyday media does their job.

In 1999 I entered the Seattle Mariners' spring-training clubhouse in Peoria, Arizona, with the intention of taping Ken Griffey Jr. for *Diamond Gems*. Almost immediately, Griffey said he would not do a recorded radio interview, but I would be welcome to jot down his thoughts on a notepad. Griffey explained he was boycotting all radio interviews because a Seattle shock jock, "The T Man," went on the air to proclaim he wanted to have sex with Griffey's wife. Griffey talked to "The T Man's" program director, apparently not resolving the situation. "The T Man's" rationale was that if he could have sex with Mrs. Griffey, the superstar could in turn become intimate with the shock jock's girlfriend.

Eventually, through his myriad of injuries as he was transplanted to his native Cincinnati, Griffey got over the episode. In 2004, he finally gave me the ten minutes for the radio interview.

Denver program director Tim Spence said shock jocks like "The T Man" could not last long in sports radio.

"I would say that as long as it's not personal, there really is plenty of opportunity for talent to entertain the audience," he said. "Most talent that are around for a long period of time and make a name for themselves in a marketplace do so on credibility and entertainment. 'Credible' . . . knowing what he's talking about. 'Entertainment' . . . somebody who understands how to have fun, talk sports, and relate to the audience."

Yet despite the ideals expressed by Spence, the Griffey episode showed how far-reaching the sometimes low-brow media culture of talk radio had become. Not only were the players angered, but the media who depended on their cooperation were adversely affected. The bad apples were spoiling it for the entire bunch.

Chicago Cubs media relations chief Sharon Pannozzo, for one, can't understand how sports-talk outlets can describe themselves as information providers when their main goal is entertainment.

"I don't credential entertainers," Pannozzo said. "So if you are an entertainer, anyone from your station who comes out here shouldn't get a credential. But you do send people out here to sort of provide some semblance of actual media work. You're sending people out under the guise that you are a media outlet. You can't say you're entertainers. You're one or the other. *The Today Show* provides entertainment and news. I don't see them on the air saying negative things about individuals.

"It's all about professionalism. If you're going to interview somebody on a radio station, that's one thing. But when your goal is to get listeners, to be inflammatory, that's a whole different part of it. Unfortunately, these people don't ever have to come here, and don't."

Some big league players, and even an executive like Minnesota Twins general manager Terry Ryan, solve the problem by simply not listening to local sports-talk radio, opting instead for the national, guest-intensive ESPN-Radio syndicated shows.

"If I was not an athlete, I'd probably listen to it all the time," said Cardinals ace Mark Mulder. "But [as a player] away from the field, I don't want to listen."

"I've learned not to listen to it very much," former reliever Rod Beck said. "People are calling in to have their own twist on things. That runs your freakin' ego. Around trade deadline, I listen to it to find out what teams are doing. But to listen about players, it can ruin your mental approach. Things that are said can be bad for the internal workings of the clubhouse."

Duels between stations and teams and their personnel have become more frequent as the pressure for ratings increases at the stations while the gulf between baseball people and the media widens.

The controversy can be witnessed on the biggest scale, of course, in New York.

Pitcher Al Leiter, then with the Mets, had an on-air war with Mike Francesa and Chris "Mad Dog" Russo in 2004. "Russo went off on a tirade that Leiter was washed up and was old," said WFAN Mets reporter Ed Coleman. "Al was struggling, but went on to have a great second half. Chris ended up at the end of the season kind of apologizing. But that tirade holds and entertains people."

Meanwhile, WIP and the Philadelphia Phillies had some rocky times during the Larry Bowa managerial era.

"They know absolutely nothing about sports," said Bowa, who went on to work as an ESPN analyst, then Yankees bench coach, after being fired by the Phillies late in 2004. "There are people who rip and criticize and never have been to a game. You never see them. If you're a real fan, you'll know the ignorance when you hear the conversation."

The sourest relations seem to be between Mark Madden, who took a turn as a pro wrestler with the Thrillseekers tag team in Tennessee, and the Pirates. A big Pittsburgh Penguins hockey fan, Madden was persuasive enough to land a role as his market's most controversial sports-talk host. The penny-pinching Pirates deserve plenty of raps for mismanagement, and Madden did not hesitate.

"Like I often said, Kevin McClatchy [a newspaper-chain heir who doubles as Pirates owner] never earned a dollar," Madden said. "He never had a business where everything is at risk."

But Madden went far beyond fair comment and criticism in the eyes of the Pirates. He angered the one Pirates official he could least afford to alienate—normally amiable media-relations director Jim Trdinich.

"I have a rift with Trdinich," Madden said. "The Pirates don't want the media to cover them. They want the media to support them. The *Post-Gazette* coverage of the Pirates has been unreasonably upbeat. A lot of media root, root, root for the home team. This town has a disproportionate amount of cheerleaders."

Trdinich had no choice but to fire back and withhold his services after too much over-the-line Madden gab.

"He's a shock jock," Trdinich said. "He had a vendetta against me, wanted me fired—all for shtick. In the season, he bashed us to the point where he said the best thing to happen to McClatchy is he dies in a car wreck. He would talk about [the late] Willie Stargell, how he never got an autograph from him, and that he should have died a worse death. Jack Wilson goes 0 for 20, he sucks, that's fine [for criticism]. But he starts attacking players and their families, that's bad.

"In spring training [before their final fallout], we got him guests. Eventually I sent his producer an e-mail that said Mark can rip us a new asshole whether we get him a guest or not, we're not going to get him guests. We get him guests and he'd rip 'em afterward. I said screw it. He's going to bash us whether we get him guests or not.

"Be fair, be honest. But to say a guy should die, that's going too far."

Similarly, top Chicago sports-talk voice Mike North took on the Cubs' Pannozzo. North accused her of "stealing" from her employer by not offering more services to his show while he did a remote in Houston with the Cubs.

"I just laugh," Pannozzo said. "He doesn't know me. He doesn't have to show his face. I couldn't pick him out of a lineup. If your 'entertainment' resorts to me, it must be a slow day for you."

The rapport is really bad when the gabbers take on the public-relations officials on top of the uniformed personnel and the front-office honchos. But that might have been a logical culmination of a format the prized style over substance.

The fans always needed a media voice. Pre-1980s radio programming did not have a lot of room for sports talk, while newspapers did not always have "sound off, sports fans" letters columns. But the pendulum swung entirely the other way when programmers mandated caller-heavy programs orchestrated by often ballpark-averse hosts. "Carphone Joe" would be the voice of authority all over the country on radio.

Mike Murphy was certainly no stranger to Wrigley Field when he became a regular host on WSCR-AM in Chicago in 1992. He was the bugler of the famed "left field bleacher bums" in the 1960s, once doing a soft-shoe routine to dodge ninety-mile-per-hour fastballs thrown at his feet by angry Cardinals pitcher Mudcat Grant as he teetered atop the bleacher wall on June 28, 1969. Murphy knew more baseball than most fans, but advertised himself as a "fan talking to fans" while bragging he never had a press credential or seen the inside of the locker room.

Almost every time I'd come on with Murphy in 1992 and '93, I'd barely get the baseball report out of my mouth when Murphy went to the caller—and the next caller. He was simply following a management mandate, so what I had to offer became secondary. A Murphy proposal to turn my conduit to inside stuff into a paying gig, à la Bruce Levine's baseball-reporter bailiwick on rival WMVP-AM, fell on deaf ears in The Score's front office.

Years later, I tried to place *Diamond Gems* on all-sports WHIT-AM in Madison, Wisconsin. The program director said no because "we're caller-driven." He had clones everywhere in the radio business, as many dozens of hosts threw out a topic each segment and invited listeners to call in to chew over it.

In truth, only a tiny percentage of sports-talk listeners ever call the station. Some of those who do punch up the stations end up as regular callers who get monikers. A host on Tim Spence's KKFN even was an extension of the genre, billed as "Lou from Littleton."

But of the vast majority who don't call, many are simply afraid to speak on the air. Others simply aren't motivated enough beyond a casual listen to the station. Some hosts have been known to plant calls, concerned that they won't get the lines to light up.

Many sports observers wonder whether the idea of fans talking to fans, not advancing the understanding of why their teams win or lose, is tiresome. It definitely can be inaccurate. Callers simply can offer up anything on the air to see if it sticks. And when it gets personal, there's a potential problem, especially if the hosts play along for the sake of making "good radio."

Houston Astros manager Phil Garner remembered a sports-talk show in Pittsburgh.

"Some guy calls in and says he was in a bar the other night and Jim Kelly was doing cocaine," Garner said. "Well, the talk-show host doesn't do anything to discredit the guy. This could be some guy who hates Jim Kelly, lost some money betting. Where's the credibility in something like that? Unfortunately, all news sources get lumped into one big thing, so a lot of people don't differentiate between talk radio, which has little basis in fact, and other TV, radio, and newspapers."

Gene Lamont, a longtime Major League coach and former White Sox and Pirates manager, is of the same mindset.

"When a caller calls in and they are way off-base, sometimes they just let them talk," Lamont said. "They should just say, 'You're wrong.' They should tell them they're not well-versed in what they're talking about. They're just stirring the pot."

The callers are disembodied and the hosts usually are ballpark no-shows, fanning the flames of anger of those they pounce upon. Those few representatives of sports-talk stations who come to the games take the flak on the scene.

"If they don't see them," WFAN's Ed Coleman said of the hosts not coming to the locker room, "the players mention it to me all the time."

Raking in mega-profits from its pioneering all-sports format, which started in 1987, WFAN has been one of the few stations to send reporters on the road full time with baseball teams. Coleman has worked the Mets beat since 1993, while Sweeny Murti traveled with the Yankees in a job once held by Suzyn Waldman, the only female part of a baseball broadcast team. Shannon Drayer travels with the Mariners for KOMO radio in Seattle. WTAM in Cleveland used to send a reporter full time with the Indians before that team took a two-year pratfall in 2002.

At least the WFAN hosts have their own source of firsthand information—to a point.

"You can be more critical if you're not there on a daily basis," Coleman said. "They get reports from me, but they take shots on their own."

Not having reporters on the scene to brief hosts can promote egg-on-your-face situations for sports talkers. Two such incidents involved The Score's Murphy.

In 1995, he and the callers were angry when slow-footed Cubs catcher Todd Pratt failed to score on a wild pitch to tie the game. Problem was, manager Jim Riggleman already explained to reporters on the scene that his hands were tied.

"Before the game, I get notification from the trainer that [starting catcher] Rick Wilkins is not to be used in the game under any circumstances," Riggleman said. "So Todd Pratt catches the game. He's on base late in the game and I can't pinch-run because I don't have another catcher. The count's 3-2, Brian McRae's the hitter, and Pratt's running on the pitch. McRae hits a shot into right-center. The ball stuck in the ivy, so Pratt has to stop at third. There's one out.

"There's a wild pitch. Pratt starts down the line, then stops, then starts again. Now the story is: Riggleman is an idiot. If I'm listening to a show like that, I'm going to say to myself there's probably more to the story. You don't have a chance to rebut it. It's out there. That can wear on a manager."

Three years later, Rod Beck, trying for another save with the Cubs, suffered a brain cramp while he was pitching against the Giants, his old team. Hours later, Beck, who used to drink with the fans at Murphy's favorite Wrigley Field–area bar, Bernie's, followed the fans' lead by calling The Score to comment on, well, himself.

"There was a grounder hugging first base with Gracie covering. I thought Grace had it and I stopped running to first," he said. "The ball took a bad hop off his arm. He turned around and flipped blindly to first. I wasn't there. Two runs scored and we lost.

"Callers and him [Murphy] were ragging on me, saying I was too fat to get over there. So I called The Score to tell them my physical condition had nothing to do with me not being over there. I had a Gold Glover playing first. I thought it was a routine play and I mentally screwed up. I took the blame for losing the game for not being over there."

"They first didn't believe it was me," Beck said. "They quizzed me about where I played my first year in pro ball and stuff like that. I gave them my stats, where I went to high school. They finally believed it was me calling."

Far more common is the athlete being asked to call the station in a more controlled situation. Representatives of sports-talk stations are on-site at the ballparks for that purpose—booking guests. Seconds after every postgame interview session at Wrigley Field, WSCR reporter David Schuster or other colleagues intercept the game contributor to ask if he will go on live now or later. Schuster is almost like a salesman, knowing rejection is a daily part of his game.

Cubs pitcher Kerry Wood disagrees that calling in will have a positive effect on host and callers.

"You can't win that battle," he said. "That's a no-win situation. They act like they're doing us a favor when we call in, when we're doing them a favor. If we don't call in, they wouldn't have much of a show."

Whether they aggravated baseball personalities did not seem to make much of a difference anyway to a goodly portion of sports talkers. They appeared to be football lovers, first, foremost, and always. Baseball indeed got shuffled further back in the priority rankings of many sports-talk programs before and after the 1994–95 strike. The combination of the Mark McGwire–Sammy Sosa home-run race in 1998, and interest that exploded in the likes of the Yankees, Red Sox, and Cubs in recent years, forced the issue. The management, hosts, and producers had to take calls from baseball fans who never really were absent, yet never were encouraged to call in with the agenda setting that marks the opening of most talk programs.

The love of the NFL was never more apparent than in the hires of Chicago sports-talk stations starting in the early 1990s. Former Bears Dan Jiggetts, Tom Waddle, Doug Buffone, and Glen Kozlowski, and former Green Bay Packer John Jurkovic, held down regular air shifts. Ex-Bull Norm Van Lier at one point was a daily regular. But no former baseball player or executive earned a similar broadcast profile, except for the kinds of shorter contributions scattered throughout the weekly schedule from the likes of baseball character Jimmy Piersall. In 2006, Piersall co-hosted a two-hour weekly show.

Dan McNeil, a host on both WSCR-AM and WMVP-AM, professed to be a White Sox fan and was squarely on the World Series bandwagon in 2005. But in reality he was first and foremost a football fanatic. McNeil once said on the air he'd love an "all-football radio station." One afternoon in the fall of 2004, McNeil told his WMVP listeners that he had a choice between Jaguars coach Jack Del Rio and White Sox general manager Kenny Williams as guests. He picked Del Rio because his team was the Bears' next opponent and was only available for an interview at that moment.

McNeil did not return a half-dozen calls for comment on his sports preferences.

Meanwhile, WSCR's Mike North had gotten his start in broadcasting by purchasing his own time on a small foreign-language-oriented station for a weekly one-hour football handicapping program. Indeed the gambling undertone that buttresses the NFL is always present in the fall and early winter in much sports-talk programming.

"Management has never said talk more about football," WSCR host Terry Boers said. "The last couple of years were good for baseball. I love baseball. Bears calls took up Mondays and Fridays for us. Football was always a safe bet. Baseball was not a safe bet till the last couple of years. But the whole thing [football] would dry up without gambling."

Boers signed on with The Score in January 1992. He said the Cubs from 2003 on were the hottest topic he ever handled on the air. The team coming within five outs of the World Series in 2003, then enduring a controversy-filled 2004 season, lit up the phone lines like never before.

"The Cubs thing was totally separate from baseball. The last couple of years wasn't like anything I was associated with," Boers's cohost Dan Bernstein said. "The Cubs are owned by a media corporation. They so coldly and successfully built a massive multimedia machine with a newspaper, TV, cable, and radio. They are an absolute romping, stomping colossus."

You'd have hardly thought that would ever be the case more than a decade ago.

Chicago sportscaster Rory Spears worked for WSCR-AM in its first few seasons in 1992–93. The station fed off the end of the Mike Ditka era with the Bears, employing "Da Coach" with a weekly show in '92. That program became the only nongame situation to get Ditka comments in his downer 5-11 swan-song season. And the station tried to latch onto the Michael Jordan–led dynastic Bulls. But actual game-oriented calls, even in the 1993 NBA Finals, did not blow out the station phone lines.

Overall, The Score was not a baseball-friendly station in those days.

"The sports atmosphere in Chicago was such that you did the winter sports, but used baseball as a little bridge to the opening of Bears camp in July," Spears said.

Indeed, when The Score went heavy on live remotes at Dave Wannstedt's first camp as Bears coach in July 1993, it went against the flow of calls. Building over the past four seasons, the White Sox came into their own in the summer of '93. The fans wanted to talk about the Pale Hose at midsummer over the Bears, but the station insisted on forcing Bears training-camp coverage from Platteville, Wisconsin, down the listeners' throats.

The Score's ruling execs also were amateur Basketball Joneses, Spears said. "My feeling was that Ron Gleason, [station manager] Harvey Wells, and Seth Mason seemed to have a big concern about basketball," he said. "I thought it was amazing that in 1994, the first year without Michael Jordan, I remember a memo coming out from Ron that made sure the station was frequently using a stringer down in Indianapolis for the Knicks-Pacers series. It was amazing to see them use a stringer for that. They wanted to keep the listener focus on basketball."

Mason, who was part of the founding management group of The Score in 1991, before they cashed out six years later, claimed he "liked all three sports" and did not favor basketball over the others. "We had problems generating interest in the Bulls in the regular season," he said. "Football was number one, it was just the sport that had the biggest reach into fandom. We would stick with the subject of the day. If the Cubs were hot, we'd talk about that."

But according to Spears, Mason forced a change in talk topics during the Knicks-Pacers playoff series in 1994. Mike Murphy was carrying on a natural flow of diamond conversation one afternoon. The callers all talked baseball and did not drift into other sports. Suddenly Mason called from home and told Spears and his fellow producer to book a basketball guest—quickly. Thumbing through the media guides, Spears tracked down a Knicks writer on his off-time, working around the house, and sweet-talked him into coming on immediately.

Mason denied trying to dump baseball talk in favor of basketball. "Murph wanted to talk baseball twelve months a year," he said. "I told him he should respect it [other sports] and not push baseball so hard in the off-season."

In other markets, baseball must run up against an irresistible tide of football talk.

Philadelphia Daily News national baseball writer Paul Hagen said the overwhelming emphasis on Eagles talk on WIP-AM persuades sports editors driving into the office that football coverage is the desire of Philadelphia fans. But WIP's big names suggested they are only going with the flow.

"Philly was a more football-centric town since the last time the Phils won the World Series," WIP GM Marc Rayfield said. "Philly was a baseball town then. The city made a decision that they were more interested in the Eagles than in any other team.

"We talk Eagles from the draft to the Super Bowl. It's a pretty long window of time. What you hope you have is a competitive baseball season. Philly so desperately wants the Phillies to win."

WIP talker Howard Eskin is a regular at Phillies games, but concedes he has to talk Eagles to satisfy the fans.

"I don't believe [a big pro-Eagles format] is the case," said Eskin. "When I started, there was nothing better than baseball. The Phillies haven't instilled the confidence that it's trying to do all it takes to be a winner. The confidence of the town waned. It has become an Eagles town. I wish WIP was that powerful. The Phillies [front office] doesn't like WIP talking football a lot."

When the Colorado Rockies failed to keep improving after their relatively successful early seasons, they lost their chance to keep within hailing distance of the mega-popular Broncos.

"Denver is a Broncos' town without a question," KKFN program director Tim Spence said. "The next level of conversation usually revolves around the Avalanche or the Nuggets (based upon time of year and season). The Rockies have been and will be for at least the next year a distant topic of conversation. People are interested, but not even close to the level of the Cubs or any team that has a following or yearly interest."

No matter the overemphasized subject matter or low-rent conversational style, few controls existed on sports-talk programming until Big Brother stepped in. The coarseness of language was starting to move into George Carlin's old seven-dirty-words gig when Janet Jackson's untimely nipple exposure at the Super Bowl in 2004 made the conservatives in Washington DC elect to roll the standards back about fifteen to twenty years.

"The FCC after Janet Jackson scared me," Pittsburgh's Mark Madden said. "My show started out insane. It's toned down. Shock for shock's case gets boring. I've never been suspended, never been fined."

But you can't really hold Madden down.

"We have fake guests," he said. "I really do what I like."

Employed now by CBS radio, Chicago's Boers and Bernstein now have some layers of corporate checks above them to tone down their boys-club language.

"It's a different show in a lot of ways," Boers said. "Big Brother is watching. It's mostly language."

The duo were instructed not to use the word "piss" on air. "It's more a matter of volume," Bernstein said. "If you say 'douchebag' once, don't say it ten times. Same with 'asswipe.'"

Founding WSCR exec Seth Mason claims he established some limits early on.

"We wanted them to be as entertaining as possible, but not use profanity gratuitously," Mason said. "'Suck' has made its way into the dictionary. 'Asswipe' is another word. They should use common sense. At times I would say to a couple of the guys, you're going back to it [guttural words] so often, you're using it so often. At times, Terry [Boers] thought it was his job to do that."

At some point, the thinking-person's sports fan, not just the knee-jerk caller who wants to propose a trade of every backup player on his favorite team for a coveted superstar, will want the sports talkers of the world to offer more than rollicking humor with sports in a supporting role. Baseball is fun at its basics, but the demeaning parts of the game have been officially repudiated. No need to transfer that aspect to one or two radio stations in every city of size.

In the end, the baseball fans can vote not with their feet, but with their push buttons.

"It's all how the public perceives it," said the Cubs' Kerry Wood. "Everything these people say on the air doesn't mean it's right. Real baseball fans can form their own opinions and know better when they listen to these types of shows."

FOURTEEN

No More Harry Carays

Marty Brennaman and Ken "Hawk" Harrelson are bookends as baseball broadcasters.

"The worst word in my profession is *we*, that famous French word meaning 'yes,'" said Brennaman. "You can't tell that I'm cryin' and pissin' and moanin' if they're losing. That's not my style. One thing we all aspire to have when I walk away from this business, if they never say anything else good about me, the one thing they will say, 'He had credibility.'"

That credibility, of course, is aimed squarely at the listeners.

"That's the only thing I care about," Brennaman said. "I've told players, I don't broadcast for you, your wife, your mom, your dad, or your friends, or their friends. I broadcast for the people who turn on the radio each night in Lima, Ohio, or Paintsville, Kentucky, and places like that. If they didn't like my work, I'd be gone a long time ago.

"Take it with all due respect, take [the New York Yankees'] John Sterling as an announcer," Brennaman said. "He's as big a homer and as big a rooter as ever lived. I'm not critical of his style. Could I do that? Not on my worst day could I root for a team like that. Do I want the Reds to win? Hell, yeah, I want them to win. It makes my job easier. It's always better to say nice things about people than be critical."

Nearly three hundred miles northwest of Brennaman's Cincinnati Reds' home base at the Great American Ballpark, Harrelson tries to bust his vocal chords at the latest White Sox highlight, in the tried-and-true tradition of many past Chicago baseball announcers.

"The greatest compliment they can pay me is being the ultimate homer," Harrelson said. "That's the ultimate compliment. I want them to win every game. When I do a Cubs game [playing the White Sox at U.S. Cellular Field], the best compliment I can get is all the Cubs fans are pissed off at me.

"An umpire puts a hard-on for our manager [a dispute between Hunter Wendelstedt and Ozzie Guillen] and causes our manager to be suspended for two games. He blew the call. That upsets me. I busted [baseball disciplinarian] Bob Watson's balls on the air. I wanted to protect this ball club. A lot of announcers, the only stat they care about is the length of the game. I don't care how long we sit here as long as we win a game."

Harrelson will use silence as a communicator. If a questionable choice of a pinch hitter is announced, Harrelson said he will pause, then say, " 'Well, Ozzie must have a hunch.' That's my way of saying I didn't like the move. But to hammer people . . . I'll let people use their imagination. They give the viewer zero credit for knowing what's going on."

Somewhere in between Brennaman and Harrelson are the majority of baseball announcers. And if the truth be known, they will stay in that safe, middle ground. Not many will go as far as to shamelessly root for the team they cover. But even fewer will move toward Brennaman's tell-it-like-it-is style.

"I've always been candid," young veteran announcer Wayne Hagin, most recently with the St. Louis Cardinals, said. "I have not been a homer. I was not brought up as a homer as a listener. People always said Harry Caray was a homer. He was not. He told it like it is long before Howard Cosell did.

"There are three responsibilities I have. First responsibility I have is to the listeners. Number two is to the sponsor. Number three is to the ball club. As long as you are fair and you criticize the performance, not the performer. There were times I felt Harry Caray criticized the performer, not the performance."

But there's one absolute certainty in the baseball broadcasting atmosphere of the early twenty-first century. No more Harry Carays can develop, period. Brennaman is the closest to that style, yet he could not duplicate the overpowering personality Caray developed through employment with four teams over fifty-three seasons from 1945 to 1997. No announcer ever will be allowed to become bigger than the team he covers, a status Caray achieved first with the White Sox, then magnified by five with the crosstown, wealthier, higher-profile Cubs.

Caray was the sleep-deprived, beer-soaked bon vivant, proud of his damn-the-consequences verbal style that skewered errant players and promoted a cast of hangers-on and saloon proprietors. He could mangle names, including calling George Bell "George Bush," while being so politically incorrect that any other announcer would have been busted and lucky to be rehired in Missoula. Caray revved it up as a near-exclusive fan conduit to the Cardinals on radio well into the TV era, reached a crescendo in a kind of guerilla-theater-on-the-air with color analyst partner Jimmy Piersall with the White Sox, and strode bigger than the franchise in a slightly toned-down, but still candid dotage with the Cubs.

When Caray died one and a half months before the 1998 season, his mold also was tossed away. Only Brennaman and a handful of other brave voices of the game can fend off the unspoken directive of self-censorship. Baseball announcers are now squeezed between a firm corporate mentality that features careful oversight of their work and an increasingly sensitive cadre of millionaire players that brook no on-air criticism. Yet at the same time, the announcers cannot fudge the truth because the cameras do not lie. And with double or triple the number of cameras and replays compared to the 1960s, every player foible or blown call is replayed and freeze-framed from every conceivable angle.

Talk about the walls ready to close in while the announcer is trying to keep both eyes and all his concentration on the field.

"I would hate to work for an organization where I have to measure every word coming out of my mouth for fear there would be repercussions," said Brennaman. "I honestly feel there are guys with my job in the Major Leagues who have to deal with that."

But even Brennaman knows there are ultimate lines that cannot be crossed.

"You don't have total freedom," Harrelson said. "I have common-sense restraint. In 1975 I did not have to worry about what I said, whether it was positive or negative toward the Red Sox. You were talking about $10 million, $12 million, $15 million payrolls. Those were big payrolls [at the time]. Now you have close to $200 million payrolls. Now the game has changed toward entertainment dollars. You have announcers sitting up there doing 155 games who are negative toward a ball club. That's not going to work anymore.

"Harry was the last of that breed you'll see."

Mind you, Caray did not have a totally unfettered style without paying the price. He aggravated a gaggle of Cardinals players in ultimate, Middle American St. Louis before owner Gussie Busch fired him amid rumors that Caray had an affair with the owner's daughter-in-law. Caray was fired by White Sox owner John Allyn, but was back on the air the next season when Allyn sold out to iconoclast Bill Veeck, who conceived of Caray's seventh-inning singalong. Caray quickly became disenchanted with Veeck successors Jerry Reinsdorf and Eddie Einhorn and jumped to the Cubs. Yet Tribune Company broadcasting chief Jim Dowdle and Cubs general manager Dallas Green counseled Caray to dial down his act amid a much more conservative corporate culture.

Nearly a decade after the end of Caray's run, would-be imitators likely would be crushed between team-management pressure and player rebellion. And despite the need for candid broadcasting of baseball, the fans aren't likely to come to their aid.

"I give the fan credit for knowing what the hell is going on," Harrelson said. "The fan has changed dramatically in the last twenty to twenty-five years. The viewer is so much more knowledgeable and sophisticated than twenty-five years ago. You're getting more and more females in the audience. Today there's too much other shit going on TV. People will not watch baseball unless they understand that. I will not go on there and tell you that's not what you saw. There are some announcers who will do that. They're insulting your intelligence."

It's commonly perceived that Harrelson serves at the pleasure and critical ear of Reinsdorf, a media junkie. And if the truth be known, a suddenly critical Harrelson style that included shots at management would end quickly. But the former outfielder, general manager, and eternal golf fiend knows his limits and doesn't exceed them. When he did once, taking umpiring crews to task for perceived prejudice against the Sox, he was summoned to the principal's office.

"The umpires didn't like Reinsdorf because they felt Jerry was instrumental in ousting Fay Vincent, who they thought was an umpires' commissioner," Harrelson said. "There was no accountability. Al Clark and these guys were sticking it right up our ass. I had enough of it. Jerry called me into the office and said I was getting on them too hard."

On the job in Cincinnati since 1974, Brennaman has earned his leeway, but knows he still raises the hackles of the team bosses.

"[Reds president] John Allen has said it on more than one occasion," he said. "He laughingly said that opinions and comments by Marty Brennaman on Reds radio are not the opinions of management and ownership. He laughs, but I know he means every single word of it. They let me do my job."

"I had problems in the early 1980s. If Dick Wagner had not been fired [as GM], I would have been fired. He had all he wanted from me. I tried to get a contract extension from him in 1981, and he said he would not negotiate contracts in the season."

Brennaman set an August 15, 1981, deadline and vowed if a contract had not been executed, he'd quit. But Wagner was fired on July 11. "We never had another word with one another," he said. "I'm convinced if he had kept his job, I wouldn't have been there in 1982. That hurdle was overcome, and I haven't had any problems since."

Other broadcasters, like thirty-seven-year Kansas City Royals voice Denny Matthews and Wayne Hagin, said they've never had prior censorship or management second-guessing.

"I've done it for twenty-four years and nobody's ever told me to tone it down, to change my style," Hagin said. "I think they honestly respect my viewpoint. One time [as Colorado Rockies announcer], I said the visiting team was running up to the batter's box with great delight because they wanted to hit at Coors Field so badly. [Rockies GM] Bob Gebhard took that as an insult to his pitching. I told him after the game, Geb, that all had to do with Coors Field, not the players."

But Hagin and his brethren now know that players wield increased clout with their guaranteed mega-bucks payouts and thus can take steps toward getting voices dislodged from the booth. Teams can fire announcers more easily than they can dispatch players.

Caray was in constant hot water with players, reaching a peak with the White Sox. Third baseman Bill Melton and Caray nearly tussled at the Pfister Hotel in Milwaukee. Melton's children were booed at old Comiskey Park, while their frustrated father asked for a trade. Players' wives and friends monitored the broadcasts, reported back to the clubhouse, and confrontations ensued. With no apparent provocation, Jimmy Piersall tried to choke Rob Gallas, then the Sox beat writer for the suburban *Chicago Daily Herald*. Piersall also called baseball wives "horny broads" on a TV special. Caray took on White Sox managers Chuck Tanner and Tony La Russa. La Russa gathered his coaches together, went to a TV studio after one game, and appeared to threaten Piersall. To this day, Melton and La Russa can barely talk about Caray. Yet Caray's overpowering popularity among the listening audience carried him through the rough spots.

But in another era, the actual breakup of a popular announcing team can be linked to player criticism and management's inability to quell the rebellion.

After a two-year absence prompted by illness, mega-popular Cubs TV analyst Steve Stone—who had teamed with Caray for fifteen seasons—returned to the booth in tandem with Caray grandson Chip Caray in 2003. He and the Cubs seemed on top of their game. Stone's first-guessing style and the Cubs' improved play, which brought them within five outs of a World Series, seemed a perfect match.

Yet below the surface, tensions fermented. Under new manager Dusty Baker, the clubhouse developed a bit of an "us versus them" mentality. Winning hides warts. And in 2003 Cubs players grumbled about Stone's fair-comment-and-criticism analysis. The jibes never went public. Reliever Joe Borowski said he and his teammates kept them in-house. A year later, a rumor circulated that the players were so upset at Stone and Chip Caray that they convened a meeting to bar the announcers from the team's National League East division-clinching celebration in the Wrigley Field clubhouse. Borowski said that report was false, and it would have been difficult to gather all the players together anyway for something less vital than money.

An unlikely catalyst named Kent Mercker helped crack open the tensions on August 27, 2004.

After one early season loss, Stone said the Cubs were not hustling, but no public reaction surfaced, probably because the game was on the West Coast and the comments were late at night. Then, in July, a Moises Alou postgame, off-handed comment that the broadcast-ers gave more credit to the team's well-publicized pitchers instead of the lineup was blown up far out of proportion. A rumor then surfaced that the players did not want Stone and Caray to ride on the team plane, but that was shot down quickly.

Nothing more surfaced until Mercker, a media-friendly, good clubhouse guy, got upset at Caray's crediting Astros pitcher Roy Oswalt with a decent outing, giving up six runs in a 15–7 victory on a warm, windy day at Wrigley Field.

Oswalt had previously angered the Cubs by throwing at catcher Michael Barrett after Aramis Ramirez slugged a homer five days ear-lier. During Oswalt's first at bat on August 27, Barrett jumped out of his crouch behind the plate and confronted him, so tensions fur-ther inflamed. Six innings later, listening to Caray's praise of Oswalt while his own arm was icing up in the clubhouse, Mercker commit-ted a serious breach of baseball etiquette by calling the press box, desiring to convey his displeasure to Caray.

But it was Stone who leaked the Mercker call to the *Chicago Tri-bune*. On August 28, Mercker said he asked Cubs public relations director Sharon Pannozzo, who had taken his call the previous day, to inform Stone he was in the wrong with the in-game critique of the announcer. The apology, though, was too late. The genie was out of the bottle.

Two other Mercker-Stone meetings in the next three weeks be-came a wild basis for controversy. In one instance, Mercker sup-posedly upbraided Stone as the former was boarding the Cubs team charter just before takeoff. In another, Mercker was accused of swearing at Stone as the two passed in a hotel elevator in Pittsburgh. Such actions, again, were out of character for Mercker.

The conflict was exacerbated because Stone, imitating most sports-talk-show hosts and many columnists, rarely ventured into the Cubs clubhouse for personal chats. Disputes such as the one with Mercker could be settled one-on-one, out of sight and earshot of the media, if Stone had been a regular clubhouse visitor. But when Stone came down to the field in Chicago, he usually made a right turn toward the visitors' dugout to confer with the opposing man-ager and star players. A year later, when Stone was a baseball analyst for all-sports WSCR-Radio, he rarely showed up at the ballpark even though he lived in Chicago during the season.

Such a style was in marked contrast to Marty Brennaman, who will eagerly own up to his on-air verbiage in person the next day.

"The Reds players through the years would have loved to kill me if they could get away with it. But I walk down the middle of that clubhouse every day. If anybody's got anything to say, they don't have to look for me. Guys I most respect are guys if they took issue with me, they came up and asked, 'How can you say something like that?' Then we have a discussion about that."

In one instance, Reds outfielder Eric Davis committed himself to going for second and was thrown out by twenty feet with the Reds down a run in the ninth.

"I was all over him," Brennaman said. "He was the first out of the inning. The next day he jumped me in the clubhouse. We argued for fifteen minutes, and we said, 'Let's agree to disagree.' The next day it was as if nothing happened."

But without the broadcaster-player meetings in the clubhouse, the Cubs controversy kept churning through the final month of 2004. Chip Caray reportedly became disenchanted by the players grumbling about the on-air comments and wanted nothing to do with complainers as his own contract ran out. The final straw came on September 30, when Stone first-guessed that Dusty Baker should have ordered an intentional walk to Reds catcher Javier Valentin in the twelfth inning. Baker didn't, and Valentin drove in the winning run with a double that effectively knocked the Cubs out of postseason contention. Minutes later, Stone participated in an edgy postgame interview with Baker.

"I told Dusty there is no black and white in baseball," Stone said. "There's gray. There's just a move you're paid to make and I'm paid to analyze."

Charges and countercharges filled the airwaves and newspapers over the next week. Stone met with Cubs president Andy MacPhail. On the season's final day, Caray announced he was leaving to join his father, Skip Caray, in the Atlanta Braves broadcast booth. Baker and Cubs general manager Jim Hendry held teleconferences with reporters after the final game to claim they had nothing against Stone, who soon announced he was departing. Stone replacement

Bob Brenly ended up with a higher salary than his predecessor, partly to ensure that a big, credible name would replace the popular analyst.

"The Chip and Steve situation was unadulterated bullshit," Brennaman said.

Mercker had goofed. Feathers were ruffled that should not have been. Stone did nothing wrong except not settling disputes in private rather than leaking the stories to the media. He had hardly been inflammatory in his broadcast style.

"I don't second-guess people," Stone said. "I made a trademark of first-guessing. I say what I think should happen, lay out what I believe should happen. I work for the fan. He's sitting at home, doing exactly what I'm doing.

"The one thing Harry [Caray] always said is when you're looking at that camera, and you're talking to the people at home, the one thing that you have to always do is make sure you're being honest with them. If you deviate from that, they're going to pick it up. That camera doesn't hide anything. In the years I've broadcast, I've felt that, number one, I've told the truth on the air. Number two, I tell it consistently. When it's good, I say it. When it's bad, I say it. There's nobody going to out-prepare me, nobody going to out-work me.

"I've always felt that if you have something to say, say it. Honesty and integrity are not something you trade for money or your job."

If Mercker was a surprising source of discord with broadcasters, consider the surprise early in the 2005 season when baseball ambassador Luis Gonzalez went off on Thom Brennaman, Marty Brennaman's son.

Tossed out early in the Arizona Diamondbacks' 4–3 loss to the Washington Nationals on May 9, Gonzalez watched the younger Brennaman's telecast from the clubhouse, like Mercker.

"Listening [to the broadcast], it just gets frustrating because I'm a player and I know what guys go through every day down there, and we all go through struggles during the season," Gonzalez told the *Arizona Republic*.

"What bothers me is that sometimes the people who are quick to criticize . . . when that player is going good they're the first ones to say, 'Oh, man, you're the greatest player.' They're the first ones to pat you on the back and say, 'Hey, buddy, good job.' "

Gonzalez said if broadcasters work for a team, they should espouse the company line.

"When you work for a company, you're a company man," he said. "I play for the Diamondbacks. I'm not going to go out there and talk bad about the Diamondbacks. They're my employers. I think that's just what frustrates us sometimes."

Unlike Mercker and Stone, Gonzalez and Brennaman met before the next game.

Talking one-on-one to the players before or after games goes a long way. Just ask former Cubs ace Rick Sutcliffe, now a star ESPN analyst.

"I'm no different than when I played," Sutcliffe said. "I really don't give a shit whether anybody likes me or not. I'm all about respect. I didn't care as a teammate whether you liked me or not. I wanted you to respect me, and in turn I hope to respect you.

"The same thing works for me as a broadcaster now. I'm in every clubhouse before every game, and I'm in the winning clubhouse after every game. You can always find me. If I say something you don't like, I'm accountable. I'm there. Once every two weeks, somebody's upset with something I said, and we figure it out. Either I'm telling the truth and you have to deal with it, or wait a minute, I got it wrong. And if I did, I'll more than compensate for it."

Marty Brennaman seconds the concept of mea culpa for announcers.

"I've gone on the air to apologize for being wrong," he said. "I criticized George Foster in Shea Stadium in 1977 for dropping two fly balls. I killed him on the air. I found out later that he was playing with a 104-degree temperature. He was as sick as a dog. The biggest mistake we can make is not correcting a mistake."

The sheer number of former players tabbed as color analysts might cut down on honesty and analysis of players who may have been former teammates. Former Minnesota Twins ace Bert Blyleven long has been a staple on his old team's broadcasts. He is not afraid to call out players for errors of commission or omission.

"I can be honest," said Blyleven. "I'm honest because I've played the game. I know what it takes to go through a tough season. I grew up listening to Vin Scully and Jerry Doggett. But there was only one Vin Scully. He was the best ever.

'On the TV side, if someone makes an error, I'll say that's a play that should be made. I have said a guy is not hustling, if he's not running out a ball. Jacque Jones hit a ball to second, he didn't hustle from home to first. It's a bang-bang play and he's not hustling down the line."

The analyst's style is affected by the region of the country. The biggest homers seem to reside in the Midwest, headquarters of the "red states" of baseball journalism. A laid-back style seems to predominate on the West Coast. Former New York Mets and San Francisco Giants announcer Ted Robinson, who used to work with the San Francisco Giants, said Harry Caray's in-your-face style simply overwhelmed listeners during his one season broadcasting the Oakland Athletics in 1970.

'Jerry Reinsdorf, a Brooklyn native, was astonished when he first came to Chicago to attend law school at Northwestern. He listened to baseball announcers like Jack Brickhouse cheering for their teams. Raised in the Red Barber–Vin Scully straight-reporting model, Reinsdorf tried to apply that to his White Sox via Don Drysdale, similar in style to Scully, in the early 1980s. It did not take with the fans. Eventually "Hawk" Harrelson, who partnered early with Drysdale, took over the lead Sox job and let loose with a partisan call.

"Budweiser has different formulas in certain sections of the country," Harrelson said. "Oscar Mayer has different formulas. They're subtle, but they're there. Boston and New York are different, even in the East. Phil Rizzuto was the ultimate homer, but you can't do that in Boston.

"With Vin Scully, there's no way in the world that Dodgers fans will want anything different than him. They were born with it. Certain styles over the years have been created and that's the way it is."

Regional differences and individual team traditions shape what the audience expects from announcers even more than management oversight or player critiques. But too many younger announcers have tried a cookie-cutter approach, mimicking the all-time greats instead of letting their own personalities come through in their deliveries. Twins announcer John Gordon claims that many up-and-comers attempt to sound like Vin Scully.

"Vin told me, 'When you walk in and close the door, you come in already unique than anyone else,'" Wayne Hagin said. "You have to be yourself. Don't create yourself to be like that. Chris Berman copied 'back, back, back, back' from Red Barber. He copied a lot of things from a lot of broadcasters. Nicknames was one thing he came up with that was very unique.

"Whoever you are, that's what you have to be on the air. Too many guys are not."

Worse yet, like so many others in baseball media, the eyes of many announcers are already on the next job, in the next city, rather than being the best one can possibly be in the here and now.

"Young guys look upon this as a springboard to a big-paying job with a network," Marty Brennaman said. "I don't think that you're ever again going to see guys who stay with the same club up to fifty-five years, like Vin Scully, Ernie Harwell, Harry Caray, Bob Uecker, Jack Buck, and myself. I never aspired to a major network, and I turned down jobs in many major markets. To me there's no more prideful thing than to say how many teams you have broadcast for . . . one? Nobody will even come close to that [Scully's longevity with the Dodgers]. The most amazing thing in our business is that a man can be with one club that long."

The announcer will last only as long as he honestly connects with his audience. If the fans were disenchanted with certified homer "Hawk" Harrelson, Jerry Reinsdorf would have shown him the door years ago. You cannot force an announcer down the audience's throats.

"I don't walk a tightrope," Harrelson said. "I will give my opinion on issues. The comments I make on decisions made by the manager in the game are only good before the play. I like to say as little as possible in a telecast if it's a good ballgame, there's nothing an announcer can say to enhance it. To sit up there and pontificate on how smart you are is bullshit. Let the fan enjoy the game.

"Curt Gowdy said he did a Rose Bowl between Washington and Ohio State. He got forty thousand letters in the next month. Twenty thousand were from Washington fans crucifying him for being against that school. Twenty thousand were from Ohio State fans crucifying him for being against them. To me, there has to be some connection between the broadcaster and fan."

The listeners will know when the announcer has achieved the kind of balancing act desired by them, team management, and players. After thirty-seven years of working Kansas City Royals games, Denny Matthews feels he has done just that.

"You can tell it like it is and not hit the guy over the head with it," Matthews said.

"If I'm not giving you an accurate description, I ain't doing the job. It's [losing] not hard at all. I don't take it personally. What you must avoid is the big picture. You take each game as it comes. Out of 162 games, there are some really good games, some really bad games, and a lot in between. You do the best job possible."

But in the end, as in libel and slander cases, the announcer's only defense is the truth. How much of the truth, and its various shades, is permissible on the air is up for question in an era of overly sensitive eyes and ears.

Marty Brennaman has a simple measuring stick when he ends each Reds broadcast.

"As far as walking out of the booth and feeling like I gave it my best shot, yes," he said. "Do I have bad nights or days? Yes. I walk out of the booth and I say to myself, 'That was a shitty broadcast. I did a bad job.' But not because I hid the truth or made excuses. I don't believe in that. Thank God I work for people who allow it to be done the way it should be done."

FIFTEEN

Old versus New Media

A huge migration away from newspaper readership seemed to be picking up steam in the first half-decade of the twenty-first century. Waiting to absorb the defectors were the usual broadcast suspects plus a cornucopia of Internet properties, ranging from well-funded sites with the ESPN brand to homespun blogs that featured analysis right out of left field.

The baseball fan had choices of information of which his father and grandfather could never conceive. Too many choices, in fact. The Internet was at the same stage of development as was radio in the mid-1920s or TV in, say, 1953: a wondrous new technology in a rapidly expanding mode that wouldn't fully mature until several decades down the line.

Could the summer-game rooter really get down-and-dirty, in-depth, inside-story comprehensive coverage from the new media compared to the clunky paper, off-the-presses and delivered via truck or car to your front door?

Internet is immediate, even graphically spectacular. But the way the biggest purveyor of daily baseball coverage set up its business, its chronicling of each team's goings-on was not as unfettered as the old-fashioned newspaper dampened down by corporate conservatism and cost cutting.

National sites are comprehensive in the big picture, but can't zero in on any one team. And, naturally, the Eastern bias of their headquarters will crop up in selection of content.

Numbers-crunching sites can dissect and analyze baseball statistics like never before, but they often cut out the human aspect of the game. That has to be factored in before a complete, accurate analysis of a player's ebb and flow can be put down in stone. Usually, the online analysts did not have access to the players, managers, and coaches, instead relying on front-office types they could hunt up via phone or e-mail. Part of the story, but not all.

Bloggers also had to pay their way into ballparks and could not gain access to the field or locker room. While some of their analysis was intelligent and measured, too much else came off as the same kind of blather the "Carphone Joes" spewed over sports-talk radio.

Television, the oldest of the "new" media, still functioned as just a highlights-and-headlines service. Time constraints and newsroom philosophies put the emphasis on the short sound bite and reporters asking the ballplayer, "Tell us about your homer in the fifth," instead of real incisive questions. Except for occasional features on pre- and postgame shows on cable channels, the fans couldn't learn appreciably more about their favorite players and teams.

The old, old media—newspapers—still remained the best source of inside-baseball information in an era when fewer eyes cast their way and fewer hands got dirty from stray newsprint.

Even stalwart newspaper readers found part of their traditional reading time diverted to online scanning and e-mail as the latter began to displace the phone as the preferred method of person-to-person communication. Ditto with the explosion of TV channels, each scrambling for a niche.

Newspaper daily circulation had been falling since the 1980s. In 1982, daily newspaper circulation was 62.4 million, according to the Newspaper Association of America. But the decline accelerated rapidly from 2001 to 2005. According to Gawker.com, a 15 percent decline was recorded in the five-year period from 55,578,046 to 47,374,033. In 2004, 54.1 percent of adults read a newspaper each day, a massive drop from 77.6 in 1970.

Only a tiny fraction was due to the circulation scandals that began popping up around the country in 2003–5, in which executives under withering pressure cooked the books in numbers or even used their own marketing funds to buy up thousands of copies to keep the circulation up.

"I don't see any bright spots and I don't see any reasonable expectation this is going to change anytime soon," said John Morton, a longtime newspaper industry analyst. "The Internet may have exacerbated the trend, but this is a problem that existed long before the Internet became ubiquitous."

Tribune Company flagship newspapers that once boasted of selling more than a million copies daily were hard hit in a six-month decline going into 2005, according to the Audit Bureau of Circulation. The *Chicago Tribune* said its average weekday circulation fell 6.9 percent, to 573,743, and the Sunday edition fell 4.7 percent, to 953,815. The *Los Angeles Times* reported that its daily circulation fell 6.5 percent, to 907,997, and Sunday circulation fell 7.9 percent.

Executives and pundits alike fretted that young readers simply were not picking up newspapers and would never get into the habit.

"Most people form their newspaper reading habit from eighteen and twenty-five and they hold it, they don't increase it as they get older," Steven Duke, project manager of Northwestern University's Readership Institute, told Herald.com on December 12, 2004.

"People have now become accustomed to getting their news when, where, and how they want it. Newspapers are going to have to redefine themselves."

News consumers could get almost all their information from the Internet, as easy and convenient as a mouse click. Up-to-the-minute, and more often than not, free.

But if they were baseball fans, they couldn't totally sate themselves from cyberspace.

Dinn Mann believed he was giving his readers as much as possible. As top editor of MLB.com—the Internet service covering all baseball teams featuring text, real audio, and access to video—longtime former newspaper sports editor Mann beat the drum that his sprawling operation could meet every fan's information needs.

MLB.com was the centralized operation of all team Web sites, which were formerly operated locally before they were consolidated under one umbrella company in 2001. Major League Baseball itself invested into partial ownership of the umbrella company.

"They want to become the wire service for Major League Baseball," said Mike Fannin, a former Mann newspaper sports department aide who now is sports editor of the *Kansas City Star*.

To be sure, a fan can obtain a feast of multimedia coverage of his favorite team on MLB.com, which operates under the umbrella of Major League Advanced Media. Writers can double the length of newspaper stories, hemmed in by tightening news holes, and write almost to their hearts' content in cyberspace. Both game stories and notes features are liberal in length. Video and audio packages of game highlights and interviews also can be easily accessed on the site. By paying basic subscription fees, fans also can listen to live game broadcasts and talk shows specifically designed for MLB.com.

But as much as Mann suggested he operated under few restrictions, his in-the-field writers said they cannot post everything they hear or see around their teams. Not bound by any inch counts or word limits, they nevertheless cannot out-report the old media because of limits of sensibility.

MLB.com reporters can be handcuffed on reporting information that is still in the speculative stage and is not yet confirmed by teams. The reporter has to act as a kind of self-censor. If not, a site editor will do it for them. After all, MLB is in a way their boss.

Even wording has to be careful. The *San Jose Mercury News*'s Chris Haft recalled how he could not use the word "demotion" while working for Reds.com in describing the busting of assistant GM Doc Rodgers.

"You could write 'reassigned,' 'moved,' 'took the position of,' but it was clearly a demotion," Haft said.

Almost everything a standard newspaper can print is covered by MLB.com. And in the increasing number of one-newspaper towns, MLB.com's reporter is the only traveling competition for the remaining print beat writer.

"We have tackled controversial issues," Astros.com reporter Alyson Footer, a former public relations official with Houston, said.

But caveats do exist.

"Sometimes we have to approach it in a different way," Footer said. "Every situation is different. If there's something out there, a controversial topic, we can't ignore it. News is news.

"There are times when it comes to rumors [such as the 2004 firing of Astros manager Jimy Williams], there are ways to approach it—attribute it to [other media] reports, get a statement from club that they don't have a comment. We do not use anonymous sources, we have much stricter policies. We can't throw things out there."

Longtime newspaper veteran Dick Kaegel, who left the *Kansas*

City Star to cover the Royals for MLB.com, seconded that analysis. So did Haft.

"There were times we had to tone it down," he said. "We were told to restrain ourselves. You really couldn't be too negative. I know when the Reds hired Dave Miley as manager, that actually Brian Grail was their first choice. Dan O'Brien [Reds GM] was overruled, and it was tough to get that in print.

"Sure you have to be delicate working in the newspaper business. There were certain no-no's. But in newspapers you maybe have a little license to push the envelope a bit. That was definitely discouraged [at MLB.com]. The mantra there was to 'celebrate baseball.' I don't necessarily have a problem with that. But there were a couple of times where I maybe felt a little hamstrung."

The "sensitivity of an issue" and a "club's feelings" often dictate how—and if—stories are played on MLB.com, Footer said.

Mann insists his reporters are not hamstrung.

"I've never had an owner tell me to take something off their site," he said. "If it's been taken off, it's an inaccuracy. There's nothing that's off-limits. But we'll take the high road. Sometimes we'll tackle stories in a reactionary fashion instead of a breaking [news] fashion.

"We don't censor our fans' message boards. We're not light in our approach, but we're not mean-spirited. We're a little bit like the broadcasters who do the game. Many have informative and enlightened things to say. It's a text-based version of what they say."

Mann said he has made MLB.com a more honest operation journalistically compared to when each team ran its own Web site prior to 2001.

"I don't think anyone will tell you there are any severe handcuffs about topics," he said. "When our group walked in the door [to centralize the operation], there were taboo topics. What I had to try to do was establish a separation of church and state. Otherwise, there was no credibility."

"If you talk to fans, they feel they get good coverage on MLB.com. These things don't happen every day. Day-by-day coverage is as thorough as anyone else's, sometimes more thorough. We can be a little more creative. Off-the-wall, off-field features that newspapers can't tackle.

"I consider my competition newspapers. I do not consider other online sources my competition."

Haft and Kansas City's Fannin figure that Mann eventually will strike the right balance.

"He's a veteran newspaper guy," Haft said. "He knows what he's doing."

"He has very good business instincts," Fannin said.

Those other sources to which Mann referred are a cornucopia of national sites and blogs, none of which focus on daily team-by-team coverage or have legitimate access to baseball newsmakers.

ESPN.com, biggest of the sports sites, is nationally focused and doesn't really have a team-by-team presence, essentially falling into the Eastern-oriented emphasis of national media. CBSSportsLine.com gamely stayed in the business despite financial difficulties. Fox Sports.com tried to jump into the fray in 2000, but laid off its entire writing staff within three years.

The major challenge—in fact, still a huge hurdle at the midpoint of the new century's first decade—was convincing major advertisers that the huge number of hits on each site could be translated into willing eyes scanning ads. All that really resulted in was a much more fragmented media landscape with the advertisers divvying up their spending into smaller slices.

A modest flow of ad dollars actually went to some bloggers, if that can be believed. The art of creating personal Web sites and fan sites has multiplied infinitely in the twenty-first century. Fans who previously were limited to gabbing their way past producers at talk stations now can pontificate or rant without limit on the Internet.

A portion of analysis is thoughtful, intelligent, even ahead of the curve found in established media.

"Some of the bloggers and fans on message boards know more about baseball or their respective teams than some of the writers I've run across," White Sox beat writer Scot Gregor of the suburban Chicago *Daily Herald* told *Chicago Sports Review* in February 2005.

Yet too much other information is unchecked criticism and wild rumor, with no controls or editing. Any fan can post seemingly anything, no matter how far out of left field the origination.

One Cubs fan Web site posted a fan's tale of two star players settling a challenge to each other, "way back when," by allowing the winner of the challenge to have sex with the other player's wife in the Wrigley Field broadcast booth after a game. According to this tall tale, fans across the street could gape at the wife's bare bottom bouncing up and down in the booth. Such a *Penthouse*-style contribution would be rejected at any legitimate publication or site where normal standards of truth in reporting are used, particularly to defend against libel suits. The Web master no doubt had never taken a "Law of the Press" course in college.

Recognizing the wild inaccuracies that gather online, *Chicago Tribune* Cubs beat writer Paul Sullivan disagreed with Gregor in the *Chicago Sports Review* article, claiming he never reads all the Internet content.

"Sometimes people will e-mail me a link to a fan site where someone is drilling me for something I wrote," Sullivan said. "I've learned never to respond. Some of these people are downright nuts. No offense to you, but everyone with a pc and a printer believes they're a writer. That's the worst aspect of the Internet age—everyone has something to say and a blog to say it in."

Taking the highbrow ground online were a collection of baseball junkies and stats wonks, who formed the *Baseball Prospectus* in the mid-1990s to analyze teams, players, and executives. The *Prospectus* has expanded past cottage-industry status to put out a late-winter annual, dissecting the entire game for the forthcoming season.

In addition, the *Prospectus*'s featured writer Will Carroll, based in Indianapolis, somehow has gleaned an impressive collection of contacts in the game that enables him to beat the daily newspapers on stories. Carroll went on to pen a 2005 book on the insidious infiltration of drugs into baseball.

"It's a combination of things [grist for their material]," said longtime *Prospectus* analyst Chris Kahrl. "We spend a lot of time talking to people in the industry. Our real interest is player performance. We're not so much interested in the human side of the story. At the end of the day, we're not on the same page as the people in sports journalism who can talk about causation and get inside people's heads.

"Journalists are not trained to analyze. They just regurgitate information, present daily bits of information. There are people in every single organization who talk to us. I'm not interested in quoting people or getting scoops. I'm more interested in understanding how an organization thinks and what it wants to do going forward."

However, like MLB.com, the *Prospectus* analysts can present most, but not all, the potential story. Although Kahrl said most of her colleagues watch "an insane number of games each year" and have their phone calls and e-mails responded to by team officials, they don't have press box and clubhouse access. Baseball's always been about far more than one-dimensional statistics, which can be manipulated in any direction an analyst desires. The game is played by flesh-and-blood people with eminently human motivations. And that has a primo effect on performance and teams' motivations.

For instance, since the *Prospectus* did not have access to the Cubs clubhouse in 2004–5, the analyst wouldn't have known about the extremely uptight personality of LaTroy Hawkins. They could ruminate all day and night about how Hawkins tries to force in too-hittable strikes on 0-and-2 counts, but they couldn't possibly know unless they tried talking to the man that Hawkins was too stiff emotionally and a mite too suspicious of the world to try to save games with just a one-run lead.

"I really stress the extent to which people in the [baseball] industry read what's going on in the analysis industry," Kahrl said. "The industry is better informed than the media."

If both the most controversial and human elements of baseball, important in the entire context, may be left out by the online information purveyors, the entire length and breadth of understanding baseball is largely absent from daily TV coverage.

The mature (not old or new) medium of television, which the majority of consumers now regard as their primary source of information, cannot really be more than a highlights-and-sound-bites service. But once, it had pretensions of being much more.

Chet Coppock remembers the day when he was under management fiat to compete not only with other sportscasters, but also newspapers. Most recently Coppock plied his trade as weekend host at the Sporting News Radio Network. But in 1981, he was nightly sportscaster at Chicago's WMAQ-TV, going up against video rivals Johnny Morris and Tim Weigel.

"In 1981, [WMAQ-TV news director] Paul Beavers gave orders to break stories," Coppock recalled. "When I got beat, he demanded news. He demanded stories be broken."

Coppock also had time to be more than a headline-and-highlights service on the traditionally jam-packed 10:00 p.m. newscast.

"I had three and a half minutes at 10:00 p.m.," he said. "Big news, I could stretch to four minutes. Three and a half was more than adequate. I had 35 percent highlights, 40 percent news, 25 percent commentary.

"In Indianapolis [WISH-TV] in the late 1970s, I had six and a half minutes on the 6:00 p.m. news.

"Now it's two and a quarter minutes for sports at 10:00 p.m. It's thank-you Warner [Saunders], a happy face, Sox won, happy face, Cubs lost, show an elephant on skates and throw it back [to the news anchor]."

"The business changed before the 1980s came to a close," Coppock said.

"Sales managers became convinced through [consultant] Frank Magid that sports was a detriment to the 10:00 p.m. news. They began to tell people weather was significantly more important than sports at 10:00 p.m.

"What I find to be odd is that now, years after the fact, electronic media on a 6:00 and 10:00 p.m. basis is so vulnerable, the sportscasters are told just be cute, just be funny, don't offend anybody. They feel sports won't gain viewers, but they can lose viewers."

A few network affiliates are throwbacks. Those are mostly Fox or Time-Warner outlets who can put on a full hour of news at 9:00 or 10:00 p.m., local times, after network programming has ended. One such outlet is KRIV-TV, Houston's Fox affiliate. Sportscaster Mark Berman enjoys more than enough time on his sportscast to break stories, present interviews, and play the usual parade of highlights.

"Our news director demands we cover the news," Berman said. "Generally speaking, most TV reporters don't report. They're headline guys."

Most recently, I rarely have seen TV anchors or reporters working clubhouses without their camera operators. They are not seen conversing with players or coaches in noninterview situations in true beat fashion, gathering background, and getting to know the players. And when the anchors and reporters do ask questions, it's often framed as a request to elicit the desired sound bite. "Tell us about your performance" or "Talk to us about your home run in the fifth." Rarely is a question posed with the angle of "why" or "how."

Cameras crowd small interview rooms and around the top interview subjects at their lockers with the sole purpose of getting pictures and sound, and crowding out those questioners that really want to get to the bottom of things. Cameras are used as a wedge to get into the right position and move others out of the way. If a non-TV person gets in the line of sight of a camera operator and his subject, the operator will press down on the individual's shoulder without so much of an "excuse me" to get the shot unimpeded. It's a miracle more fights don't break out between reporters and camera operators as a result.

"The difficulty is we so often sell the sizzle, not the steak," said Cincinnati Reds announcer George Grande, who in another incarnation was the first *SportsCenter* anchor seen on the air when ESPN signed on in 1979.

"The good thing is you get highlights you never got before," Grande said. "The bad thing is you don't tell the story of the game. In telling the story of the game, you want to show the bunt that got the guy in scoring position."

Grande, who prepped in the business just down the hall from Walter Cronkite at CBS News, was one of the minority of broadcasters trying to go in-depth with his 1980s weekly ESPN show *Inside Baseball*. Other mentors, like Vin Scully, Milton Richman, and Dick Young, taught Grande to honor the game, aim for the scoop, report something no one else had, and be fair.

"We tried to be in-depth on *Inside Baseball*," Grande said.

But eventually that program gave way to *Baseball Tonight*, the game's top nightly highlights extravaganza. Analysis and reporting in recent years has often given way to on-air verbal rasslin' matches between panelists like John Kruk and Harold Reynolds.

In the end, perhaps all forms of media can complement one another. But one cannot completely take the place of another. New cannot perform the complete functions of the old. At the same time, old cannot go where new can go, live and in color.

Old, in the form of newspapers, cannot practically be replaced as the most complete form of baseball coverage unless the new media continue to evolve into something they are not at the present.

Jim Rygelski, longtime St. Louis journalist and baseball historian, summed up the old versus new media debate with a December 4, 2004, essay.

"Here's yet one more reason why you should get your news primarily from a daily newspaper.

"Y'all probably saw the story on TV Thursday about the auctioning of the bat Babe Ruth used to hit the first-ever home run in Yankee Stadium. Fifteen seconds or so about only the price ($1.2 million), that it was to an unnamed buyer, and marked the third time that more than a million had been paid for a piece of sports memorabilia. Yes, that price is obscene, and the person who bought it surely could have found a more humanitarian way of spending his money.

"However, a nine-paragraph, Associated Press story in the *St. Louis Post-Dispatch* (and undoubtedly in many other daily newspapers across the nation) told a much fuller story, as newspaper stories inevitably do over TV. I offer this just as an example of what depth one gets by reading.

"The AP story repeated the facts of the TV report, but added all this: The full price was $1,265,000 plus a 15 percent commission added for the Chicago-based auction house that bought it for the anonymous East Coast collector. It noted that Babe hit the home run in the third inning of the first game every played in Yankee Stadium, April 18, 1923, against the Boston Red Sox. The Yankees won the game 4–1.

"Ruth shortly after donated the bat to the *Los Angeles Evening Herald* for a high school home-run-hitting contest. He inscribed on the barrel of the bat: 'To the Boy Home Run King of Los Angeles,' and signed it 'Babe Ruth, N.Y., May 7, 1923.' The high schooler who won it, Victor Orsatti, kept it until his death sixty-one years later. He willed it to a caretaker, who kept it under her bed until it was auctioned. A portion of the proceeds from the sale will go to a baseball program at a Mexican orphanage.

"You could have read the entire AP story in less than two minutes. Look at the human factor it brings out. You can also absorb its contents rather than having them shot at you by a rat-a-tat-tat voice on the screen.

"Anyway, TV's okay, but don't depend on it primarily or, especially, solely. Subscribe to a daily paper (I work for a weekly, so I have no personal economic interest in this, just a spiritual one). Read. Read, read, read. Then read some more.

"I trust I'm preaching to the choir."

Afterword

Baseball is the most media-accessible and, in turn, fan-accessible sport that's ever been created. Problem is, the players who play the game, the executives who govern it, and the media who cover it don't know a good thing when they have it in their firm grasp.

Say a game begins at 1:20 p.m. The home locker room will typically open at 9:50 a.m., three and a half hours before the first pitch. Even if the clubhouse is closed during batting practice after 10:30 or 10:45, players, coaches, and the manager usually can be tracked down for a quick quote or informal conversation around the cage—if the media member isn't too busy gossiping with a colleague or simply killing the grass. Then, after batting practice is over at 11:50, the locker room reopens for up to forty-five minutes. If a reporter can't cop a few one-on-ones during this open window, he or she really isn't trying.

Contrast this arrangement with the NFL. Locker rooms are closed pregame. Reporters have to gather their material at practice in dribs and drabs during the week, usually in tightly controlled group interviews. Head coaches almost never can be interviewed one-on-one. Access to their defensive and offensive coordinators also is increasingly choreographed. There's no sitting around a dugout bench or leaning against the cage chewing the fat with these militarized coaching minds.

Meanwhile, the NBA prides itself on being a media-friendly league. Not so fast. Reporters have a short window after practice between games to interview players and coaches, usually on the court, with little if any locker-room access. Before a common 7:30 p.m. NBA tipoff time, the locker room will be open from 6:00 to 6:45 p.m. Yet players know that media window all too well. More often than not, they'll retire to the trainer's room or players lounge, or go onto the court to shoot.

Gone is the sight of Michael Jordan sitting by his cubicle lacing his shoes and sorting tickets on the floor in a cramped Chicago Stadium locker room before a 1991 playoff game against the Knicks—with nobody interviewing him! An enterprising author could have done a book chapter with His Airness while all the visiting New York writers were down the hall chowing down on Chef Hans's dinner, instead of picking the all-time star's brain. Five years later, with four rings in his possession and a spacious United Center locker room rife with hiding places at his beck and call, Jordan was usually nowhere to be found between 6:00 and 6:45 p.m.

Many of Jordan's successors took the cue and zipped their lips before games, if you could even find them in media-accessible areas.

"Jordan cut it back substantially the bigger he got," said the *Chicago Tribune*'s Sam Smith, author of *The Jordan Rules*, the most revealing book about Jordan's reign with the Bulls. "In his Second Coming [from 1995] on, he no longer did pregame interviews, no longer did one-on-ones. When David Halberstam came around to do a book, he never talked to him one-on-one. Here's Halberstam, not some beat writer or columnist, one of the most accomplished writers of our era."

In addition to copying Jordan's shaved head and baggy shorts, the Kevin Garnetts of the post-Jordan era made sure their thoughts were recorded in only snippet form postgame.

"Larry Bird came to the arena three hours before the game to shoot and you could talk to him anytime," Smith said. "Same with Magic [Johnson]. They came at a time when the NBA was in trouble and there was talk of teams going out of business. That group understood they were in it together, to promote the product and promote themselves. Now there's a complete separation between the players, the media, and the public, and it's not ever going to come back. The commissioner [David Stern] doesn't want to alienate the players. He's decided it's not a major-enough issue to push it any further."

If the NBA lets its own advocacy of openness slide, imagine the policy of the mega-popular NFL. Only the hardest-working pro football reporters can develop the kind of one-on-one relationships that are classically prized in journalism.

The tradeoff is regularly scheduled media access, but all done in a group fashion. Those reporters who crave a nine-to-five schedule on weekdays will covet the football beat. The only reason they have to arrive three hours before a game is to beat the incoming crowd and traffic. They also know when they'll get out of the stadium. There's no football equivalent to the seventeen-inning game or a three-hour rain delay.

The NFL has been steadily cutting one-on-one access since the 1970s. Jerry Izenberg of the *Newark Star-Ledger*, one of four reporters in 2005 to have covered all thirty-eight Super Bowls, told *Editor and Publisher* in 2005 that he could interview players in their hotel rooms before the first six Super Bowls through 1972. He even had lunch with a Chiefs linebacker the day before Super Bowl I.

"Now you don't get near them at all, it's like a Gestapo," Izenberg said.

Green Bay Packers radio voice Wayne Larrivee also witnessed the sea change. When he began as the Kansas City Chiefs radio announcer, "the NFL was the best in promoting itself and its players. But since the NFL took over the top pedestal in sports, it's become a very difficult league to deal with. What has happened is the league has gotten so big and popular there's a certain amount of arrogance.

"NFL team PR directors used to take media-outlet directors to dinner. They used to advance the games with the PR director. You'd get a shot with the PR people. In the old AFC West, we'd have a spring meeting where the PR directors would bring in local media and coaches would be there. We'd have two and a half days of visiting and talking to people. Now you have very little contact from team to team. When I call people, I'm very lucky to get a call back. It's very [network] TV oriented."

Larrivee is still the TV voice of the Bulls on WGN, and once handled two seasons' worth of Cubs telecasts. The NFL is toughest to work.

"I find you have to break through the all the orchestration [to get information and talk individually with players]," he said. Even as the voice of the Packers, he did not have a close relationship with legend-in-his-own-time quarterback Brett Favre.

The increasing bunker mentality was carried to an extreme when Nick Saban took over the coaching reins of the Dolphins early in 2005. The team made their media room at their Davie, Florida, training base off-limits for everyday use in the off-season. Trying to tightly control the flow of information, Saban had made his assistant coaches off-limits to the media during his Louisiana State days.

No wonder Larrivee has fondest memories of the pregame baseball routine.

"Baseball was great," he said. "I enjoyed that aspect of it. There were some real good guys I got to know over the years, hanging out two hours before the game. There's a whole different pace to baseball that I enjoyed. From a lifestyle standpoint, you have to be married to baseball, going to all the different cities. But I think baseball's got a personal charm, it's a personal thing. It comes out in all the writing and broadcasting about the game."

Offering a similar opinion was Clark Spencer, who had split the Marlins beat for the *Miami Herald*.

"I've done every sport except the NBA," said Spencer. "I just like baseball. Baseball has a slow ebb and flow to it that makes it a lot easier. I wouldn't like to cover a sport like the NFL where the window of access is very small. You're only covering sixteen games. In baseball, you've got twenty-five guys. In basketball, only twelve, but there's only five or six guys you're paying attention to. You're not paying attention to the third-string point guard. At some point in the season, that twenty-fifth guy on the baseball team is going to do something that merits attention."

Given such testimony about its contrast with other sports, why would baseball want to chop down a good thing it had going? Its top minds have given it serious thought, and it's starting to move into action.

Starting in the 1990s, some sentiment surfaced to decrease the total amount of pregame access accorded to baseball media. Hal McCoy of the *Dayton Daily News*, the game's senior beat writer, heard it from a high level almost a decade ago.

"In 1997, as BBWAA president, Dave Dombrowski [then general manager of the Florida Marlins] asked me to breakfast one day," McCoy said. "He asked if the writers would be against cutting down clubhouse access to an hour [total] before the game. It would be like the NBA. I said absolutely not. He was speaking for all the general managers. The idea came out of the GM meetings.

"These guys didn't understand it's to their benefit. They said it's getting too crowded and distracting in the locker room. That's hogwash. They don't understand, the more access we have, the more coverage they get. You know they would like to do it, but the BBWAA would fight it. I don't think overall access will be cut like that."

No serious top-level effort to cut access has surfaced since then, although many media members believe it's not far from the front of the honchos' thinking. More recently, Cubs media relations director Sharon Pannozzo suggested a shorter pregame session where the players are assured of being available. But one of Pannozzo's counterparts said practicality would be an overriding issue.

"If we limit it to an hour, we as PR people have to make sure all the players are in there for an hour," Reds media relations director Rob Butcher said. "Problem is, they're not. Part of a pro athlete's job is to deal with the media, like it or not. You have to learn how to deal with it."

However, total access has become an issue in a crowded old ballpark like Wrigley Field, which has inadequate facilities for both players and media. With media hordes descending on a projected World Series contender, Pannozzo barred TV cameras from the clubhouse before games, while mandating that reporters could not stand around waiting for interviews close to the players' lunchroom, at one end of the cramped clubhouse. But at the other extreme, all media were allowed in a tiny interview room that was too small to handle the mob and got uncomfortably hot when the ancient air conditioner had to be turned off when an interviewee began speaking.

"Before you didn't need controls," Pannozzo said. "Things pretty much ran okay. Things went pretty smoothly. Now the press box isn't designed to hold them, the clubhouse is not designed to hold them. You make concessions and you do have to change. People in this town are not used to change. Things were always done a certain way. In the whole ballpark, you had made changes slowly."

At the same time, Pannozzo's media relations staff had not been increased to handle the extra load. Interns handle what should be full timers' duties.

"We're still sitting here with the same-sized staff as 1982," Pannozzo said. "Quite frankly, we're not equipped to win [with the present staff]. L.A. has a big staff—six people. We're staffed the same number of people to get the job done based on the fact we're going to have a losing season, when you don't have a lot of coverage. Twenty years ago, you didn't have Fox, you didn't have regular ESPN. By volume alone, you're staffed to lose."

That modest-sized staff also had to handle a blizzard of messages.

"Before voice mail, people calling you had to get you [or leave a written message]," Pannozzo said. "In 1982 when I started, our phone system had no voice mail. Now you have a cell phone for Chicago and a separate cell phone for spring training in Arizona. You have your office phone back in Chicago and your phone in Arizona. Now you also have e-mail. If you're doing your job, you've got to give them an e-mail response. I get a hundred e-mails per day. The sheer volume has exploded due to technological advances."

While some seriously think about closing the door, others believe in a more open policy in which players and team officials are media savvy. Over the last two decades some teams have begun media-training programs in which players are taught about handling interview situations.

One of the oldest programs was practiced by the Pittsburgh Pirates by media relations chief Jim Trdinich.

"I started in 1989 with Rick Cerrone on our staff," he said. "We would meet with the nonroster guys, the first- and second-year guys, in groups of four or five in spring training. We put out an eight-page pamphlet on how to deal with the media and public. We now get with the minor leaguers in spring training. We get with the first-year guys, tell them who covers our team, what to expect. We tell starting pitchers to tip their cap when coming off the mound. If they go to places to hide, I just go get the guy. We tell them it's just five minutes of your time. We try to nip it in the bud. By not saying anything, you say a lot."

The Cleveland Indians also are longtime practitioners of media training.

"We do it with our top prospects in the winter," media relations director Bart Swain said. "We get them acclimated to the city and the media. We work with them once a week on different techniques.

We have actual media sessions and do mock interviews. The big thing about this business is trust."

The sessions helped ace pitcher C. C. Sabathia. "C. C. needed to be more expansive, give longer answers, and make eye contact," Swain said. "No question it has had a positive effect."

Yet another media-training-savvy organization is the White Sox.

"The first year we did it was 1997," White Sox vice president Scott Reifert said. "We did the Major Leaguers. The team was young enough to do it. We did it in January before SoxFest [annual fan convention]. We'd bring in media trainers in English and Spanish. We'd do mock interviews and have the players interview each other. Some guys learned it and enjoyed it, but some guys were never comfortable with it. At least they were exposed to it."

The White Sox media training even extended to front-office honchos. More recently, Reifert would hang around pregame interviews of manager Ozzie Guillen and general manager Kenny Williams. Sometimes they get signals from Reifert, who always is in an analyzing mode.

"After every interview he [Williams] does, we sit down and go through it," Reifert said. "Kenny and I have a sign [to wrap up interviews] and I give him the sign. One of the things he said early on is that 'I get very impassioned, we need a sign and we need a way for you to give me the sign.'"

In 2004 an angry Williams verbally banished young pitcher Jon Rauch from the White Sox organization after Rauch left the clubhouse before the end of a game in which he was routed early.

"We talked about it afterward," Reifert said. "If we say and do this, this will be the result. Kenny wanted to send a message that way. Was it done on purpose? You betcha. Jon Rauch isn't pitching here anymore."

Williams is emotional, but Guillen is often off-the-wall.

"He's crazy like a fox," Reifert said. "I'm not going to say, 'This is what you'd say.' I'd recommend a tactic like this. I never want to be writing a script for a guy, because people can read through that."

Media training also provided work for outside firms such as Highland Park, Illinois–based Speaking Specialists. Headed by former all-news-station-anchor Sue Castorino and husband, former sportscaster Randy Minkoff, the firm specialized in training corporate executives for public speaking, before the Kansas City Royals called in 1999.

"The Royals had us working with all their players," Castorino said. "After one session, one player came up and said, 'This is helping me, I'm glad I paid attention.' His name was Johnny Damon."

Speaking Specialists also has worked with the Reds, Marlins, Braves, and Brewers. In the sessions, props like microphones and bright lights are used.

"We tell them you're going to get good questions, dumb questions, questions out of left field," Castorino said. "After we do [mock] sports interviews, we do news-feature questions.

"If someone gets burned even once, they're reluctant. We have to go in and do damage control time and again. They'll say, 'I never said it [in an interview].' We ask them, 'Did you let the reporters put words in your mouth?' We help them understand the difference between the beat reporter and the columnist."

Castorino and Minkoff also try to bridge the cultural gap with baseball's huge pool of Spanish-speaking players.

"We do international sessions and work with Latin players separately," Castorino said. "We show tapes in Spanish and English. Sometimes they're reluctant."

Dealing with female reporters is part of the training in all languages.

"They ask, 'Do I shake your hand, do I hold back?'" Castorino said of the Latin players. Her response to all: "This is our job, treat us respectfully."

In contrast, Rob Butcher did not conduct formal media training with the Reds or in his former job with the New York Yankees.

"I address the team in spring training and during the season, I do go over that stuff," Butcher said. "But we don't walk through situations. We just say here's what to expect. I say they have a job to do and their job is just as important as yours.

"Mainly, from the time a player is drafted, he deals with media. Kids in high school deal with media. It's not as big a shock as ten years ago. You grow up through the [farm] system, you have more and more media. It's not as necessary as it used to be.

"The best thing we can do is let them know what to expect and get them to cooperate with media. I'm not saying take them to dinner.

But be professional, cooperate with them. There will come a day when a writer has a chance to bury you or not bury you. If they like you and you've treated them wonderfully, they won't bury you."

In the end, however, all the media training in the world won't close the widening gap between baseball people and those who cover them unless both sides understand what's at stake.

The media training must emphasize to players that they need to be the game's top salesmen in a crowded sports and media world. No longer is baseball the preeminent sport that stands out over struggling pro football and basketball leagues in the manner of the perceived glory years of the mid-twentieth century. The megabucks that players receive are hard-earned by teams through sponsorships and ever-increasing ticket prices.

"Baseball can't be so arrogant as to think they're always going to be a front-page story," said Bob Dvorchak, former Pirates beat writer for the *Pittsburgh Post-Gazette*. "They've got to reestablish their relevance to readers and sports fans in this country. Football is a juggernaut and is marketed so well. It plays once a week. Baseball has got to be marketed better."

The wild-card playoff format has helped keep baseball in the news throughout September. Still, the game now not only has to battle overwhelming coverage of football, but even high school sports mandated, particularly in the Midwest, by editors grasping for straws in a bewilderingly competitive media world.

"If a city has a losing [baseball] team, it gets pushed back [in the paper]," said Hal McCoy. "I'm fortunate. I may only get a little corner of the front page and it jumps to inside. I still get page 1."

At the same time, editors and program directors have to take their baseball coverage more seriously. The fans want it, but won't flood phone lines and e-mails in the same manner of high school athletes' mothers who crave to add to junior's scrapbook. The media managers, who often aren't rooted in their communities as they move around in search of better jobs, are more frequently dispatching inexperienced, apathetic, or cynical folks to cover the game. Those who grew up as baseball fans are often in the minority. Knowledgeability and passion for the game often play second fiddle to surviving office politics.

"For quality baseball coverage, particularly in print, the fans will get what they demand," said sports-talk-show host Dan Bernstein of WSCR-AM in Chicago. "The fans will gravitate toward the writers they feel are giving them the best, most independent information.

"It's a battle we always fight between a fan who just wants to be happy—there are plenty of lobotomized fans out there—and the ones who are the critical-thinking fans. Those [latter] fans here are always asking why, asking for answers, for reasons, asking what those players are doing to earn every dollar the fans are pouring into Tribune Company coffers. The team has to meet them halfway.

"The fans will get the best coverage they can through this natural selection process. Those who aren't giving it to them will fade away."

University of Nebraska Press

Related sports books:

SPORTS HEROES, FALLEN IDOLS
By Stanley H. Teitelbaum

On the court and on the field, they are the world's winners, exhibiting a natural grace and prowess their adoring fans can only dream about. Yet so often, when off the field, our sports heroes lose their perspective, their balance, and their place. An evenhanded and honest look at athletes who have faltered, Teitelbaum's work helps us see past our sports stars' exalted image into what that image—and its frailty—says about our society and ourselves.

ISBN: 0-8032-4445-2; 978-0-8032-4445-0 (cloth)

BIG LEAGUES
Professional Baseball, Football, and Basketball in National Memory
By Stephen Fox

What is behind America's enduring love affair with professional baseball, football, and basketball? *Big Leagues* traces the evolution of these team sports from unlikely beginnings to multibillion-dollar businesses that still arouse widespread passion. Stephen Fox also surveys the world of fandom, examines the "big money" explosion, and dares to project the future.

ISBN: 0-8032-6896-3; 978-0-8032-6896-8 (paper)

Order online at www.nebraskapress.unl.edu or call 1-800-755-1105.
Mention the code "BOFOX" to receive a 20% discount.